"I believe in memory not as a place of arrival, but as point of departure—a catapult throwing you into present times, allowing you to imagine the future instead of accepting it. It would be absolutely impossible for me to have any connection with history if history were just a collection of dead people, dead names, dead facts. That's why I wrote *Memory of Fire* in the present tense, trying to keep alive everything that happened and allow it to happen again, as soon as the reader reads it."

EDUARDO GALEANO

guished is the Uruguayan Eduardo Galeano, who has made the genre his trademark, notably in his three-volume masterpiece, *Memory of Fire*."

—Alberto Manguel, *The Guardian*

"The Uruguayan author's vignettes stitch together tales of wonder and terror, love and war, and just about everything in between. Are these koans, fables, experiences, or testimonials? Galeano, author of the groundbreaking *Memory of Fire* trilogy, is a collector of stories, a clairvoyant reared in the cafés of Montevideo who, like [Roberto] Bolaño, carries with him a multitude. He, too, sings of the dead, the tortured, the brutalized; like Bolaño, he resuscitates an endless array of friends, comrades, and fellow travelers."

—Anderson Tepper, *Village Voice*

"An extraordinary canter through the history of the Americas."

—Isabel Fonseca

"Unquestionably Galeano's masterwork, *Memory of Fire* is a kind of secret history of the Americas, told in hundreds of kaleidoscopic vignettes that resurrect the lives of campesinos and slaves, dictators and scoundrels, poets and visionaries."

—Scott Sherman, *The Atlantic*

"A massive fresco of Latin American history since the pre-Columbian era to modern times."

—Isabel Allende

"He has merged Homer and Herodutus and, like them, has demonstrated that a tale well told, particularly a collective one, is an oracle that we could do well to heed."

—Gregory Rabassa

"Passionate and lyrical, lucidly visual . . . Galeano parades the subjects of history before us in a dazzling frieze."

—*New Statesman*

"[A]n epic work of literary creation . . . there could be no greater vindication of the wonders of the lands and people of Latin America."

—*Washington Post*

"Galeano's outrage is tempered by intelligence, an ineradicable sense of humor, and hope. . . . [A] compelling book."

—*Los Angeles Times*, front-page review

Eduardo Galeano

MEMORY OF FIRE

I. GENESIS

Part One of a Trilogy

Translated
by Cedric Belfrage

NATION
BOOKS
New York

Translator's Acknowledgment

Translation is a field in which two heads are better than one. I am grateful to Mark Fried for making himself so freely available to cooperate in this work.

Translation copyright© 1985 by Cedric Belfrage
First published as a Norton paperback 1998,
reprinted by arrangement with Pantheon Books
Paperback reprinted in 2010 by Nation Books,
A Member of the Perseus Books Group

Nation Books is a co-publishing venture of the Nation Institute and the Perseus Books Group.

Books published by Nation Books are available at special discounts for bulk purchases in the United States by corporations, institutions, and other organizations. For more information, please contact the Special Markets Department at the Perseus Books Group, 2300 Chestnut Street, Suite 200, Philadelphia, PA 19103, or call (800) 810-4145, ext. 5000, or e-mail special.markets@perseusbooks.com.

Text design by Marsha Cohen

Originally published in 1982 in Spain as *Memoria del fuego, I. Los nacimientos*, by Siglo Veintiuno de España Editores, S.A. Copyright © by Siglo Veintiuno de España Editores, S.A; copyright © by Siglo Veintiuno de España Editores, S.A; copyright © by Eduardo Galeano. Originally published in hardcover by Pantheon Books, a division of Random House, Inc., in 1985.

Cataloging-in-Publication data for this book are available from the Library of Congress.

ISBN 0-393-31773-0 (v. 1)
Nation Books paperback ISBN 978-1-56858-444-7

Contents

Preface   XV

First Voices / 1

The Creation   3
Time   3
The Sun and the Moon   4
The Clouds   5
The Wind   5
The Rain   6
The Rainbow   7
Day   8
Night   8
The Stars   9
The Milky Way   10
The Evening Star   10
Language   11
Fire   11
The Forest   12
The Cedar   12
The Guaiacum Tree   13
Colors   13
Love   14
The Rivers and the Sea   14
The Tides   15
Snow   16
The Flood   16
The Tortoise   17
The Parrot   18
The Hummingbird   18
The Night Bird (Urutaú)   19
The Ovenbird   20
The Crow   20
The Condor   21
The Jaguar   21
The Bear   22
The Crocodile   23
The Armadillo   23
The Rabbit   24

The Snake   25
The Frog   26
The Bat   26
Mosquitos   27
Honey   27
Seeds   28
Corn   28
Tobacco   29
Maté   29
Cassava   30
The Potato   31
The Kitchen   31
Music   32
Death   33
Resurrection   34
Magic   34
Laughter   35
Fear   35
Authority   36
Power   36
War   37
Parties   38
Conscience   38
The Sacred City   39
Pilgrims   40
The Promised Land   40
Dangers   41
The Spider Web   41
The Prophet   42

Old New World / 43

1492: *The Ocean Sea* The Sun Route to the Indies   45
1492: *Guanahaní* Columbus   45
1493: *Barcelona* Day of Glory   46
1493: *Rome* The Testament of Adam   47
1493: *Huexotzingo* Where Is the Truth? Where Are the Roots? 48
1493: *Pasto* Everybody Pays Taxes   48
1493: *Santa Cruz Island* An Experience of Miquele de Cuneo
        from Savona   49
1495: *Salamanca* The First Word from America   50
1495: *La Isabela* Caonabó   50
1496: *La Concepción* Sacrilege   51
1498: *Santo Domingo* Earthly Paradise   51
        The Language of Paradise   52

1499: *Granada*   Who Are Spaniards?   52
1500: *Florence*   Leonardo   53
1506: *Valladolid*   The Fifth Voyage   54
1506: *Tenochtitlán*   The Universal God   54
1511: *Guauravo River*   Agüeynaba   55
1511: *Aymaco*   Becerrillo   56
1511: *Yara*   Hatuey   57
1511: *Santo Domingo*   The First Protest   57
1513: *Cuareca*   Leoncico   58
1513: *Gulf of San Miguel*   Balboa   59
1514: *Sinú River*   The Summons   59
1514: *Santa María del Darién*   For Love of Fruit   60
1515: *Antwerp*   Utopia   61
1519: *Frankfurt*   Charles V   61
1519: *Acla*   Pedrarias   62
1519: *Tenochtitlán*   Portents of Fire, Water, Earth, and Air   63
1519: *Cempoala*   Cortés   64
1519: *Tenochtitlán*   Moctezuma   65
1519: *Tenochtitlán*   The Capital of the Aztecs   67
   Aztec Song of the Shield   68
1520: *Teocalhueyacan*   "Night of Sorrow"   68
1520: *Segura de la Frontera*   The Distribution of Wealth   69
1520: *Brussels*   Dürer   70
1520: *Tlaxcala*   Toward the Reconquest of Tenochtitlán   70
1521: *Tlatelolco*   Sword of Fire   71
1521: *Tenochtitlán*   The World Is Silenced in the Rain   71
1521: *Florida*   Ponce de León   72
1522: *Highways of Santo Domingo*   Feet   72
1522: *Seville*   The Longest Voyage Ever Made   73
1523: *Cuzco*   Huaina Cápac   74
1523: *Cuauhcapolca*   The Chief's Questions   75
1523: *Painala*   Malinche   76
1524: *Quetzaltenango*   The Poet Will Tell Children the Story of
   This Battle   77
1524: *Utatlán*   The Vengeance of the Vanquished   78
1524: *Scorpion Islands*   Communion Ceremony   78
1525: *Tuxkahá*   Cuauhtémoc   79
1526: *Toledo*   The American Tiger   80
1528: *Madrid*   To Loosen the Purse Strings   81
1528: *Tumbes*   Day of Surprises   81
1528: *Bad Luck Island*   "People Very Generous with What They
   Have . . ."   82
1531: *Orinoco River*   Diego de Ordaz   83
   Piaroa People's Song About the White Man   83
1531: *Mexico City*   The Virgin of Guadelupe   84
1531: *Santo Domingo*   A Letter   84
1531: *Serrana Island*   The Castaway and the Other   85

1532: *Cajamarca*   Pizarro   87
1533: *Cajamarca*   The Ransom   88
1533: *Cajamarca*   Atahualpa   89
1533: *Xaquixaguana*   The Secret   90
1533: *Cuzco*   The Conquerors Enter the Sacred City   91
1533: *Riobamba*   Alvarado   91
1533: *Quito*   This City Kills Itself   92
1533: *Barcelona*   The Holy Wars   92
1533: *Seville*   The Treasure of the Incas   93
1534: *Riobamba*   Inflation   94
1535: *Cuzco*   The Brass Throne   94
1536: *Mexico City*   Motolinía   95
1536: *Machu Picchu*   Manco Inca   96
1536: *Valley of Ulúa*   Gonzalo Guerrero   96
1536: *Culiacán*   Cabeza de Vaca   97
1537: *Rome*   The Pope Says They Are Like Us   98
1538: *Santo Domingo*   The Mirror   98
1538: *Valley of Bogotá*   Blackbeard, Redbeard, Whitebeard   99
1538: *Masaya Volcano*   Vulcan, God of Money   100
1541: *Santiago de Chile*   Inés Suárez   101
1541: *Rock of Nochistlán*   Never   102
1541: *Old Guatemala City*   Beatriz   103
1541: *Cabo Frío*   At Dawn, the Cricket Sang   104
1542: *Quito*   El Dorado   104
1542: *Conlapayara*   The Amazons   105
1542: *Iguazú River*   In Broad Daylight   106
1543: *Cubagua*   The Pearl Fishers   106
1544: *Machu Picchu*   The Stone Throne   107
         War Song of the Incas   107
1544: *Campeche*   Las Casas   107
1544: *Lima*   Carvajal   108
1545: *Royal City of Chiapas*   The Bad News Comes from
         Valladolid   110
1546: *Potosí*   The Silver of Potosí   110
1547: *Valparaíso*   The Parting   111
         Song of Nostalgia, from the Spanish Songbook   112
1548: *Xaquixaguana*   The Battle of Xaquixaguana Is Over   112
1548: *Xaquixaguana*   The Executioner   113
1548: *Xaquixaguana*   On Cannibalism in America   114
1548: *Guanajuato*   Birth of the Guanajuato Mines   115
1549: *La Serena*   The Return   116
         The Last Time   116
1552: *Valladolid*   He Who Always Took the Orders Now Gives
         Them   117
1553: *The Banks of the San Pedro River*   Miguel   117
         A Dream of Pedro de Valdivia   118
1553: *Tucapel*   Lautaro   119

1553: *Tucapel* Valdivia   119
1553: *Potosí* Beauty and the Mayor   120
      To the Strains of the Barrel Organ a Blind Man Sings to Her
          Who Sleeps Alone   121
1553: *Potosí* The Mayor and the Gallant   121
1554: *Cuzco* The Mayor and the Ears   122
1554: *Lima* The Mayor and the Bill Collector   122
1554: *Mexico City* Sepúlveda   123
1556: *Asunción, Paraguay* Conquistadoras   124
1556: *Asunción, Paraguay* "The Paradise of Mahomet"   125
      Womanizer Song, from the Spanish Songbook   125
1556: *La Imperial* Mariño de Lobera   126
1558: *Cañete* The War Goes On   127
      Araucanian Song of the Phantom Horseman   128
1558: *Michmaloyan* The Tzitzimes   128
1558: *Yuste* Who Am I? What Have I Been?   129
1559: *Mexico City* The Mourners   130
      Advice of the Old Aztec Wise Men   130
1560: *Huexotzingo* The Reward   131
1560: *Michoacán* Vasco de Quiroga   132
1561: *Villa de los Bergantines* The First Independence of
          America   133
1561: *Nueva Valencia del Rey* Aguirre   134
1561: *Neuva Valencia del Rey* From Lope de Aguirre's Letter to
          King Philip II   136
1561: *Barquisimeto* Order Restored   136
1562: *Maní* The Fire Blunders   137
1563: *Arauco Fortress* The History That Will Be   138
1564: *Plymouth* Hawkins   138
1564: *Bogotá* Vicissitudes of Married Life   139
1565: *Road to Lima* The Spy   140
1565: *Yauyoa* That Stone Is Me   141
      Prayer of the Incas, Seeking God   141
1565: *Mexico City* Ceremony   142
1566: *Madrid* The Fanatic of Human Dignity   143
1566: *Madrid* Even If You Lose, It's Still Worthwhile   143
1568: *Los Teques* Guaicaipuro   144
1568: *Mexico City* The Sons of Cortés   145
1569: *Havana* St. Simon Against the Ants   145
1571: *Mexico City* Thou Shalt Inform On Thy Neighbor   146
1571: *Madrid* Who Is Guilty, Criminal or Witness?   147
1572: *Cuzco* Túpac Amaru I   147
      The Vanquished Believe: 148
1574: *Mexico City* The First *Auto-da-Fé* in Mexico   148
1576: *Guanajuato* The Monks Say: 149
1576: *Xochimilco* The Apostle Santiago *versus* the Plague   150
1577: *Xochimilco* St. Sebastian *versus* the Plague   151

1579: *Quito*   Son of Atahualpa   151
1580: *Buenos Aires*   The Founders   152
1580: *London*   Drake   153
1582: *Mexico City*   What Color Is a Leper's Skin?   154
1583: *Copacabana*   God's Aymara Mother   154
1583: *Santiago de Chile*   He Was Free for a While   155
1583: *Tlatelolco*   Sahagún   155
1583: *Ácoma*   The Stony Kingdom of Cíbola   156
       Night Chant, a Navajo Poem   157
1586: *Cauri*   The Pestilence   158
1588: *Quito*   Grandson of Atahualpa   158
1588: *Havana*   St. Martial *versus* the Ants   159
1589: *Cuzco*   He Says He Had the Sun   160
1592: *Lima*   An *Auto-da-Fé* in Lima   160
1593: *Guarapari*   Anchieta   161
1596: *London*   Raleigh   162
1597: *Seville*   A Scene in Jail   163
1598: *Potosí*   History of Floriana Rosales, Virtuous Woman of
       Potosí (Abbreviated Version of the Chronicle by
       Bartolomé Arzáns de Orsúa y Vela)   164
       Spanish Couplets to Be Sung and Danced   166
1598: *Panama City*   Times of Sleep and Fate   167
1599: *Quito*   The Afro-Indians of Esmeraldas   167
1599: *Chagres River*   The Wise Don't Talk   168
1599: *La Imperial*   Flaming Arrows   169
1599: *Santa Marta*   They Make War to Make Love   169
1600: *Santa Marta*   They Had a Country   170
       Techniques of Hunting and Fishing   171
1600: *Potosí*   The Eighth Wonder of the World   172
       Prophecies   173
       Ballad of Cuzco   173
1600: *Mexico City*   Carriages   174
1601: *Valladolid*   Quevedo   174
1602: *Recife*   First Expedition Against Palmares   175
1603: *Rome*   The Four Parts of the World   176
1603: *Santiago de Chile*   The Pack   176
1605: *Lima*   The Night of the Last Judgment   177
1607: *Seville*   The Strawberry   178
1608: *Puerto Príncipe*   Silvestre de Balboa   178
1608: *Seville*   Mateo Alemán   179
1608: *Córdoba*   The Inca Garcilaso   180
1609: *Santiago de Chile*   How to Behave at the Table   180
1611: *Yarutini*   The Idol-Exterminator   181
1612: *San Pedro de Omapacha*   The Beaten Beats   182
1613: *London*   Shakespeare   182
1614: *Lima*   Minutes of the Lima Town Council: Theater
       Censorship Is Born   183

1614: *Lima*   Indian Dances Banned in Peru   183
1615: *Lima*   Guamán Poma   184
1616: *Madrid*   Cervantes   185
1616: *Potosí*   Portraits of a Procession   186
1616: *Santiago Papasquiaro*   Is the Masters' God the Slaves' God?   189
1617: *London*   Whiffs of Virginia in the London Fog   190
1618: *Lima*   Small World   192
1618: *Luanda*   Embarcation   193
1618: *Lima*   Too Dark   194
1620: *Madrid*   The Devil's Dances Come from America   195
1622: *Seville*   Rats   197
1624: *Lima*   People for Sale   198
1624: *Lima*   Black Flogs Black   199
1624: *Lima*   The Devil at Work   199
1624: *Seville*   Last Chapter of the "Life of the Scoundrel"   201
1624: *Mexico City*   A River of Anger   202
1625: *Mexico City*   How Do You Like Our City?   203
1625: *Samayac*   Indian Dances Banned in Guatemala   204
1626: *Potosí*   A Wrathful God   205
1628: *Chiapas*   Chocolate and the Bishop   206
1628: *Madrid*   Blue Blood for Sale   207
       Song About the Indies Hand, Sung in Spain   208
1629: *Las Cangrejeras*   Bascuñán   208
1629: *Banks of the Bío-Bío River*   Putapichun   209
1629: *Banks of River Imperial*   Maulicán   210
1629: *Repocura Region*   To Say Good-Bye   211
1630: *Motocintle*   They Won't Betray Their Dead   212
1630: *Lima*   María, Queen of the Boards   213
1631: *Old Guatemala*   A Musical Evening at the Concepción
       Convent   214
       Popular Couplets of the Bashful Lover   216
1633: *Pinola*   Gloria in Excelsis Deo   216
1634: *Madrid*   Who Was Hiding Under Your Wife's Cradle?   217
1636: *Quito*   The Third Half   218
1637: *Mouth of the River Sucre*   Dieguillo   219
1637: *Massachusetts Bay*   "God is an Englishman,"   220
1637: *Mystic Fort*   From the Will of John Underhill, Puritan of
       Connecticut, Concerning a Massacre of Pequot Indians   221
1639: *Lima*   Martín de Porres   222
1639: *San Miguel de Tucumán*   From a Denunciation of the Bishop
       of Tucumán, Sent to the Inquisition Tribunal in Lima   224
1639: *Potosí*   Testament of a Businessman   224
       The Indians Say: 225
1640: *São Salvador de Bahia*   Vieira   225
1641: *Lima*   Avila   226
1641: *Mbororé*   The Missions   226
1641: *Madrid*   Eternity Against History   227

1644: *Jamestown*   Opechancanough   228
1645: *Quito*   Mariana de Jesús   229
1645: *Potosí*   Story of Estefanía, Sinful Woman of Potosí
     (Abbreviation of Chronicle by Bartolomé Arzáns de
     Orsúa y Vela)   230
1647: *Santiago de Chile*   Chilean Indians' Game Banned   232
1648: *Olinda*   Prime Cannon Fodder   232
1649: *Ste. Marie des Hurons*   The Language of Dreams   233
     An Iroquois Story   234
     Song About the Song of the Iroquois   235
1650: *Mexico City*   The Conquerors and the Conquered   236
     From the Náhuatl Song on the Transience of Life   236
1654: *Oaxaca*   Medicine and Witchcraft   237
1655: *San Miguel de Nepantla*   Juana at Four   238
1656: *Santiago de la Vega*   Gage   238
1658: *San Miguel de Nepantla*   Juana at Seven   239
     Juana Dreams   239
1663: *Old Guatemala*   Enter the Printing Press   240
1663: *The Banks of the Paraíba River*   Freedom   240
     Song of Palmares   241
1663: *Serra da Barriga*   Palmares   241
1665: *Madrid*   Charles II   243
1666: *New Amsterdam*   New York   243
1666: *London*   The White Servants   244
1666: *Tortuga Island*   The Pirates' Devotions   244
1667: *Mexico City*   Juana at Sixteen   245
1668: *Tortuga Island*   The Dogs   246
1669: *Town of Gibraltar*   All the Wealth of the World   247
1669: *Maracaibo*   The Broken Padlock   248
1670: *Lima*   "Mourn for us,"   248
1670: *San Juan Atitlán*   An Intruder on the Altar   249
1670: *Masaya*   "The Idiot"   250
1670: *Cuzco*   Old Moley   250
1671: *Panama City*   On Punctuality in Appointments   251
1672: *London*   The White Man's Burden   252
     Mandingo People's Song of the Bird of Love   253
1674: *Port Royal*   Morgan   253
1674: *Potosí*   Claudia the Witch   254
1674: *Yorktown*   The Olympian Steeds   255
1676: *Valley of Connecticut*   The Ax of Battle   255
1676: *Plymouth*   Metacom   256
1677: *Old Road Town*   Death Here, Rebirth There   256
1677: *Pôrto Calvo*   The Captain Promises Lands, Slaves, and
     Honors   257
1678: *Recife*   Ganga Zumba   257
     Yoruba Spell Against the Enemy   258
1680: *Santa Fe, New Mexico*   Red Cross and White Cross   259

1681: *Mexico City*   Juana at Thirty   260
1681: *Mexico City*   Sigüenza y Góngora   260
1682: *Accra*   All Europe Is Selling Human Flesh   261
1682: *Remedios*   By Order of Satan   262
1682: *Remedios*   But They Stay On   263
1682: *Remedios*   By Order of God   264
1688: *Havana*   By Order of the King   265
1691: *Remedios*   Still They Don't Move   265
1691: *Mexico City*   Juana at Forty   266
1691: *Placentia*   Adario, Chief of the Huron Indians, Speaks to
          Baron de Lahontan, French Colonizer in Newfoundland   269
1692: *Salem Village*   The Witches of Salem   269
1692: *Guápulo*   Nationalization of Colonial Art   271
1693: *Mexico City*   Juana at Forty-Two   271
1693: *Santa Fe, New Mexico*   Thirteen Years of Independence   272
          Song of the New Mexican Indians to the Portrait That
             Escapes from the Sand   272
1694: *Macacos*   The Last Expedition Against Palmares   273
          Lament of the Azande People   274
1695: *Serra Dois Irmãos*   Zumbí   275
1695: *São Salvador de Bahia*   The Capital of Brazil   276
1696: *Regla*   Black Virgin, Black Goddess   277
1697: *Cap Français*   Ducasse   277
1699: *Madrid*   Bewitched   278
1699: *Macouba*   A Practical Demonstration   279
1700: *Ouro Prêto*   All Brazil to the South   279
1700: *St. Thomas Island*   The Man Who Makes Things Talk   280
          Bantu People's Song of the Fire   281
1700: *Madrid*   Penumbra of Autumn   282

The Sources   283

Index   295

Preface

I was a wretched history student. History classes were like visits to the waxworks or the Region of the Dead. The past was lifeless, hollow, dumb. They taught us about the past so that we should resign ourselves with drained consciences to the present: not to make history, which was already made, but to accept it. Poor History had stopped breathing: betrayed in academic texts, lied about in classrooms, drowned in dates, they had imprisoned her in museums and buried her, with floral wreaths, beneath statuary bronze and monumental marble.

Perhaps *Memory of Fire* can help give her back breath, liberty, and the word.

Through the centuries, Latin America has been despoiled of gold and silver, nitrates and rubber, copper and oil: its memory has also been usurped. From the outset it has been condemned to amnesia by those who have prevented it from being. Official Latin American history boils down to a military parade of bigwigs in uniforms fresh from the dry-cleaners. I am not a historian. I am a writer who would like to contribute to the rescue of the kidnapped memory of all America, but above all of Latin America, that despised and beloved land: I would like to talk to her, share her secrets, ask her of what difficult clays she was born, from what acts of love and violation she comes.

I don't know to what literary form this voice of voices belongs. *Memory of Fire* is not an anthology, clearly not; but I don't know if it is a novel or essay or epic poem or testament or chronicle or . . . Deciding robs me of no sleep. I do not believe in the frontiers that, according to literature's customs officers, separate the forms.

I did not want to write an objective work—neither wanted to nor could. There is nothing neutral about this historical narration. Unable to distance myself, I take sides: I confess it and am not sorry. However, each fragment of this huge mosaic is based on a solid documentary foundation. What is told here has happened, although I tell it in my style and manner.

This Book

is the first of a trilogy. It is divided into two parts. In one, indigenous creation myths raise the curtain on pre-Columbian America. In the other, the history of America unfolds from the end of the fifteenth century to the year 1700. The second volume of *Memory of Fire* will cover the eighteenth and nineteenth centuries. The third volume will reach up to our times.

The numbers in parentheses at the foot of each text indicate the principal works consulted by the author in search of information and reference points. The documentary sources are listed at the end.

The heading on each historical episode shows the year and place of its occurrence.

Literal transcriptions appear in italics. The author has modernized the spelling of the ancient sources cited.

Acknowledgments

to Jorge Enrique Adoum, Angel Berenguer, Hortensia Campanella, Juan Gelman, Ernesto González Bermejo, Carlos María Gutiérrez, Mercedes López-Baralt, Guy Prim, Fernando Rodríguez, Nicole Rouan, César Salsamendi, Héctor Tizón, José María Valverde, and Federico Vogelius, who read the drafts and made valuable comments and suggestions;

to Federico Alvarez, Ricardo Bada, José Fernando Balbi, Alvaro Barros-Lémez, Borja and José María Calzado, Ernesto Cardenal, Rosa del Olmo, Jorge Ferrer, Eduardo Heras León, Juana Martínez, Augusto Monterroso, Dámaso Murúa, Manuel Pereira, Pedro Saad, Nicole Vaisse, Rosita and Alberto Villagra, Ricardo Willson, and Sheila Wilson-Serfaty, who eased the author's access to the necessary bibliography;

to José Juan Arrom, Ramón Carande, Alvaro Jara, Magnus Mörner, Augusto Roa Bastos, Laurette Sejourné, and Eric R. Wolff, who answered queries;

to the AGKED Foundation of West Germany, which contributed to the realization of this project;

and especially to Helena Villagra, who was its implacable and beloved critic, page by page, as it was realized.

This Book

is dedicated to Grandmother Esther. She knew it before she died.

E. G.

*The dry grass will set fire
to the damp grass*

—African proverb brought
to the Americas by slaves

FIRST VOICES

The Creation

The woman and the man dreamed that God was dreaming about them.

God was singing and clacking his maracas as he dreamed his dream in a cloud of tobacco smoke, feeling happy but shaken by doubt and mystery.

The Makiritare Indians know that if God dreams about eating, he gives fertility and food. If God dreams about life, he is born and gives birth.

In their dream about God's dream, the woman and the man were inside a great shining egg, singing and dancing and kicking up a fuss because they were crazy to be born. In God's dream happiness was stronger than doubt and mystery. So dreaming, God created them with a song:

"I break this egg and the woman is born and the man is born. And together they will live and die. But they will be born again. They will be born and die again and be born again. They will never stop being born, because death is a lie."

(51)*

Time

For the Maya, time was born and had a name when the sky didn't exist and the earth had not yet awakened.

The days set out from the east and started walking.

The first day produced from its entrails the sky and the earth.

The second day made the stairway for the rain to run down.

The cycles of the sea and the land, and the multitude of things, were the work of the third day.

The fourth day willed the earth and the sky to tilt so that they could meet.

The fifth day decided that everyone had to work.

The first light emanated from the sixth day.

In places where there was nothing, the seventh day put soil; the eighth plunged its hands and feet in the soil.

* This number indicates the source consulted by the author, as listed at the end of the book.

The ninth day created the nether worlds; the tenth earmarked for them those who had poison in their souls.

Inside the sun, the eleventh day modeled stone and tree.

It was the twelfth that made the wind. Wind blew, and it was called spirit because there was no death in it.

The thirteenth day moistened the earth and kneaded the mud into a body like ours.

Thus it is remembered in Yucatán.

(208)

The Sun and the Moon

The first sun, the watery sun, was carried off by the flood. All that lived in the world became fish.

The second sun was devoured by tigers.

The third was demolished by a fiery rain that set people ablaze.

The fourth sun, the wind sun, was wiped out by storm. People turned into monkeys and spread throughout the hills.

The gods became thoughtful and got together in Teotihuacán. "Who will take on the job of dawning?"

The Lord of the Shells, famous for his strength and beauty, stepped forward. "I'll be the sun," he said.

"Who else?"

Silence.

Everybody looked at the Small Syphilitic God, the ugliest and wretchedest of all gods, and said, "You."

The Lord of the Shells and the Small Syphilitic God withdrew to the hills that are now the pyramids of the sun and the moon. There they fasted and meditated.

Afterward the gods piled up firewood, made a bonfire, and called to them.

The Small Syphilitic God ran up and threw himself into the flames. He immediately emerged, incandescent, in the sky.

The Lord of the Shells looked at the bonfire with a frown, moved forward, backward, hesitated, made a couple of turns. As he could not decide, they had to push him. After a long delay he rose into the sky. The gods were furious and beat him about the face with a rabbit, again and again, until they extinguished his glow. Thus, the arrogant Lord of the Shells became the moon. The stains on the moon are the scars from that beating.

But the resplendent sun didn't move. The obsidian hawk flew toward the Small Syphilitic God. "Why don't you get going?"

The despised, purulent, humpbacked, crippled one answered, "Because I need blood and power."

This fifth sun, the sun that moves, gave light to the Toltecs and gives it to the Aztecs. He has claws and feeds on human hearts.

(108)

The Clouds

Cloud let fall a drop of rain on the body of a woman. After nine months, she had twins.

When they grew up, they wanted to know who their father was.

"Tomorrow morning early," she said, "look toward the east. You'll see him there, up in the sky like a tower."

Across earth and sky, the twins went in search of their father.

Cloud was incredulous and demanded, "Show me that you are my children."

One of the twins sent a flash of lightning to the earth. The other, a thunderclap. As Cloud was still doubtful, they crossed a flood and came out safe.

Then Cloud made a place for them by his side, among his many brothers and nephews.

(174)

The Wind

When God made the first of the Wawenock Indians, some bits of clay remained on the earth. With these bits Gluskabe made himself.

From on high, God asked in astonishment, "Well, where did *you* come from?"

"I'm miraculous," said Gluskabe. "Nobody made me."

God stood beside him and reached out his hand toward the universe. "Look at my work," he challenged. "If you're miraculous, show me things you have invented."

"I can make wind, if you like." And Gluskabe blew at the top of his lungs.

The wind was born and immediately died.

"I can make wind," Gluskabe admitted shamefacedly, "but I can't make it stay."

Then God blew, so powerfully that Gluskabe fell down and lost all his hair.

(174)

The Rain

In the region of the great northern lakes, a little girl suddenly discovered she was alive. The wonders of the world opened her eyes and she took off at random.

Following the trail of the Menomenee nation's hunters and woodcutters, she came to a big log cabin. There lived ten brothers, birds of the thunder, who offered her shelter and food.

One bad morning, when she was fetching water from the creek, a hairy snake caught her and carried her into the depths of a rocky mountain. The snakes were about to eat her up when the little girl sang.

From far away, the thunder birds heard the call. They attacked the rocky mountain with lightning, rescued the prisoner, and killed the snakes.

The thunder birds left the little girl in the fork of a tree.

"You'll live here," they told her. "We'll come every time you sing."

Whenever the little green tree frog sings from his tree, the thunderclaps gather and it rains upon the world.

(113)

The Rainbow

The forest dwarfs had caught Yobuënahuaboshka in an ambush and cut off his head.

The head bumped its way back to the land of the Cashinahuas.

Although it had learned to jump and balance gracefully, nobody wanted a head without a body.

"Mother, brothers, countrymen," it said with a sigh, "Why do you reject me? Why are you ashamed of me?"

To stop the complaints and get rid of the head, the mother proposed that it should change itself into something, but the head refused to change into what already existed. The head thought, dreamed, figured. The moon didn't exist. The rainbow didn't exist.

It asked for seven little balls of thread of all colors.

It took aim and threw the balls into the sky one after the other. The balls got hooked up beyond the clouds; the threads gently unraveled toward the earth.

Before going up, the head warned: "Whoever doesn't recognize me will be punished. When you see me up there, say: 'There's the high and handsome Yobuënahuaboshka!' "

Then it plaited the seven hanging threads together and climbed up the rope to the sky.

That night a white gash appeared for the first time among the stars. A girl raised her eyes and asked in astonishment: "What's that?"

Immediately a red parrot swooped upon her, gave a sudden twirl, and pricked her between the legs with his sharp-pointed tail. The girl bled. From that moment, women bleed when the moon says so.

Next morning the cord of seven colors blazed in the sky.

A man pointed his finger at it. "Look, look! How extraordinary!" He said it and fell down.

And that was the first time that someone died.

(59)

Day

The crow, which now dominates the totem of the Haida nation, was the grandson of that great divine chief who made the world.

When the crow wept asking for the moon, which hung from the wall of tree trunks, his grandfather gave it to him. The crow threw it into the sky through the chimney opening and started crying again, wishing for the stars. When he got them he spread them around the moon.

Then he wept and hopped about and screamed until his grandfather gave him the carved wooden box in which he kept daylight. The great divine chief forbade him to take the box out of the house. He had decided that the world should live in the dark.

The crow played with the box, pretending to be satisfied, but out of the corner of his eye he watched the guards who were watching him.

When they weren't looking, he fled with the box in his claw. The point of the claw split passing through the chimney, and his feathers were burned and stayed black from then on.

The crow arrived at some islands off the northern coast. He heard human voices and asked for food. They wouldn't give him any. He threatened to break the wooden box.

"I've got daylight in here," he warned, "and if it escapes, the sky will never put out its light. No one will be able to sleep, nor to keep secrets, and everybody will know who is people, who is bird, and who is beast of the forest."

They laughed. The crow broke open the box, and light burst forth in the universe.

(87)

Night

The sun never stopped shining and the Cashinahua Indians didn't know the sweetness of rest.

Badly in need of peace, exhausted by so much light, they borrowed night from the mouse.

It got dark, but the mouse's night was hardly long enough for a bite of food and a smoke in front of the fire. The people had just settled down in their hammocks when morning came.

So then they tried out the tapir's night. With the tapir's night they could sleep soundly and they enjoyed the long and much-deserved rest. But when they awoke, so much time had passed that undergrowth from the hills had invaded their lands and destroyed their houses.

After a big search they settled for the night of the armadillo. They borrowed it from him and never gave it back.

Deprived of night, the armadillo sleeps during the daytime.

(59)

The Stars

By playing the flute love is declared, or the return of the hunters announced. With the strains of the flute, the Waiwai Indians summon their guests. For the Tukanos, the flute weeps; for the Kalinas it talks, because it's the trumpet that shouts.

On the banks of the Negro River, the flute confirms the power of the men. Flutes are sacred and hidden, and any woman who approaches deserves death.

In very remote times, when the women had the sacred flutes, men toted firewood and water and prepared the cassava bread. As the men tell it, the sun got indignant at the sight of women running the world, so he dropped into the forest and fertilized a virgin by slipping leaf juices between her legs. Thus was born Jurupari.

Jurupari stole the sacred flutes and gave them to the men. He taught the men to hide them and defend them and to celebrate ritual feasts without women. He also told them the secrets they were to transmit to their male children.

When Jurupari's mother found where the sacred flutes were hidden, he condemned her to death; and with the bits that remained of her he made the stars of the sky.

(91 and 112)

The Milky Way

No bigger than a worm, he ate the hearts of birds. His father was the best hunter of the Moseten people.

Soon he was a serpent as big as an arm. He kept asking for more hearts. The hunter spent the whole day in the forest killing for his son.

When the serpent got too big for the shack, the forest had been emptied of birds. The father, an expert bowman, brought him jaguars' hearts.

The serpent devoured them and grew. Then there were no more jaguars in the forest.

"I want human hearts," said the serpent.

The hunter emptied his village and its vicinity of people, until one day in a far-off village he was spotted on a tree branch and killed.

Driven by hunger and nostalgia, the serpent went to look for him.

He coiled his body around the guilty village so that no one could escape. While the men let fly all their arrows against this giant ring that had laid siege to them, the serpent rescued his father's body and grew upward. There he can still be seen undulating, bristling with luminous arrows, across the night sky.

(174)

The Evening Star

The moon, stooping mother, asked her son, "I don't know where your father is. Find him and give him word of me."

The son took off in search of the brightest of all lights. He didn't find him at noontime, when the sun of the Tarascan people drinks his wine and dances with his women to the beat of drums.

He didn't find him on the horizons and in the regions of the dead. The sun wasn't in any of his four houses.

The evening star is still hunting his father across the sky. He always arrives too early or too late.

(55)

Language

The First Father of the Guaranís rose in darkness lit by reflections from his own heart and created flames and thin mist. He created love and had nobody to give it to. He created language and had no one to listen to him.

Then he recommended to the gods that they should construct the world and take charge of fire, mist, rain, and wind. And he turned over to them the music and words of the sacred hymn so that they would give life to women and to men.

So love became communion, language took on life, and the First Father redeemed his solitude. Now he accompanies men and women who sing as they go:

We're walking this earth,
We're walking this shining earth.

(40 and 192)

Fire

The nights were icy because the gods had taken away fire. The cold cut into the flesh and words of men. Shivering, they implored with broken voices; the gods turned a deaf ear.

Once, they gave fire back and the men danced for joy, chanting hymns of gratitude. But soon the gods sent rain and hail and put out the bonfires.

The gods spoke and demanded: to deserve fire, men must cut open their chests with obsidian daggers and surrender their hearts.

The Quiché Indians offered the blood of their prisoners and saved themselves from the cold.

The Cakchiquels didn't accept the bargain. The Cakchiquels, cousins of the Quichés and likewise descended from the Mayas, slipped away on feathered feet through the smoke, stole the fire, and hid it in their mountain caves.

(188)

The Forest

In a dream, the Father of the Uitoto Indians glimpsed a shining mist. The mist was alive with mosses and lichens and resonant with winds, birds, and snakes. The Father could catch the mist, and he held it with the thread of his breath. He pulled it out of the dream and mixed it with earth.

Several times he spat on the misty earth. In the foamy mash the forest rose up, trees unfolded their enormous crowns, fruit and flowers erupted. On the moistened earth the grasshopper, the monkey, the tapir, the wild boar, the armadillo, the deer, the jaguar, and the anteater took shape and voice. Into the air soared the golden eagle, the macaw, the vulture, the hummingbird, the white heron, the duck, and the bat.

The wasp arrived in a great hurry. He left toads and men without tails and then rested.

(174)

The Cedar

The First Father conjured the world to birth with the tip of his wand and covered it with down.

Out of the down rose the cedar, the sacred tree from which flows the word. Then the First Father told the Mby'a-guaranís to hollow out the trunk and listen to what it had in it. He said that whoever could listen to the cedar, the casket of words, would know where to establish his hearth. Whoever couldn't would return to despised dust.

(192)

The Guaiacum Tree

A young woman of the Nivakle people was going in search of water when she came upon a leafy tree, Nasuk, the guaiacum, and felt its call. She embraced its firm trunk, pressing her whole body against it, and dug her nails into its bark. The tree bled.

Leaving it, she said, "How I wish, Nasuk, that you were a man!"

And the guaiacum turned into a man and ran after her. When he found her, he showed her his scratched shoulder and stretched out by her side.

(192)

Colors

White were once the feathers of birds, and white the skin of animals.

Blue now are those that bathed in a lake into which no river emptied and from which none was born. Red, those that dipped in the lake of blood shed by a child of the Kadiueu tribe. Earth-color, those that rolled in the mud, and ashen those that sought warmth in extinguished campfires. Green, those that rubbed their bodies in the foliage, white those that stayed still.

(174)

Love

In the Amazonian jungle, the first woman and the first man looked at each other with curiosity. It was odd what they had between their legs.

"Did they cut yours off?" asked the man.

"No," she said, "I've always been like that."

He examined her close up. He scratched his head. There was an open wound there. He said: "Better not eat any cassava or bananas or any fruit that splits when it ripens. I'll cure you. Get in the hammock and rest."

She obeyed. Patiently she swallowed herb teas and let him rub on pomades and unguents. She had to grit her teeth to keep from laughing when he said to her, "Don't worry."

She enjoyed the game, although she was beginning to tire of fasting in a hammock. The memory of fruit made her mouth water.

One evening the man came running through the glade. He jumped with excitement and cried, "I found it!"

He had just seen the male monkey curing the female monkey in the arm of a tree.

"That's how it's done," said the man, approaching the woman.

When the long embrace ended, a dense aroma of flowers and fruit filled the air. From the bodies lying together came unheard of vapors and glowings, and it was all so beautiful that the suns and the gods died of embarrassment.

(59)

The Rivers and the Sea

There was no water in the forest of the Chocos. God knew that the ant had it and asked her for some. She didn't want to listen. God tightened her waist, making it permanently slim, and the ant exuded the water she kept in her belly.

"Now tell me where you got it."

The ant led God to a tree that had nothing unusual about it. Frogs and men with axes worked on it for four days and four nights, but the tree wouldn't fall. A liana kept it from touching the ground.

God ordered the toucan, "Cut it."

The toucan couldn't, and for that was sentenced to eat fruit whole.

The macaw cut the liana with his hard, sharp beak.

When the water tree fell, the sea was born from its trunk and the rivers from its branches.

All of the water was sweet. It was the Devil that kept chucking fistfuls of salt into it.

(174)

The Tides

In olden times, winds blew unremittingly on Vancouver Island. Good weather didn't exist, and there was no low tide.

Men decided to kill the winds. They sent in spies. The winter blackbird failed; so did the sardine. Despite his bad vision and broken arms, it was the sea gull that managed to dodge the hurricanes mounting guard on the house of the winds.

Then men sent in an army of fish led by the sea gull. The fish hurled themselves in a body against the door. The winds, rushing out, trod on them, slipping and falling one after another on the stingray, which pierced them with his tail and devoured them.

The west wind was captured alive. Imprisoned by the men, it promised that it would not blow continuously, that there would be soft air and light breezes, and that the waters would recede a couple of times a day so that shellfish could be gathered at low tide. They spared its life.

The west wind has kept its word.

(114)

Snow

"I want you to fly!" said the master of the house, and the house took off and flew. It moved through the air in the darkness, whistling as it went, until the master ordered, "I want you to stop here!" And the house stopped, suspended in the night and the falling snow.

There was no whale blubber to light the lamps, so the master gathered a fistful of fresh snow, and the snow gave him light.

The house landed in an Iglulik village. Someone came over to greet it, and when he saw the lamp lit with snow, exclaimed, "The snow is burning!" and the lamps went out.

(174)

The Flood

At the foot of the Andes, the heads of communities had a meeting. They smoked and discussed.

The tree of abundance reared its rich crown far above the roof of the world. From below could be seen the high branches bent by the weight of fruit, luxuriant with pineapples, coconuts, papayas, guanábanas, corn, cassava, beans . . .

Mice and birds enjoyed the feast. People, no. The fox went up and down giving himself banquets, sharing with no one. Men who tried to make the climb crashed to the ground.

"What shall we do?"

One of the chiefs conjured up an ax in his sleep. He awoke with a toad in his hand and struck it against the enormous trunk of the tree of abundance, but the little creature merely vomited up its liver.

"That dream was lying."

Another chief, in a dream, begged the Father of all for an ax. The Father warned that the tree would get its own back but sent a red parrot. Grasping the parrot, the chief struck the tree of abundance. A rain of food fell to the ground, and the earth was deafened by the noise. Then the most unusual storm burst from the depths of the rivers. The waters rose, covering the world.

Only one man survived. He swam and swam for days and nights, until he could cling to the top of a palm tree that stuck out of the water.

(174)

The Tortoise

When the Flood receded, the Oaxaca Valley was a quagmire.

A handful of mud took on life and started walking. The tortoise walked very, very slowly. He moved with his head stretched out and his eyes very open, discovering the world that the sun was bringing back to life.

In a place that stank, the tortoise saw the vulture devouring corpses.

"Take me to heaven," he said. "I want to meet God."

The vulture made him keep asking. The corpses were tasty. The tortoise stuck out his head in entreaty, then pulled it back under his shell, unable to stand the stench.

"You who have wings, take me," he begged.

Bored by his persistence, the vulture opened his huge black wings and flew off with the tortoise on his back. They flew through clouds, and the tortoise, his head tucked in, complained, "How disgusting you smell!"

The vulture pretended not to hear.

"What a stink of putrefaction!" the tortoise repeated.

He kept it up until the hideous bird lost patience, leaned over brusquely, and threw him down to earth.

God came down from heaven and put the bits together.

The shell shows where the mends were.

(92)

The Parrot

After the Flood, the forest was green but empty. The survivor shot his arrows through the trees, and the arrows hit nothing but shadows and foliage.

One evening, after much walking and searching, the survivor returned to his refuge and found roast meat and cassava cakes. The same happened the next day, and the next. From desperate hunger and loneliness, he turned to wondering whom he had to thank for his good fortune. In the morning, he hid and waited.

Two parrots appeared out of the sky. No sooner had they alit on the ground than they turned into women. They lit a fire and started cooking.

The only man chose the one with the longest hair and the finest and brightest feathers. The other woman, scorned, flew off.

The Mayna Indians, descendants of this couple, curse their ancestor when their women turn lazy or grouchy. They say it's all his fault because he chose the useless one. The other was mother and father of all the parrots living in the forest.

(191)

The Hummingbird

At dawn he greets the sun. Night falls and he's still at work. He goes buzzing from branch to branch, from flower to flower, quick and necessary like light itself. At times he's doubtful and pauses suspended in the air; at times he flies backward as no one else can. At times he's a little drunk from all the honey he has sucked. As he flies, he emits flashes of color.

He brings messages from the gods, becomes a bolt of lightning to carry out their vengeance, blows prophecies in the ears of the soothsayers. When a Guaraní child dies, he rescues its soul, which lies in the calyx of a flower, and takes it in his long needle beak to the Land Without Evil. He has known the way there since the beginning of time. Before the world was born, he already existed; he freshened the mouth of the First Father with drops of dew and assuaged his hunger with the nectar of flowers.

He led the long pilgrimage of the Toltecs to the sacred city
of Tula before bringing the warmth of the sun to the Aztecs.

As captain of the Chontals, he glides over the camps of the
enemy, assesses their strength, dive-bombs them, and kills their
chief in his sleep. As the sun of the Kekchis, he flies to the moon,
takes her by surprise in her chamber, and makes love to her.

His body is the size of an almond. He is born from an egg no
bigger than a bean, in a nest that fits inside a nut. He sleeps with
a little leaf as covering.

(40, 206, and 210)

The Night Bird (Urutaú)

"I am the daughter of misfortune," said the chief's daughter Ñeambiú, when her father forbade her love for a man of an enemy
community.

She said it and fled.

After a while they found her in the Iguazú Mountains. They
found a statue. Ñeambiú looked without seeing; her mouth was
still and her heart asleep.

The chief sent for the one who deciphers mysteries and heals
sicknesses. The whole community came out to witness the resurrection.

The shaman sought advice from maté tea and cassava wine.
He went up to Ñeambiú and lied right into her ear:

"The man you love has just died."

Ñeambiú's scream turned all the people into weeping willows.
She flew off, turned into a bird.

The screams of the urutaú, which shake the mountains at
nighttime, can be heard more than half a league away. It's difficult
to see the urutaú, impossible to hunt him. No one can catch up
with the phantom bird.

(86)

The Ovenbird

When he reached the age for the three manhood tests, this boy ran and swam better than anyone and spent nine days without food, stretched out by leather thongs, without moving or complaining. During the tests he heard a woman's voice singing to him from far away, which helped him to endure.

The chief of the community decided that the boy should marry his daughter, but he took flight and got lost in the woods of the Paraguay River, searching for the singer.

There you still meet the ovenbird. He flaps his wings powerfully and utters glad sounds when he thinks the sought-after voice is flying his way. Waiting for the one who doesn't come, he has built a house of mud, with the door open to the northern breeze, in a place secure from lightning.

Everyone respects him. He who kills the ovenbird or breaks his house draws the storm upon himself.

(144)

The Crow

The lakes were dry, the riverbeds empty. The Takelma Indians, dying of thirst, sent the male and the female crow to look for water.

The male crow got tired right away. He urinated in a bowl and said that was the water he was bringing from a far place.

The female kept on flying. She returned much later with a load of fresh water and saved the Takelma people from the drought.

As a punishment the male crow was sentenced to suffer thirst through the summers. Unable to moisten his throat, he talks in a very raucous voice while the weather is hot.

(114)

The Condor

Cauillaca was weaving cloth in the shade of a tree, and overhead soared Coniraya, who had turned into a bird. The girl paid absolutely no attention to his warblings and flutterings.

Coniraya knew that other, older, more important gods burned with desire for Cauillaca. However, he sent his seed down to her from up there, in the form of a ripe fruit. When she saw the fleshy fruit at her feet, she picked it up and bit into it. She felt a strange pleasure and became pregnant.

Afterward he turned into a person—a ragged, sad sack of a man—and pursued her all over Peru. Cauillaca fled toward the ocean with her little son on her back, and behind trekked Coniraya, furiously hunting her.

He made inquiries of a skunk. The skunk, noticing his bleeding feet and general distress, answered, "Idiot. Can't you see there's no point in following her?"

So Coniraya cursed him, "You shall wander about by night, leaving a bad smell wherever you go. When you die, no one will pick you up off the ground."

But the condor put spirit into the hunter. "Run!" he called to him. "Run and you'll catch her!"

So Coniraya blessed him, "You shall fly wherever you want. There won't be any place in the sky or on earth where you can't go. No one will get to where you build your nest. You'll never lack for food; and he who kills you will die."

After climbing a lot of mountains, Coniraya reached the coast. He was too late. The girl and her son were already an island, carved in rock, out in midocean.

(100)

The Jaguar

The jaguar was out hunting with bow and arrows when he met a shadow. He tried to catch it and couldn't. He lifted his head. The master of the shadow was young Botoque of the Kayapó tribe, who was near death from hunger on top of a rock.

Botoque had no strength to move and could only just stammer a few words. The jaguar lowered his bow and invited him to a roast meat dinner in his house. Although the lad didn't know what "roast" meant, he accepted and dropped on to the hunter's back.

"You're carrying some stranger's child," said the jaguar's wife.

"He's mine now," said the jaguar.

Botoque saw fire for the first time. He got acquainted with the stone oven and the smell of roast tapir and venison. He learned that fire illuminates and warms. The jaguar gave him a bow and arrows and taught him to defend himself.

One day Botoque fled. He had killed the jaguar's wife.

He ran desperately for a long time and didn't stop till he reached his village. There he told his story and displayed the secrets: the new weapon and the roast meat. The Kayapós decided to appropriate fire, and he led them to the remote house. Nothing was left to the jaguar of the fire except its reflection shining in his eyes.

Ever since then, the jaguar has hated men. For hunting, all he has are his fangs and claws, and he eats the flesh of his victims raw.

(111)

The Bear

The day animals and the night animals got together to decide what they would do about the sun, which then came and went whenever it liked. The animals resolved to leave the problem to fate. The winning group in the game of riddles would decide how long the world would have sunlight in the future.

They were still talking when the sun approached, intrigued by the discussion. The sun came so close that the night animals had to scatter. The bear was a victim of the general flurry. He put his right foot into his left moccasin and his left foot into his right moccasin, and took off on the run as best he could.

According to the Comanches, since then the bear walks with a lurch.

(132)

The Crocodile

The sun of the Macusi people was worried. Every day there were fewer fish in their ponds.

He put the crocodile in charge of security. The ponds got emptier. The crocodile, security guard and thief, invented a good story about invisible assailants, but the sun didn't believe it, took a machete, and left the crocodile's body all crisscrossed with cuts.

To calm him down, the crocodile offered his beautiful daughter in marriage.

"I'll be expecting her," said the sun.

As the crocodile had no daughter, he sculpted a woman in the trunk of a wild plum tree.

"Here she is," he said, and plunged into the water, looking out of the corner of his eye, the way he always looks.

It was the woodpecker who saved his life. Before the sun arrived, the woodpecker pecked at the wooden girl below the belly. Thus she, who was incomplete, was open for the sun to enter.

(112)

The Armadillo

A big fiesta was announced on Lake Titicaca, and the armadillo, who was a very superior creature, wanted to dazzle everybody.

Long beforehand, he set to weaving a cloak of such elegance that it would knock all eyes out.

The fox noticed him at work. "Are you in a bad mood?"

"Don't distract me. I'm busy."

"What's that for?"

The armadillo explained.

"Ah," said the fox, savoring the words, "for the fiesta tonight?"

"What do you mean, tonight?"

The armadillo's heart sank. He had never been more sure of his time calculations. "And me with my cloak only half finished!"

While the fox took off with a smothered laugh, the armadillo finished the cloak in a hurry. As time was flying, he had to use coarser threads, and the weave ended up too big. For this reason the armadillo's shell is tight-warped around the neck and very open at the back.

(174)

The Rabbit

The rabbit wanted to grow.

God promised to increase his size if he would bring him the skins of a tiger, of a monkey, of a lizard, and of a snake.

The rabbit went to visit the tiger. "God has let me into a secret," he said confidentially.

The tiger wanted to know it, and the rabbit announced an impending hurricane. "I'll save myself because I'm small. I'll hide in some hole. But what'll you do? The hurricane won't spare you."

A tear rolled down between the tiger's mustaches.

"I can think of only one way to save you," said the rabbit. "We'll look for a tree with a very strong trunk. I'll tie you to the trunk by the neck and paws, and the hurricane won't carry you off."

The grateful tiger let himself be tied. Then the rabbit killed him with one blow, stripped him, and went on his way into the woods of the Zapotec country.

He stopped under a tree in which a monkey was eating. Taking a knife, the rabbit began striking his own neck with the blunt side of it. With each blow of the knife, a chuckle. After much hitting and chuckling, he left the knife on the ground and hopped away.

He hid among the branches, on the watch. The monkey soon climbed down. He examined the object that made one laugh, and he scratched his head. He seized the knife and at the first blow fell with his throat cut.

Two skins to go. The rabbit invited the lizard to play ball. The ball was of stone. He hit the lizard at the base of the tail and left him dead.

Near the snake, the rabbit pretended to be asleep. Just as the snake was tensing up, before it could jump, the rabbit plunged his claws into its eyes.

He went to the sky with the four skins.

"Now make me grow," he demanded.

And God thought, "The rabbit is so small, yet he did all this. If I make him bigger, what won't he do? If the rabbit were big, maybe I wouldn't be God."

The rabbit waited. God came up softly, stroked his back, and suddenly caught him by the ears, whirled him about, and threw him to the ground.

Since then the rabbit has had big ears, short front feet from having stretching them out to break his fall, and pink eyes from panic.

(92)

The Snake

God said to him, "Three canoes will pass down the river. In two of them, death will be traveling. If you guess which one is without death, I'll liberate you from the shortness of life."

The snake let pass the first canoe, which was laden with baskets of putrid meat. Nor did he pay attention to the second, which was full of people. The third looked empty, but when it arrived, he welcomed it.

For this reason the snake is immortal in the region of the Shipaiás.

Every time he begins to get old, God presents him with a new skin.

(111)

The Frog

From a cave in Haiti came the first Taíno Indians.

The sun had no mercy on them. Suddenly, without warning, he would kidnap and transform them. He turned the one who mounted guard by night into a stone; of the fisherman he made trees, and the one who went out for herbs he caught on the road and turned into a bird that sings in the morning.

One of the men fled from the sun. When he took off, he took all the women with him.

There is no laughter in the song of the little frogs in the Caribbean islands. They are the Taíno children of those days. They say, "Toa, toa," which is their way of calling to their mothers.

(126 and 168)

The Bat

When time was yet in the cradle, there was no uglier creature in the world than the bat.

The bat went up to heaven to look for God. He didn't say, "I'm bored with being hideous. Give me colored feathers." No. He said, "Please give me feathers, I'm dying of cold."

But God had not a single feather left over.

"Each bird will give you a feather," he decided.

Thus the bat got the white feather of the dove and the green one of the parrot, the iridescent one of the hummingbird, the pink one of the flamingo, the red of the cardinal's tuft and the blue of the kingfisher's back, the clayey one of the eagle's wing, and the sun feather that burns in the breast of the toucan.

The bat, luxuriant with colors and softness, moved between earth and clouds. Wherever he went, the air became pleasant and the birds dumb with admiration. According to the Zapotec peoples, the rainbow was born of the echo of his flight.

Vanity puffed out his chest. He acquired a disdainful look and made insulting remarks.

The birds called a meeting. Together they flew up to God.

"The bat makes fun of us," they complained. "And what's more, we feel cold for lack of the feathers he took."

Next day, when the bat shook his feathers in full flight, he suddenly became naked. A rain of feathers fell to earth.

He is still searching for them. Blind and ugly, enemy of the light, he lives hidden in caves. He goes out in pursuit of the lost feathers after night has fallen and flies very fast, never stopping because it shames him to be seen.

(92)

Mosquitos

There were many dead in the Nootkas village. In each dead body there was a hole through which blood had been stolen.

The murderer, a child who was already killing before he learned to walk, received his sentence roaring with laughter. They pierced him with lances and he laughingly picked them out of his body like thorns.

"I'll teach you to kill me," said the child.

He suggested to his executioners that they should light a big bonfire and throw him into it.

His ashes scattered through the air, anxious to do harm, and thus the first mosquitos started to fly.

(174)

Honey

Honey was in flight from his two sisters-in-law. He had thrown them out of his hammock several times.

They came after him night and day. They saw him and it made their mouths water. Only in dreams did they succeed in touching him, licking him, eating him.

Their spite kept growing. One morning when the sisters-in-law were bathing, they came upon Honey on the riverbank. They ran and splashed him. Once wet, Honey dissolved.

In the Gulf of Paria it's not easy to find the lost honey. You have to climb the trees, ax in hand, open up the trunks, and do a lot of rummaging. The rare honey is eaten with pleasure and with fear, because sometimes it kills.

(112)

Seeds

Pachacamac, who was a son of the sun, made a man and a woman in the dunes of Lurín.

There was nothing to eat, and the man died of hunger.

When the woman was bent over searching for roots, the sun entered her and made a child.

Jealous, Pachacamac caught the newborn baby and chopped it to pieces. But suddenly he repented, or was scared of the anger of his father, the sun, and scattered about the world the pieces of his murdered brother.

From the teeth of the dead baby, corn grew; from the ribs and bones, cassava. The blood made the land fertile, and fruit trees and shade trees rose from the sown flesh.

Thus the women and men born on these shores, where it never rains, find food.

(57)

Corn

The gods made the first Maya-Quichés out of clay. Few survived. They were soft, lacking strength; they fell apart before they could walk.

Then the gods tried wood. The wooden dolls talked and walked but were dry; they had no blood nor substance, no memory and no purpose. They didn't know how to talk to the gods, or couldn't think of anything to say to them.

Then the gods made mothers and fathers out of corn. They molded their flesh with yellow corn and white corn.

The women and men of corn saw as much as the gods. Their glance ranged over the whole world.

The gods breathed on them and left their eyes forever clouded, because they didn't want people to see over the horizon.

(188)

Tobacco

The Cariri Indians had implored the Grandfather to let them try the flesh of wild pigs, which didn't yet exist. The Grandfather, architect of the Universe, kidnapped the little children of the Cariris and turned them into wild pigs. He created a big tree so that they could escape into the sky.

The people pursued the pigs up the tree from branch to branch and managed to kill a few. The Grandfather ordered the ants to bring down the tree. When it fell, the people suffered broken bones. Ever since that great fall, we all have divided bones and so are able to bend our fingers and legs or tilt our bodies.

With the dead boars a great banquet was made in the village.

The people besought the Grandfather to come down from the sky, where he was minding the children saved from the hunt, but he preferred to stay up there.

The Grandfather sent tobacco to take his place among men. Smoking, the people talked with God.

(111)

Maté

The moon was simply dying to tread the earth. She wanted to sample the fruit and to bathe in some river.

Thanks to the clouds, she was able to come down. From sunset until dawn, clouds covered the sky so that no one could see the moon was missing.

Nighttime on the earth was marvelous. The moon strolled through the forest of the high Paraná, caught mysterious aromas and flavors, and had a long swim in the river. Twice an old peasant rescued her. When the jaguar was about to sink his teeth into the moon's neck, the old man cut the beast's throat with his knife; and when the moon got hungry, he took her to his house. "We offer you our poverty," said the peasant's wife, and gave her some corn tortillas.

On the next night the moon looked down from the sky at her friends' house. The old peasant had built his hut in a forest clearing very far from the villages. He lived there like an exile with his wife and daughter.

The moon found that the house had nothing left in it to eat. The last corn tortillas had been for her. Then she turned on her brightest light and asked the clouds to shed a very special drizzle around the hut.

In the morning some unknown trees had sprung up there. Amid their dark green leaves appeared white flowers.

The old peasant's daughter never died. She is the queen of the maté and goes about the world offering it to others. The tea of the maté awakens sleepers, activates the lazy, and makes brothers and sisters of people who don't know each other.

(86 and 144)

Cassava

No man had touched her, but a boy-child grew in the belly of the chief's daughter.

They called him Mani. A few days after birth he was already running and talking. From the forest's farthest corners people came to meet the prodigious Mani.

Mani caught no disease, but on reaching the age of one, he said, "I'm going to die," and he died.

A little time passed, and on Mani's grave sprouted a plant never before seen, which the mother watered every morning. The plant grew, flowered, and gave fruit. The birds that picked at it flew strangely, fluttering in mad spirals and singing like crazy.

One day the ground where Mani lay split open. The chief thrust his hand in and pulled out a big, fleshy root. He grated it with a stone, made a dough, wrung it out, and with the warmth of the fire cooked bread for everyone.

They called the root *mani oca*, "house of Mani," and manioc is its name in the Amazon basin and other places.

(174)

The Potato

A chief on Chiloé Island, a place populated by sea gulls, wanted to make love like the gods.

When pairs of gods embraced, the earth shook and tidal waves were set moving. That much was known, but no one had seen them.

Anxious to surprise them, the chief swam out to the forbidden isle. All he got to see was a giant lizard, with its mouth wide open and full of foam and an outsized tongue that gave off fire at the tip.

The gods buried the indiscreet chief in the ground and condemned him to be eaten by the others. As punishment for his curiosity, they covered his body with blind eyes.

(178)

The Kitchen

In the center of the wood, a woman of the Tillamook people came upon a cabin that was throwing out smoke. Curious, she approached and went in.

Fire burned amid stones in the center of the cabin. From the ceiling hung a number of salmons. One fell on her head. The woman picked it up and hung it back in place. Once again the fish fell and hit her on the head. Again she hung it back up, and again it fell.

The woman threw on the fire the roots she had gathered to eat. The fire burned them up in a flash. Furious, she struck the fire several times with the poker, so violently that the fire was almost out when the master of the house arrived and stayed her arm.

The mysterious man revived the flames, sat down beside the woman, and explained to her, "You didn't understand."

By striking the flames and dispersing the embers she had been on the point of blinding the fire, and that was a punishment it didn't deserve. The fire had eaten up the roots because it thought the woman was offering them to it. And before that, it was the fire that had caused the salmon to fall several times on the woman's head, not to hurt her but to tell her that she could cook it.

"Cook it? What's that?"

So the master of the house taught the woman how to talk to the fire, to roast the fish on the embers, and eat it with relish.

(114)

Music

While the spirit Bopé-joku whistled a melody, corn rose out of the ground, unstoppable, luminous, and offered giant ears swollen with grains.

A woman was picking them and doing it wrong. Tugging hard at an ear, she injured it. The ear took revenge by wounding her hand. The woman insulted Bopé-joku and cursed his whistling.

When Bopé-joku closed his lips, the corn withered and dried up. The happy whistlings that made the cornfields bloom and gave them vigor and beauty were heard no more. From then on the Bororo people cultivated corn with pain and effort and reaped wretched crops.

Spirits express themselves by whistling. When the stars come out at night, that's how the spirits greet them. Each star responds to a note, which is its name.

(112)

Death

The first of the Modoc Indians, Kumokums, built a village on the banks of a river. Although it left the bears plenty of room to curl up and sleep, the deer complained that it was very cold and there wasn't enough grass.

Kumokums built another village far from there and decided to spend half of every year in each. For this he divided the year into two parts, six moons of summer and six of winter, and the remaining moon was dedicated to moving.

Life between the two villages was as happy as could be, and births multiplied amazingly; but people who died refused to get out, and the population got so big that there was no way to feed it.

Then Kumokums decided to throw out the dead people. He knew that the chief of the land of the dead was a great man and didn't mistreat anybody.

Soon afterward Kumokums's small daughter died. She died and left the country of the Modocs, as her father had ordered.

In despair, Kumokums consulted the porcupine.

"You made the decision," said the porcupine, "and now you must take the consequences like anyone else."

But Kumokums journeyed to the far-off land of the dead and claimed his daughter.

"Now your daughter is my daughter," said the big skeleton in charge there. "She has no flesh or blood. What can she do in your country?"

"I want her anyway," said Kumokums.

The chief of the land of the dead thought for a long time.

"Take her," he yielded, and warned, "She'll walk behind you. On approaching the country of the living, flesh will return to cover her bones. But you may not turn around till you arrive. Understand? I give you this chance."

Kumokums set out. The daughter walked behind him.

Several times he touched her hand, which was more fleshy and warm each time, and still he didn't look back. But when the green woods appeared on the horizon he couldn't stand the strain and turned his head. A handful of bones crumbled before his eyes.

(132)

Resurrection

After five days it was the custom for the dead to return to Peru. They drank a glass of chicha and said, "Now I'm eternal."

There were too many people in the world. Crops were sown at the bottom of precipices and on the edge of abysses, but even so, the food wouldn't go around.

Then a man died in Huarochirí.

The whole community gathered on the fifth day to receive him. They waited for him from morning till well after nightfall. The hot dishes got cold, and sleep began closing eyelids. The dead man didn't come.

He came the next day. Everyone was furious. The one who boiled most with indignation was his wife, who yelled, "You good-for-nothing! Always the same good-for-nothing! All the dead are punctual except you!"

The resurrected one stammered some excuse, but the woman threw a corncob at his head and left him stretched out on the floor. Then the soul left the body and flew off, a quick, buzzing insect, never to return.

Since that time no dead person has come back to mix with the living and compete for their food.

(14)

Magic

An extremely old Tukuna woman chastised some young girls who had denied her food. During the night she tore the bones out of their legs and devoured the marrow, so the girls could never walk again.

In her infancy, soon after birth, the old woman had received from a frog the powers of healing and vengeance. The frog had taught her to cure and kill, to hear unhearable voices and see unseeable colors. She learned to defend herself before she learned to talk. Before she could walk she already knew how to be where she wasn't, because the shafts of love and hate instantly pierce the densest jungles and deepest rivers.

When the Tukunas cut off her head, the old woman collected
her own blood in her hands and blew it toward the sun.

"My soul enters you, too!" she shouted.

Since then anyone who kills receives in his body, without
wanting or knowing it, the soul of his victim.

(112)

Laughter

The bat, hanging from a branch by his feet, noticed a Kayapó
warrior leaning over the stream.

He wanted to be his friend.

He dropped on the warrior and embraced him. As he didn't
know the Kayapó language, he talked to him with his hands. The
bat's caresses drew from the man the first laugh. The more he
laughed, the weaker he felt. He laughed so much that finally he
lost all his strength and fell in a faint.

When the villagers learned about it, they were furious. The
warriors burned a heap of dry leaves in the bats' cave and blocked
up the entrance.

Afterward they had a discussion. The warriors resolved that
laughter should be used only by women and children.

(111)

Fear

These incredible bodies called to them, but the Nivakle men dared
not enter. They had seen the women eat: they swallowed the flesh
of fish with the upper mouth, but chewed it first with the lower
mouth. Between their legs they had teeth.

So the men lit bonfires, called to the women, and sang and
danced for them.

The women sat around in a circle with their legs crossed.

The men danced all through the night. They undulated, turned,

and flew like smoke and birds. When dawn came they fell fainting
to the ground. The women gently lifted them and gave them water
to drink.

Where they had been sitting, the ground was all littered with
teeth.

(192)

Authority

In remote times women sat in the bow of the canoe and men in
the stern. It was the women who hunted and fished. They left the
villages and returned when they could or wanted. The men built
the huts, prepared the meals, kept the fires burning against the
cold, minded the children, and tanned skins for clothes.

Such was life for the Ona and Yagan Indians in Tierra del
Fuego, until one day the men killed all the women and put on the
masks that the women had invented to scare them.

Only newly born girls were spared extermination. While they
grew up, the murderers kept repeating to them that serving men
was their destiny. They believed it. Their daughters believed it,
too, likewise the daughters of their daughters.

(91 and 178)

Power

In the lands where the Juruá River is born, Old Meanie was lord
of the corn. He gave out the grains roasted, so that no one could
plant them.

The lizard succeeded in stealing a raw grain from him. Old
Meanie caught her and ripped off her jaw and fingers and toes;
but she had managed to conceal the grain behind her back molar.
The lizard afterward spat out the raw grain on the common land.
Her jaw was too big and her fingers and toes too long to be com-
pletely torn off.

Old Meanie was also lord of the fire. The parrot sneaked up

close to it and started screeching her lungs out. Old Meanie threw at her everything that was handy, and the little parrot dodged the projectiles until she saw a lighted stick flying her way. Then she picked it up with her beak, which was an enormous as a toucan's, and fled. A trail of sparks followed her. The embers, fanned by the wind, burned her beak, but she had already reached the trees when Old Meanie beat his drum and let loose a rainstorm.

The parrot managed to leave the burning stick in the hollow of a tree under the care of the other birds and flew back into the downpour. The water relieved her burns, but her beak, shortened and curved, still shows a white scar from the fire.

The birds protected the stolen fire with their bodies.

(59)

War

At dawn, the trumpet call announced from the mountain that it was time for crossbows and blowguns.

At nightfall, nothing remained of the village except smoke.

A man lay among the dead without moving. He smeared his body with blood and waited. He was the only survivor of the Palawiyang people.

When the enemy moved off, that man got up. He contemplated his destroyed world. He walked among the people who had shared hunger and food with him. He sought in vain some person or thing that hadn't been wiped out. The terrifying silence dazed him. The smell of fire and blood sickened him. He felt disgusted to be alive, and he threw himself back down among his own.

With the first light came the vultures. There was nothing left in that man except fog and a yearning to sleep and let himself be devoured.

But the condor's daughter opened a path through the circling birds of prey. She beat her wings hard and dived. He grabbed onto her feet, and the condor's daughter took him far away.

(54)

Parties

An Inuit, bow in hand, was out hunting reindeer when an eagle unexpectedly appeared behind him.

"I killed your two brothers," said the eagle. "If you want to save yourself you must give a party in your village so everyone can sing and dance."

"A party? Sing, what's that? What's dance?"

"Come with me."

The eagle showed him a party. There was a lot of good food and drink. The drum beat as hard as the heart of the eagle's old mother, its rhythm guiding her children from her house across the vast expanses of ice and mountain. Wolves, foxes, and other guests danced and sang until sunup.

The hunter returned to his village.

A long time afterward he learned that the eagle's old mother and all the oldsters of the eagle world were strong and handsome and swift. Human beings had finally learned to sing and dance, and had sent them, from afar, from their own parties, gaieties that warmed the blood.

(174)

Conscience

When the waters of the Orinoco lowered, canoes brought the Caribs with their battle-axes.

No one had a chance against the sons of the jaguar. They leveled villages and made flutes from their victims' bones. They feared nobody. The only thing that struck panic into them was a phantom born in their own hearts.

The phantom lay in wait for them behind the trees. He broke their bridges and placed in their paths tangled lianas. He traveled by night. To throw them off the track, he walked backward. He was on the slope from which rocks broke off, in the mud that sank beneath their feet, in the leaf of the poisonous plant, in the touch of the spider. He knocked them down with a breath, injected fever through their ears, and robbed them of shade.

He was not pain, but he hurt. He was not death, but he killed. His name was Kanaima, and he was born among the conquerors to avenge the conquered.

(54)

The Sacred City

Wiracocha, who had fled from the darkness, ordered the sun to send a daughter and a son to earth to light the way for the blind.

The sun's children arrived on the banks of Lake Titicaca and set out through the Andean ravines. They carried a golden staff. Wherever it sank in at the first blow, they would there found a new kingdom. From the throne they would act like their father, who gives light, clarity, and warmth, sheds rain and dew, promotes harvests, multiplies flocks, and never lets a day pass without visiting the world.

They tried everywhere to stick in the golden staff, but the earth bounced it back. They scaled heights and crossed cataracts and plateaus. Whatever their feet touched was transformed; arid ground became fertile, swamps dried, and rivers returned to their beds. At dawn, wild geese escorted them; in the evening, condors.

Finally, beside Mount Wanakauri, the sun's children stuck in the staff. When the earth swallowed it, a rainbow rose in the sky.

Then the first of the Incas said to his sister and wife:

"Let us call the people together."

Between the mountains and the prairie, the valley was covered with scrub. No one had a house. The people lived in holes or in the shelter of rocks, eating roots, and didn't know how to weave cotton or wool to keep out the cold.

Everyone followed the sun's children. Everyone believed in them. Everyone knew, by the brilliance of their words and eyes, that the sun's children were not lying, and accompanied them to the place where the great city of Cuzco, still unborn, awaited them.

(76)

Pilgrims

The Maya-Quichés came from the east.

When they first reached the new lands, carrying their gods on their backs, they were scared that there would be no dawn. They had left happiness back in Tulán and arrived out of breath after a long and painful trek. They waited at the edge of the Izmachí forest, silent, huddled together, without anybody sitting down or stretching out to rest. But time passed and it went on being dark.

At last the morning star appeared in the sky.

The Quichés hugged each other and danced; and afterward, says the sacred book, *the sun rose like a man.*

Since then the Quichés gather at the end of each night to greet the morning star and watch the birth of the sun. When the sun is first about to peep out, they say:

"That's where we come from."

(188)

The Promised Land

Sleepless, naked, and battered, they journeyed night and day for more than two centuries. They went in search of the place where the land extends between canes and sedges.

Several times they got lost, scattered, and joined up again. They were buffeted by the winds and dragged themselves ahead lashed together, bumping and pushing each other. They fell from hunger and got up and fell again and got up again. In the volcanic region where no grass grows, they ate snake meat.

They carried the banner and the cloak of the god who had spoken to the priests in sleep and promised a kingdom of gold and quetzal feathers. *You shall subject all the peoples and cities from sea to sea,* the god had announced, *and not by witchcraft but by valor of the heart and strength of the arm.*

When they approached the luminous lake under the noonday sun, for the first time the Aztecs wept. There was the little island of clay: on the nopal cactus, higher than the rushes and wild grasses, the eagle spread his wings.

Seeing them come, the eagle lowered his head. These outcasts, massed on the edge of the lake, filthy, trembling, were the chosen, those who in remote times had been born out of the mouths of the gods.

Huitzilopochtli welcomed them. *"This is the place of our rest and our greatness,"* his voice resounded. *"I order that the city which will be queen of all others be called Tenochtitlán. This is Mexico!"*

(60 and 210)

Dangers

He who made the sun and the moon warned the Taínos to watch out for the dead.

In the daytime the dead hid themselves and ate guavas, but at night they went out for a stroll and challenged the living. Dead men offered duels and dead women, love. In the duels they vanished at will; and at the climax of love the lover found himself with nothing in his arms. Before accepting a duel with a man or lying down with a woman, one should feel the belly with one's hand, because the dead have no navels.

The lord of the sky also warned the Taínos to watch out even more for people with clothes on.

Chief Cáicihu fasted for a week and was worthy of his words. *Brief shall be the enjoyment of life,* announced the invisible one, he who has a mother but no beginning. *Men wearing clothes shall come, dominate, and kill.*

(168)

The Spider Web

Waterdrinker, priest of the Sioux, dreamed that outlandish creatures were weaving a huge spider web around his people. He awoke knowing that was how it was going to be and said to his people,

*When this happens, you shall live in square gray houses, in a barren
land, and beside those square gray houses you shall starve.*

(152)

The Prophet

Stretched out on his mat, the priest-jaguar of Yucatán listened to
the gods' message. They spoke to him through the roof, sitting
astride of his house, in a language that no one else knew.

Chilam Balam, he who was the mouth of the gods, remembered what had not yet happened:

*"Scattered through the world shall be the women who sing
and the men who sing and all who sing . . . No one will escape,
no one will be saved . . . There will be much misery in the years
of the rule of greed. Men will turn into slaves. Sad will be the face
of the sun . . . The world will be depopulated, it will become small
and humiliated . . ."*

(25)

OLD NEW WORLD

1492: *The Ocean Sea*

The Sun Route to the Indies

The breezes are sweet and soft, as in spring in Seville, and the sea is like a Guadalquivir river, but the swell no sooner rises than they get seasick and vomit, jammed into their fo'c'sles, the men who in three patched-up little ships cleave the unknown sea, the sea without a frame. Men, little drops in the wind. And if the sea doesn't love them? Night falls on the caravels. Whither will the wind toss them? A dorado, chasing a flying fish, jumps on board and the panic grows. The crew don't appreciate the savory aroma of the slightly choppy sea, nor do they listen to the din of the sea gulls and gannets that come from the west. That horizon: does the abyss begin there? Does the sea end?

Feverish eyes of mariners weatherbeaten in a thousand voyages, burning eyes of jailbirds yanked from Andalusian prisons and embarked by force: these eyes see no prophetic reflections of gold and silver in the foam of the waves, nor in the country and river birds that keep flying over the ships, nor in the green rushes and branches thick with shells that drift in the sargassos. The bottom of the abyss—is that where hell starts to burn? Into what kind of jaws will the trade winds hurl these little men? They gaze at the stars, seeking God, but the sky is as inscrutable as this never-navigated sea. They hear its roar, mother sea, the hoarse voice answering the wind with phrases of eternal condemnation, mysterious drums resounding in the depths. They cross themselves and want to pray and stammer: "Tonight we'll fall off the world, tonight we'll fall off the world."

(52)

1492: *Guanahaní*

Columbus

He falls on his knees, weeps, kisses the earth. He steps forward, staggering because for more than a month he has hardly slept, and beheads some shrubs with his sword.

Then he raises the flag. On one knee, eyes lifted to heaven, he pronounces three times the names of Isabella and Ferdinand. Beside him the scribe Rodrigo de Escobedo, a man slow of pen, draws up the document.

From today, everything belongs to those remote monarchs: the coral sea, the beaches, the rocks all green with moss, the woods, the parrots, and these laurel-skinned people who don't yet know about clothes, sin, or money and gaze dazedly at the scene.

Luis de Torres translates Christopher Columbus's questions into Hebrew: "Do you know the kingdom of the Great Khan? Where does the gold you have in your noses and ears come from?"

The naked men stare at him with open mouths, and the interpreter tries out his small stock of Chaldean: "Gold? Temples? Palaces? King of kings? Gold?"

Then he tries his Arabic, the little he knows of it: "Japan? China? Gold?"

The interpreter apologizes to Columbus in the language of Castile. Columbus curses in Genovese and throws to the ground his credentials, written in Latin and addressed to the Great Khan. The naked men watch the anger of the intruder with red hair and coarse skin, who wears a velvet cape and very shiny clothes.

Soon the word will run through the islands:

"Come and see the men who arrived from the sky! Bring them food and drink!"

(52)

1493: Barcelona
Day of Glory

The heralds announce him with their trumpets. The bells peal and the drums beat out festive rhythms. The admiral, newly returned from the Indies, mounts the stone steps and advances on the crimson carpet amid the silken dazzle of the applauding royal court. The man who has made the saints' and sages' prophecies come true reaches the platform, kneels, and kisses the hands of the queen and the king.

From the rear come the trophies: gleaming on trays, the bits of gold that Columbus had exchanged for little mirrors and red caps in the remote gardens newly burst from the sea. On branches and dead leaves are paraded the skins of lizards and snakes; and behind them, trembling and weeping, enter the beings never before seen. They are the few who have survived the colds, the measles, and the disgust for the Christians' food and bad smell. Not naked, as they were when they approached the three caravels and were captured, they have been covered up with trousers, shirts, and a few parrots that have been put in their hands and on their heads and shoulders. The parrots, robbed of their feathers by the foul winds of the voyage, look as moribund as the men. Of the captured women and children, none has survived.

Hostile murmurs are heard in the salon. The gold is minimal, and there is not a trace of black pepper, or nutmeg, or cloves, or ginger; and Columbus has not brought in any bearded sirens or men with tails, or the ones with only one eye or foot—and that foot big enough when raised to be protection from the fierce sun.

(44)

1493: Rome

The Testament of Adam

In the dim light of the Vatican, fragrant with oriental perfumes, the pope dictates a new bull.

A short time has passed since Rodrigo Borgia, of Xátiva, Valencia, took the name Alexander VI. Not a year yet since the day he bought for cash the seven votes he was short in the Sacred College, and could change a cardinal's purple for the ermine cape of the supreme pontiff.

Alexander devotes more time to calculating the price of indulgences than to meditating on the mystery of the Holy Trinity. Everyone knows that he prefers very brief Masses, except for the ones his jester Gabriellino celebrates in a mask in his private chambers, and everyone knows that the new pope is capable of rerouting the Corpus Christi procession to pass beneath a pretty woman's balcony.

He is also capable of cutting up the world as if it were a chicken: he raises a hand and traces a frontier, from head to tail of the planet, across the unknown sea. God's agent concedes in perpetuity all that has been or is being discovered, to the west of that line, to Isabella of Castile and Ferdinand of Aragon and their heirs on the Spanish throne. He entrusts them to send good, God-fearing, erudite, wise, expert men to the islands and mainlands discovered or to be discovered, to instruct the natives in the Catholic faith and teach them good customs. Whatever is discovered to the east will belong to the Portuguese crown.

Anguish and euphoria of sails unfurled: in Andalusia Columbus is already preparing a second voyage to the regions where gold grows in bunches on the vines and precious stones await in the craniums of dragons.

(180)

1493: Huexotzingo

Where Is the Truth? Where Are the Roots?

This is the city of music, not of war: Huexotzingo, in the valley of Tlaxcala. In a flash the Aztecs attack and damage it, and take prisoners to sacrifice to their gods.

On this evening, Tecayehuatzin, king of Huexotzingo, has assembled the poets from other areas. In the palace gardens, the poets chat about the flowers and songs that come down to earth, a region of the fleeting moment, from within the sky, and that only last up there in the house of the Giver of life. The poets talk and doubt:

Can it be that men are real?
Will our song
Still be real tomorrow?

The voices follow one another. When night falls, the king of Huexotzingo thanks them and says good-bye:

We know something that is real
The hearts of our friends.

(108)

1493: Pasto

Everybody Pays Taxes

Even these remote heights far to the north are reached by the Inca Empire's tax collector.

The Quillacinga people have nothing to give, but in this vast kingdom all communities pay tribute, in kind or in labor time. No one, however far off and however poor, can forget who is in charge.

At the foot of the volcano, the chief of the Quillacingas steps forward and places a bamboo cylinder in the hands of the envoy from Cuzco. The cylinder is full of live lice.

(57 and 150)

1493: Santa Cruz Island

An Experience of Miquele de Cuneo from Savona

The shadow of the sails spreads across the sea. Gulfweed and jellyfish, moved by the waves, drift over the surface toward the coast.

From the quarterdeck of one of the caravels, Columbus contemplates the white beaches where he has again planted the cross and the gallows. This is his second voyage. How long it will last he doesn't know; but his heart tells him that all will come out well, and why wouldn't the admiral believe it? Doesn't he have the habit of measuring the ship's speed with his hand against his chest, counting the heartbeats?

Belowdecks in another caravel, in the captain's cabin, a young girl shows her teeth. Miquele de Cuneo reaches for her breasts, and she scratches and kicks him and screams. Miquele received her a while ago. She is a gift from Columbus.

He lashes her with a rope. He beats her hard on the head and stomach and legs. Her screams become moans, the moans become wails. Finally all that can be heard are the comings and goings of sea gulls and the creak of rocked timbers. From time to time waves send a spray through-the porthole.

Miquele hurls himself upon the bleeding body and thrusts, gasps, wrestles. The air smells of tar, of saltpeter, of sweat. Then the girl, who seems to have fainted or died, suddenly fastens her nails in Miquele's back, knots herself around his legs, and rolls him over in a fierce embrace.

After some time, when Miquele comes to, he doesn't know where he is or what has happened. Livid, he detaches himself from her and knocks her away with his fist.

He staggers up on deck. Mouth open, he takes a deep breath of sea breeze. In a loud voice, as if announcing an eternal truth, he says, "These Indian woman are all whores."

(181)

1495: Salamanca

The First Word from America

Elio Antonio de Nebrija, language scholar, publishes here his "Spanish-Latin Vocabulary." The dictionary includes the first Americanism of the Castilian language:

Canoa: Boat made from a single timber.

The new word comes from the Antilles.

These boats without sails, made of the trunk of a ceiba tree, welcomed Christopher Columbus. Out from the islands, paddling canoes, came the men with long black hair and bodies tattooed with vermilion symbols. They approached the caravels, offered fresh water, and exchanged gold for the kind of little tin bells that sell for a copper in Castile.

(52 and 154)

1495: La Isabela

Caonabó

Detached, aloof, the prisoner sits at the entrance of Christopher Columbus's house, He has iron shackles on his ankles, and handcuffs trap his wrists.

Caonabó was the one who burned to ashes the Navidad fort that the admiral had built when he discovered this island of Haiti. He burned the fort and killed its occupants. And not only them: In these two long years he has castigated with arrows any Spaniards he came across in Cibao, his mountain territory, for their hunting of gold and people.

Alonso de Ojeda, veteran of the wars against the Moors, paid him a visit on the pretext of peace. He invited him to mount his horse, and put on him these handcuffs of burnished metal that tie his hands, saying that they were jewels worn by the monarchs of Castile in their balls and festivities.

Now Chief Caonabó spends the days sitting beside the door, his eyes fixed on the tongue of light that invades the earth floor at dawn and slowly retreats in the evening. He doesn't move an eyelash when Columbus comes around. On the other hand, when Ojeda appears, he manages to stand up and salute with a bow the only man who has defeated him.

(103 and 158)

1496: La Concepción

Sacrilege

Bartholomew Columbus, Christopher's brother and lieutenant, attends an incineration of human flesh.

Six men play the leads in the grand opening of Haiti's incinerator. The smoke makes everyone cough. The six are burning as a punishment and as a lesson: They have buried the images of Christ and the Virgin that Fray Ramón Pané left with them for protection and consolation. Fray Ramón taught them to pray on their knees, to say the Ave Maria and Paternoster and to invoke the name of Jesus in the face of temptation, injury, and death.

No one has asked them why they buried the images. They were hoping that the new gods would fertilize their fields of corn, cassava, boniato, and beans.

The fire adds warmth to the humid, sticky heat that foreshadows heavy rain.

(103)

1498: Santo Domingo

Earthly Paradise

In the evening, beside the Ozama River, Christopher Columbus writes a letter. His body creaks with rheumatism, but his heart jumps for joy. The discoverer explains to Their Catholic Majesties *that which is plainly evident:* Earthly Paradise is on the nipple of a woman's breast.

He realized it two months ago, when his caravels entered the

Gulf of Paria. *There ships start rising gently toward the sky* . . .
Navigating upstream to where the air has no weight, Columbus
has reached the farthest limit of the Orient. *In these the world's
most beautiful lands,* the men show cleverness, ingenuity, and
valor, and the extremely beautiful women wear only their long hair
and necklaces of many pearls wound around their bodies. The
water, sweet and clear, awakens thirst. Winter does not punish
nor summer burn, and the breeze caresses what it touches. The
trees offer fresh shade and, within arm's reach, fruits of great
delectability that arouse hunger.

But beyond *this greenness and this loveliness* no ship can go.
This is the frontier of the Orient. Here waters, lands, and islands
end. Very high and far away, the Tree of Life spreads its enormous
crown and the source of the four sacred rivers bubbles up. One of
them is the Orinoco, *which I doubt if such a great and deep river
is known in the world.*

The world is not round. The world is a woman's tit. The nipple
begins in the Gulf of Paria and rises to a point very close to the
heavens. The tip, where the juices of Paradise flow, will never be
reached by any man.

(53)

The Language of Paradise

The Guaraos, who live in the suburbs of Earthly Paradise, call the
rainbow *snake of necklaces* and the firmament *overhead sea.* Lightning is *glow of the rain.* One's friend, *my other heart.* The soul,
sun of the breast. The owl, *lord of the dark night.* A walking cane
is a *permanent grandson;* and for "I forgive," they say *I forget.*

(17)

1499: Granada
Who Are Spaniards?

The mosques remain open in Granada, seven years after the surrender of this last redoubt of the Moors in Spain. The advance of
the cross behind the victory of the sword is slow. Archbishop Cisneros decides that Christ cannot wait.

"Moors" is the Christian Spaniards' name for Spaniards of Islamic culture, who have been here for eight centuries. Thousands and thousands of Spaniards of Jewish culture have been condemned to exile. The Moors will likewise get the choice between baptism and exile; and for false converts burn the fires of the Inquisition. The unity of Spain, this Spain that has discovered America, will not result from the sum of its parts.

By Archbishop Cisneros's order the Muslim sages of Granada troop off to prison. Lofty flames devour Islamic books—religion and poetry, philosophy and science—the only copies guarding the words of a culture that has irrigated these lands and flourished in them.

From on high, the carved palaces of the Alhambra are mute witnesses of the enslavement, while its fountains continue giving water to the gardens.

(64, 218, and 223)

1500: Florence

Leonardo

He is just back from the market with various cages on his back. He puts them on the balcony, opens the little doors, and the birds make off. He watches the birds lose themselves in the sky, fluttering joyously, then sits down to work.

The noon sunshine warms his hand. On a wide board Leonardo da Vinci draws the world. And in the world that Leonardo draws appear the lands that Columbus has found toward the sunset. The artist invents them, as previously he has invented the airplane, the tank, the parachute, and the submarine, and he gives them form as previously he has incarnated the mystery of virgins and the passion of saints: He imagines the body of America, which still doesn't have that name, and sketches it as new land and not as part of Asia.

Columbus, seeking the Levant, has found the West. Leonardo guesses that the world has grown.

(209)

1506: Valladolid

The Fifth Voyage

Last night he dictated his last testament. This morning he asked if the king's messenger had arrived. Afterward, he slept. Nonsense mutterings and groans. He still breathes, but stertorously, as if battling against the air.

At court, no one has listened to his entreaties. He returned from the third voyage in chains, and on the fourth there was no one to pay attention to his titles and dignities.

Christopher Columbus is going out knowing that there is no passion or glory that does not lead to pain. On the other hand, he does not know that within a few years the banner that he stuck for the first time into the sands of the Caribbean will be waving over the empire of the Aztecs, in lands yet unknown, and over the kingdom of the Incas, under the unknown skies of the Southern Cross. He does not know that with all his lies, promises, and ravings, he has still fallen short. The supreme admiral of the ocean sea still believes he has reached Asia from the rear.

The ocean will not be called the Sea of Columbus; nor will the new world bear his name, but that of his Florentine friend Amerigo Vespucci, navigator and pilot master. But it was Columbus who found dazzling color that didn't exist in the European rainbow. Blind, he dies without seeing it.

(12 and 166)

1506: Tenochtitlán

The Universal God

Moctezuma has conquered in Teuctepec.

Fire rages in the temples. The drums beat. One after another, prisoners mount the steps toward the round, sacrificial stone. The priest plunges the obsidian dagger into each breast, lifts up the heart, and shows it to the sun, which rises above the blue volcanoes.

To what god is the blood offered? The sun demands it, to be born each day and travel from one horizon to the other. But the ostentatious death ceremonies also serve another god who does not appear in the codices nor in the chants.

If that god did not reign over the world, there would be no slaves nor masters nor vassals nor colonies. The Aztec merchants could not wrest a diamond for a bean from the defeated peoples, nor an emerald for a grain of corn, nor gold for sweetmeats, nor cacao for stones. The carriers would not be crossing the immensity of the empire in long lines with tons of tribute on their backs. The common people would dare to put on cotton tunics and would drink chocolate and audaciously wear the forbidden quetzal feathers and gold bracelets and magnolias and orchids reserved for the nobility. Then the masks hiding the warrior chiefs' faces would fall, the eagle's beak, the tiger's jaws, the plumes that wave and sparkle in the air.

The steps of the great temple are stained with blood, and skulls accumulate in the center of the plaza. Not only so that the sun should move, no; also so that that secret god should decide instead of man. In homage to that god, across the sea inquisitors fry heretics on bonfires or twist them in the torture chambers. It is the God of Fear. The God of Fear, who has rat's teeth and vulture's wings.

(60)

1511: Guauravo River

Agüeynaba

Three years ago, Captain Ponce de León arrived at this island of Puerto Rico in a caravel. Chief Agüeynaba opened his home to him, offered him food and drink and the choice of one of his daughters, and showed him the rivers from which gold was taken. He also gave him his name. Juan Ponce de León started calling himself Agüeynaba, and Agüeynaba received in exchange the name of the conquistador.

Three days ago the soldier Salcedo came alone to the banks of the Guauravo River. The Indians offered their backs for him to cross on. When they reached midstream, they let him fall and held him down against the river bottom until he stopped kicking. Afterward they laid him out on the grass.

Salcedo is now a glob of purple contorted flesh squeezed into a suit of armor, attacked by insects and quickly putrefying in the sun. The Indians look at it, holding their noses. Night and day they have been begging the stranger's pardon, for the benefit of the doubt. No point in it now. The drums broadcast the good news: *The invaders are not immortal.*

Tomorrow will come the rising. Agüeynaba will head it. The chief of the rebels will go back to his old name. He will recover his name, which has been used to humiliate his people.

"Co-qui, co-qui," cry the little frogs. The drums calling for struggle drown out their crystal-counterpoint singsong.

(1)

1511: Aymaco

Becerrillo

The insurrection of chiefs Agüeynaba and Mabodamaca has been put down and all the prisoners have gone to their deaths.

Captain Diego de Salazar comes upon the old woman hidden in the underbrush and does not run his sword through her. "Here," he says to her, "take this letter to the governor, who is in Caparra."

The old woman opens her eyes slightly. Trembling, she holds out her fingers.

And she sets off. She walks like a small child, with a baby-bear lurch, carrying the envelope like a standard or a flag.

While the old woman is still within crossbow range, the captain releases Becerrillo. Governor Ponce de León has ordered that Becerrillo should receive twice the pay of a crossbowman, as an expert flusher-out of ambushes and hunter of Indians. The Indians of Puerto Rico have no worse enemy.

The first arrow knocks the old woman over. Becerrillo, his ears perked up, his eyes bulging, would devour her in one bite.

"Mr. Dog," she entreats him, "I'm taking this letter to the governor."

Becerrillo doesn't know the local language, but the old woman shows him the empty envelope.

"Don't do me harm, Mr. Dog."

Becerrillo sniffs at the envelope. He circles a few times the trembling bag of bones that whines words, lifts a paw, and pees on her.

(166)

1511: Yara

Hatuey

In these islands, in these Calvaries, those who choose death by hanging themselves or drinking poison along with their children are many. The invaders cannot avoid this vengeance, but know how to explain it: the Indians, *so savage that they think everything is in common*, as Oviedo will say, *are people by nature idle and vicious, doing little work. For a pastime many killed themselves with venom so as not to work, and others hanged themselves with their own hands.*

Hatuey, Indian chief of the Guahaba region, has not killed himself. He fled with his people from Haiti in a canoe and took refuge in the caves and mountains of eastern Cuba.

There he pointed to a basketful of gold and said: "This is the god of the Christians. For him they pursue us. For him our fathers and our brothers have died. Let us dance for him. If our dance pleases him, this god will order them not to mistreat us."

They catch him three months later.

They tie him to a stake.

Before lighting the fire that will reduce him to charcoal and ash, the priest promises him glory and eternal rest if he agrees to be baptized. Hatuey asks:

"Are there Christians in that heaven?"

"Yes."

Hatuey chooses hell, and the firewood begins to crackle.

(102,103, and 166)

1511: Santo Domingo

The First Protest

In the log-walled, palm-roofed church, Antonio de Montesinos, Dominican friar, hurls thunder from the pulpit. He denounces the extermination:

"By what right and by what justice do you hold the Indians in such cruel and horrible bondage? Aren't they dying, or better said, aren't you killing them, to get gold every day? Are you not

obliged to love them as yourselves? Don't you understand this, don't you feel it?"

Then Montesinos, head high, makes his way through the astounded multitude.

A murmur of fury swells up. They didn't bargain for this, these peasants from Estremadura and shepherds from Andalusia who have repudiated their names and histories and, with rusty arquebuses slung over their shoulders, left at random in search of the mountains of gold and the nude princesses on this side of the ocean. A Mass of pardon and consolation was what was needed by these adventurers bought with promises on the steps of Seville Cathedral, these flea-bitten captains, veterans of no battle, and condemned prisoners who had to choose between America and jail or gallows.

"We'll denounce you to King Ferdinand! You'll be deported!"

One bewildered man remains silent. He came to these lands nine years ago. Owner of Indians, gold mines, and plantations, he has made a small fortune. His name is Bartolomé de las Casas, and he will soon be the first priest ordained in the New World.

(103)

1513: Cuareca

Leoncico

Their muscles almost burst through the skin. Their yellow eyes never stop flashing. They pant. They snap their jaws and bite holes in the air. No chain can hold them when they get the command to attack.

Tonight, by order of Captain Balboa, the dogs will sink their teeth into the naked flesh of fifty Indians of Panama. They will disembowel and devour fifty who were guilty of the abominable sin of sodomy, *who only lacked tits and wombs to be women.* The spectacle will take place in this mountain clearing, among the trees that the storm uprooted a few days ago. By torchlight the soldiers quarrel and jockey for the best places.

Vasco Núñez de Balboa chairs the ceremony. His dog Leoncico heads up God's avengers. Leoncico, son of Becerrillo, has a body crisscrossed with scars. He is a past master of capturings and quarterings. He gets a sublieutenant's pay and a share of each gold or slave booty.

In two days' time Balboa will discover the Pacific Ocean.

(81 and 166)

1513: Gulf of San Miguel

Balboa

With water up to his waist, he raises his sword and yells to the four winds.

His men carve an immense cross in the sand. The scribe Valderrábano registers the names of those who have just discovered the new ocean, and Father Andrés intones the *Te Deum Laudamus*.

Balboa discards his fifteen kilos of armor, throws his sword far away, and jumps in.

He splashes about and lets himself be dragged by the waves, dizzy with a joy he won't feel again. The sea opens for him, embraces him, rocks him. Balboa would like to drink it dry.

(141)

1514: Sinú River

The Summons

They have crossed much water and time and are fed up with heat, jungles, and mosquitos. They carry out, however, the king's instructions: not to attack the natives without first summoning them to surrender. St. Augustine authorizes war against those who abuse their liberty, because their liberty would make them dangerous if they were not tamed; but as St. Isidore well says, no war is just without a previous declaration.

Before they start the rush for the gold, for nuggets possibly as big as eggs, lawyer Martín Fernández de Enciso reads, complete with periods and commas, the ultimatum that the interpreter translates painfully by fits and starts.

Enciso speaks in the name of King Ferdinand and Queen Juana, his daughter, tamers of barbarous peoples. He makes it known to the Indians of the Sinú that God came to the world and left St. Peter as his representative, that St. Peter's successor is the holy father and that the holy father, lord of the universe, has awarded to the king of Castile all the lands of the Indies and of this peninsula.

The soldiers bake in their armor. Enciso slowly and meticulously summons the Indians to leave these lands since they don't belong to them, and if they want to stay to pay their highnesses tribute in gold in token of obedience. The interpreter does his best.

The two chiefs listen, sitting down and without blinking, to the odd character who announces to them that in case of refusal or delay he will make war on them, turn them into slaves along with their women and children, and sell and dispose of them as such and that the deaths and damages of that just war will not be the Spaniards' responsibility.

The chiefs reply, without a glance at Enciso, that the holy father has indeed been generous with others' property but must have been drunk to dispose of what was not his and that the king of Castile is impertinent to come threatening folk he doesn't know.

Then the blood flows.

Subsequently the long speech will be read at dead of night, without an interpreter and half a league away from villages that will be taken by surprise. The natives, asleep, won't hear the words that declare them guilty of the crime committed against them.

(78, 81, and 166)

1514: Santa María del Darién

For Love of Fruit

Gonzalo Fernández de Oviedo, a new arrival, tries out the fruit of the New World.

The guava seems to him much superior to the apple.

The guanábana is pretty to look at and offers a white, watery pulp of very mild flavor, which, however much you eat of it, causes neither harm nor indigestion.

The mamey has a finger-licking flavor and smells very good. *Nothing better exists,* he finds.

But he bites into a medlar, and an aroma unequaled even by musk invades his head. *The medlar is the best fruit,* he corrects himself, *and nothing comparable can be found.*

Then he peels a pineapple. The golden pine smells as peaches would like to and is able to give an appetite to people who have forgotten the joys of eating. Oviedo knows no words worthy of describing its virtues. It delights his eyes, his nose, his fingers, his tongue. *This outdoes them all, as the feathers of the peacock outshine those of any bird.*

(166)

1515: Antwerp

Utopia

The New World adventures bring the taverns of this Flemish port to the boil. One summer night, on the waterfront, Thomas More meets or invents Rafael Hithloday, a sailor from Amerigo Vespucci's fleet, who says he has discovered the isle of Utopia off some coast of America.

The sailor relates that in Utopia neither money nor private property exists. There, scorn for gold and for superfluous consumption is encouraged, and no one dresses ostentatiously. Everybody gives the fruits of his work to the public stores and freely collects what he needs. The economy is planned. There is no hoarding, which is the son of fear, nor is hunger known. The people choose their prince and the people can depose him; they also elect the priests. The inhabitants of Utopia loathe war and its honors, although they fiercely defend their frontiers. They have a religion that does not offend reason and rejects useless mortifications and forcible conversions. The laws permit divorce but severely punish conjugal betrayals and oblige everyone to work six hours a day. Work and rest are shared; the table is shared. The community takes charge of children while their parents are busy. Sick people get privileged treatment; euthanasia avoids long, painful agonies. Gardens and orchards occupy most of the space, and music is heard wherever one goes.

(146)

1519: Frankfurt

Charles V

A half century has passed since Gutenberg's death, and printeries multiply all over Europe; they publish the Bible in Gothic letters, and gold and silver price quotations in Gothic numerals. The monarch devours men, and men shit gold coins in Hieronymus Bosch's garden of delights; and Michaelangelo, while painting and sculpting his athletic saints and prophets, writes: *The blood of Christ is sold by the spoonful*. Everything has its price: the pope's throne and the monarch's crown, the cardinal's cape and the bishop's miter. Indulgences, excommunications, and titles of nobility are bought. The Church deems lending at interest a sin, but the holy father mortgages Vatican lands to the bankers; and on the banks of the Rhine, the crown of the Holy Empire is offered to the highest bidder.

Three candidates dispute the heritage of Charlemagne. The electors swear by the purity of their votes and cleanliness of their hands and pronounce their verdict at noon, the hour of the Angelus: they sell the crown of Europe to the king of Spain, Charles I, son of the seducer and the madwoman and grandson of the Catholic monarchs, for 850,000 florins, which Germany's bankers Függer and Welser plunk down on the table.

Charles I turns himself into Charles V, emperor of Spain, Germany, Austria, Naples, Sicily, the Low Countries, and the immense New World, defender of the Catholic faith, and God's warrior vicar on earth.

Meanwhile, the Muslims threaten the frontiers, and Martin Luther nails up his defiant heresies on the door of a Wittemberg church. A prince must have war as his sole objective and thought, Macchiavelli has written. At age nineteen, the new monarch is the most powerful man in history. On his knees, he kisses the sword.

(116, 209, and 218)

1519: Acla

Pedrarias

Noise of sea and drums. Night has fallen, but there is light from the moon. Around the plaza, fish and dried ears of corn hang from the straw roofs.

Enter Balboa, chained, hands bound behind his back. They untie him. Balboa smokes his last cigar. Without saying a word, he places his neck on the block. The executioner raises the ax.

From his house, Pedro Arias de Avila peers furtively through the cane wall. He is sitting on the coffin that he brought from Spain. He uses the coffin as a chair or a table, and once a year,

year after year, covers it with candles, during the requiem that celebrates his resurrection. They call him Pedrarias the Buried ever since he got up out of this coffin, wrapped in a shroud, as nuns sang the office of the dead and relatives sobbed uncontrollably. Previously they had called him Pedrarias the Gallant, because of his invincibility in tournaments, battles, and gallantries; and now, although he is nearing eighty, he deserves the name of Fury of the Lord. When Pedrarias wakes up shaking his white mane because he lost a hundred Indians at dice the night before, his glance is better avoided.

Ever since he landed on these beaches, Pedrarias has distrusted Balboa. Balboa being his son-in-law, he doesn't kill him without a trial. There are not too many lawyers around here, so the judge is also counsel and prosecutor; the trial, long.

Balboa's head rolls on the sand.

It was Balboa who had founded this town of Acla, among trees twisted by the winds. On the day Acla was born, a black bird of prey dived from above the clouds, seized the steel helmet from Balboa's head, and took off, cawing.

Here Balboa was building, piece by piece, the brigantines that would be launched to explore the new sea he had discovered.

The job will be completed by the executioner. He will found an enterprise of conquest, and Pedrarias will be his partner. The executioner, who came with Columbus on his last voyage, will be a marquis with twenty thousand vassals in the mysterious kingdoms to the south. His name is Francisco Pizarro.

(81 and 141)

1519: Tenochtitlán

Portents of Fire, Water, Earth, and Air

One day long ago, the soothsayers flew to the cave of the mother of the god of war. The witch, who had not washed for eight centuries, did not smile or greet them. Without thanking them, she accepted their gifts—cloth, skins, feathers—and listened sourly to their news. *Mexico*, the soothsayers told her, *is mistress and queen, and all cities are under her orders*. The old woman grunted her sole comment: *The Aztecs have defeated the others*, she said, *and others will come who will defeat the Aztecs*.

Time passed.

For the past ten years, portents have been piling up.

A bonfire leaked flames from the middle of the sky for a whole night.

A sudden three-tongued fire came up from the horizon and flew to meet the sun.

The house of the god of war committed suicide, setting fire to itself. Buckets of water were thrown on it, and the water enlivened the flames.

Another temple was burned by a flash of lightning one evening when there was no storm.

The lake in which the city is situated turning into a boiling cauldron. The waters rose, white-hot, towering with fury, carrying away houses, even tearing up foundations.

Fishermen's nets brought up an ash-colored bird along with the fish. On the bird's head there was a round mirror. In the mirror, Emperor Moctezuma saw advancing an army of soldiers who ran on the legs of deer, and he heard their war cries. Then the soothsayers who could neither read the mirror nor had eyes to see the two-headed monsters that implacably haunted Moctezuma's sleeping and waking hours were punished. The emperor shut them up in cages and condemned them to die of hunger.

Every night the cries of an unseen woman startle all who sleep in Tenochtitlán and in Tlatelolco. *My little children*, she cries, *now we have to go far from here!* There is no wall that the woman's cry does not pierce: *Where shall we go, my little children?*

(60 and 210)

1519: Cempoala

Cortés

Twilight of soaring flames on the coast of Veracruz. Eleven ships are burning up; burning, too, the rebel soldiers who hang from the yardarm of the flagship. While the sea opens its jaws to devour the bonfires, Hernán Cortés, standing on the beach, presses on the pommel of his sword and uncovers his head.

Not only the ships and the hanged have met their end; now there is no going back, no more life than what is born tomorrow, either gold and glory or the vulture of defeat. On the Veracruz beach have been sunk the dreams of those who would have liked to return to Cuba to sleep the colonial siesta in net hammocks, wrapped in women's hair and cigar smoke: the sea leads to the past and the land to danger. Those who could afford it will go forward on horseback, the others on foot: seven hundred men into Mexico, toward the mountains and the volcanos and the mystery of Moctezuma.

Cortés adjusts his feathered headpiece and turns his back on the flames. In one gallop he makes it to the native village of Cempoala, while night is still falling. He says nothing to the men. They will find out as they go.

He drinks wine alone in his tent. Perhaps he thinks about the men he has killed without confession or the women he has bedded without marriage since those student days in Salamanca that seem so far off, or his lost years as a bureaucrat in the Antilles during the waiting time. Perhaps he thinks about Governor Diego Velázquez, who will soon be quivering with rage in Santiago de Cuba. Certainly he smiles if he thinks about that soporific fool, whose orders he will never again obey; or about the surprise that awaits the soldiers whom he hears laughing and cursing at games of dice and cards.

Something of this runs in his head, or maybe the fascination and panic of the days to come; then he looks up, sees her at the door, recognizes her against the light. Her name was Malinali or Malinche when the chief of Tabasco made her a gift to him. She has been known as Marina for a week.

Cortés speaks a few words while she waits, perfectly still. Then in a single movement the girl loosens her hair and clothing. A cascade of colored cloths falls between her bare feet, and the glow of her body silences him.

A few paces away by the light of the moon, the soldier Bernal Díaz del Castillo records the day's events. He uses a drum as a table.

(56 and 62)

1519: Tenochtitlán

Moctezuma

Great mountains have arrived, moving over the sea, off the coasts of Yucatán. The god Quetzalcóatl has come back. The people kiss the bows of the ships.

Emperor Moctezuma mistrusts his own shadow.

"What shall I do? Where will I hide?"

Moctezuma would like to turn into a stone or a stick. The court jesters cannot distract him. Quetzalcóatl, the bearded god, he who loaned the land and the beautiful songs, has come to demand what is his.

In olden times, Quetzalcóatl had departed for the east after burning his house of gold and his house of coral. The handsomest birds flew to open the way for him. He put out to sea on a raft of snakes and was lost to sight sailing into the dawn. Now he has returned. The bearded god, the plumed serpent has returned hungry.

The earth shakes. In the stewpots the birds dance as they boil. *No one will remain,* the poet had said. *No one, no one, truly no one alive on the earth.*

Moctezuma has sent great offerings of gold to the god Quetzalcóatl, helmets filled with gold dust, golden ducks, golden dogs, golden tigers, golden necklaces, and wands and bows and arrows, but the more gold the god eats, the more he wants; and he is advancing toward Tenochtitlán, dissatisfied. He marches between the great volcanos, and behind him come other bearded gods. The hands of the invaders send forth thunder that stuns and fire that kills.

"What shall I do? Where will I hide?"

Moctezuma lives with his head buried in his hands.

Two years ago, when there were already omens aplenty of the god's return and vengeance, Moctezuma sent his soothsayers to the cave of Huémac, king of the dead. The soothsayers descended into the depths of Chapultepec with a retinue of dwarfs and hunchbacks and delivered to Huémac on the emperor's behalf an offering of skins of recently flayed prisoners. Huémac sent word back to Moctezuma:

"Don't fool yourself. Here there's no rest or joy."

And he told him to fast and to sleep without a woman.

Moctezuma obeyed. He made a long penitence. The eunuchs shut tight the quarters of his wives; the cooks forgot about his favorite dishes. But things got worse. The black crows of distress came in flocks. Moctezuma lost the protection of Tlazoltéotl, the goddess of love, also the goddess of shit, she who eats our nastiness so that love is possible; and thus the soul of the solitary emperor was drowned in garbage and blackness. He sent more messengers to Huémac on several occasions with entreaties and gifts, until finally the king of the dead gave him an appointment.

On the night arranged, Moctezuma went to meet him. His boat headed for Chapultepec. The emperor stood in the bow, and the mist over the lake opened up for his flamingo plume.

Shortly before reaching the foot of the mountain, Moctezuma heard the sound of oars. A canoe appeared, moving rapidly, and somebody shone out for an instant in the black mist, naked and alone, his paddle raised like a lance.

"Is that you, Huémac?"

Whoever it was kept moving nearer until he almost grazed the emperor. He looked into the emperor's eyes as no man can look. "Coward!" he said to him and disappeared.

(60, 200, and 210)

1519: Tenochtitlán

The Capital of the Aztecs

Dumbfounded by the beauty of it, the conquistadors ride down the causeway. Tenochtitlán seems to have been torn from the pages of Amadís, *things never heard of, never seen, nor even dreamed* . . . The sun rises behind the volcanos, enters the lake, and breaks the floating mist into shreds. The city—streets, canals, high-towered temples—glitters before them. A multitude comes out to greet the invaders, silent and unhurried, while innumerable canoes open furrows in the cobalt waters.

Moctezuma arrives on a litter, seated on a soft jaguar skin, beneath a canopy of gold, pearls, and green feathers. The lords of the kingdom go ahead sweeping the ground he will tread.

He welcomes the god Quetzalcóatl:

"*Thou hast come to occupy thy throne,*" he says. "*Thou hast come amid clouds, amid mists. I am not seeing thee in dreams. I am not dreaming. Unto thy land hast thou come . . .*"

Those who accompany Quetzalcóatl receive garlands of magnolias, necklaces of flowers around their necks, on their arms, on their breasts: the flower of the shield and the flower of the heart, the flowers of fine perfume and of golden hue.

Quetzalcóatl is a native of Estremadura who landed on American shores with his whole wardrobe on his back and a few coins in his purse. He was nineteen when he set foot on the wharf at

Santo Domingo and asked: *Where is the gold?* He is now thirty-four and a captain of great daring. He wears armor of black iron and leads an army of horsemen, lancers, crossbowmen, riflemen, and fierce dogs. He has promised his soldiers: *"I will make you in a very short time the richest men of all who ever came to the Indies."*

Emperor Moctezuma, who opens the gates of Tenochtitlán, will soon be finished. In a short while he will be called *woman of the Spaniards*, and his own people will stone him to death. Young Cuauhtémoc will take his place. *He* will fight.

(60 and 62)

Aztec Song of the Shield

*On the shield, the virgin gave birth
to the great warrior.
On the shield, the virgin gave birth
to the great warrior.*

*On the mountain of the serpent, the conqueror,
amid the mountains,
with war paint
and with eagle shield.*

*No one, for sure, could face him,
The ground began to spin
when he put on his war paint
and raised his shield.*

(77)

1520: Teocalhueyacan

"Night of Sorrow"

Hernán Cortés reviews the few survivors of his army while Malinche sews the torn flags.

Tenochtitlán is behind them. Behind, too, as if bidding them farewell, the column of smoke spewed by the volcano Popocatépetl, which no wind seemed able to bend.

The Aztecs have recovered their city, the roofs bristling with bows and lances, the lake covered with battle canoes. The conquistadors fled in disorder, pursued by a storm of arrows and stones, while war drums, yells, and curses stunned the night.

These wounded, mutilated, dying men left to Cortés saved themselves by using corpses as a bridge: They crossed to the other shore stepping on horses that slipped and drowned and on soldiers killed by arrows and stones or drowned by the weight of the gold-filled sacks that they could not bring themselves to leave behind.

(62 and 200)

1520: Segura de la Frontera

The Distribution of Wealth

Murmurings and scufflings in the Spaniards' camp. The soldiers have no alternative. They must surrender the gold bars saved from the disaster. Anyone hiding something will be hanged.

The bars come from the works of Mexico's goldsmiths and sculptors. Before being turned into booty and melted into ingots, this gold was a serpent about to strike, a tiger about to jump, an eagle about to soar, or a dagger that snaked and flowed like a river in the air.

Cortés explains that this gold is mere bubbles compared with what awaits them. He takes out the fifth part for the king, another fifth for himself, plus the shares due to his father and the horse that died under him, and gives almost all the rest to the captains. Little or nothing remains for the soldiers who have licked this gold, bitten it, weighed it in their hands, slept with their heads pillowed on it, told it their dreams of revenge.

Meanwhile, branding irons mark the faces of Indian slaves newly captured in Tepeaca and Huaquechula.

The air smells of burned flesh.

(62 and 205)

1520: Brussels

Dürer

These things must be emanations from the sun, like the men and women who made them in the remote land they inhabit: helmets and girdles, feather fans, dresses, cloaks, hunting gear, a gold sun and a silver moon, a blowgun, and other weapons of such beauty that they seem made to revive their victims.

The greatest draftsman of all the ages does not tire of staring at them. This is part of the booty that Cortés seized from Moctezuma: the only pieces that were not melted into ingots. King Charles, newly seated on the Holy Empire's throne, is exhibiting to the public the trophies from his new bits of world.

Albrecht Dürer doesn't know the Mexican poem that explains that the true artist finds pleasure in his work and talks with his heart, because he has one that isn't dead and eaten by ants. But seeing what he sees, Dürer hears those words and finds that he is experiencing the greatest happiness of his half century of life.

(108)

1520: Tlaxcala

Toward the Reconquest
of Tenochtitlán

The year is close to its end. As soon as the sun comes out, Cortés will give the order to march. His troops, pulverized by the Aztecs, have been rehabilitated in a few months under the protection of their Indian allies of Tlaxcala, Huexotzingo, and Texcoco. An army of fifty thousand natives is under his orders, and new soldiers have come from Spain, Santo Domingo, and Cuba, well provided with horses, arquebuses, crossbows, and cannon. To fight on the water when they reach the lake, Cortés will have sails, iron fittings, and masts to equip three brigantines. The Huexotzingo Indians will lay down the timbers.

The first light throws the volcanic skyline into relief. Beyond, rising out of the prodigious waters, Tenochtitlán awaits defiantly.

(56)

1521: Tlatelolco

Sword of Fire

Blood flows like water; the drinking water is acid with blood. To eat, only earth remains. They fight house by house, over the ruins and over the dead, day and night. Almost three months of battle without letup. Only dust and the stink of corpses to breathe; but still drums beat in the last towers, bells tinkle on the ankles of the last warriors. The strength-giving battle cries and chants continue. The last women take up battle-axes from the fallen and until they collapse keep hammering on shields.

Emperor Cuauhtémoc summons the best of his captains. He puts on the long-feathered owl headpiece and takes up the sword of fire. With this sword in his fist, the god of war had emerged from his mother's belly, back in the most remote of times. With this serpent of sunbeams, Huitzilopochtli had decapitated his sister the moon and had cut to pieces his four hundred brothers, the stars, because they didn't want to let him be born.

Cuauhtémoc orders: *"Let our enemies look on it and be struck with terror."*

The sword of fire opens up an avenue. The chosen captain advances, alone, through the smoke and debris.

They fell him with a single shot from an arquebus.

(60, 107, and 200)

1521: Tenochtitlán

The World Is Silenced in the Rain

Suddenly, all at once, the cries and the drums cease. Gods and men have been defeated. With the gods' death, time has died. With the men's death, the city has died. This warrior city, she of the white willows and white rushes, has died fighting as she lived. No more will conquered princes of all the regions come in boats through the mist to pay her tribute.

A stunning silence reigns. And the rain begins to fall. Thunder and lightning fill the sky, and it rains all through the night.

The gold is piled into huge baskets. Gold of shields and insignia of war, gold of the masks of gods, lip and ear pendants, ornaments, lockets. The gold is weighed and the prisoners priced. *One of these wretches is hardly worth two handfuls of corn* . . . The soldiers gather to play dice and cards.

Fire burns the soles of Emperor Cuauhtémoc's feet, anointed with oil, while the world is silent, and it rains.

[60, 107, and 200)

1521: Florida

Ponce de León

He was old, or felt he was. There wouldn't be enough time, nor would the weary heart hold out. Juan Ponce de León wanted to discover and win the unconquered world that the Florida islands had announced. He wanted to dwarf the memory of Christopher Columbus by the grandeur of his feats.

Here he landed, following the magic river that crosses the garden of delights. Instead of the fountain of youth, he has met this arrow that penetrates his breast. He will never bathe in the waters that restore energy to the muscles and shine to the eyes without erasing the experience of the mature spirit.

The soldiers carry him in their arms toward the ship. The conquered captain murmurs complaints like a newborn baby, but his years remain many and he is still aging. The men carrying him confirm without astonishment that here a new defeat has occurred in the continuous struggle between the alwayses and the nevers.

(166)

1522: Highways of Santo Domingo

Feet

The rebellion, the first by black slaves in America, has been smashed. It had broken out in the sugar mills of Diego Columbus, son of the discoverer. Fire had spread through the mills and plantations of the whole island. The blacks had risen up with the few surviving Indians, armed with sticks and stones and sugar-cane lances that broke against armor in futile fury.

Now from gallows scattered along the highways hang women and men, the young and the old. At the traveler's eye level dangle feet by which he can guess what the victims were before death came. Among these leathery limbs, gashed by toil and tread, are frisky feet and formal feet; prisoner feet and feet that still dance, loving the earth and calling for war.

(166)

1522: Seville

The Longest Voyage Ever Made

No one thought they were still alive, but last night they arrived. They dropped anchor and fired all their guns. They didn't land right away, nor let themselves be seen. In the morning they appeared on the wharf. Shaking and in rags, they entered Seville carrying lighted torches. The crowd opened up, amazed, for this procession of scarecrows headed by Juan Sebastián de Elcano. They stumbled ahead, leaning on each other for support, from church to church, fulfilling pledges, always pursued by the crowd. They chanted as they went.

They had left three years ago, down the river in five elegant ships that headed west, a bunch of adventurers who had come together to seek the passage between the oceans, and fortune and glory. All fugitives, they put to sea in flight from poverty, love, jail, or the gallows.

Now the survivors talk of storms, crimes, and marvels. They have seen seas and lands without map or name; six times they have crossed the zone where the world boils, without ever getting burned. To the south they have encountered blue snow and in the sky, four stars forming a cross. They have seen the sun and the moon moving backward and fish flying. They have heard of women whom the wind impregnates and met some black birds like crows that rush into the open jaws of whales and devour their hearts. On one very remote island, they report, live little people half a meter tall, with ears that reach down to their feet. So long are their ears that when they go to bed, one serves as pillow and the other as blanket. They also report that when the Molucca Indians saw the small boats launched from the ships, they thought those boats were small daughters of the ships, that the ships gave them birth and suckled them.

The survivors say that in the South of the South, where the lands open up and the oceans embrace, the Indians light huge bonfires night and day to keep from dying of cold. Those Indians are such giants, they say, that our heads hardly reached their waists.

Magellan, who headed the expedition, caught two of them by putting iron fetters on their ankles and wrists as adornments; but later one died of scurvy and the other of heat.

They say that they had no alternative to drinking stagnant water, holding their noses, and that they ate sawdust, hides, and the rats that showed up to dispute with them the last wormy biscuits. Anyone who died of hunger they threw overboard, and as they had no stones to sink them, the corpses remained floating on the water: Europeans with faces to heaven and Indians face down. When they got to the Moluccas, one sailor traded the Indians a playing card, the king of diamonds, for six fowls, but couldn't even take a bite of them, so swollen were his gums.

They have seen Magellan weep—tears in the eyes of the tough Portuguese navigator when the ships entered the ocean never before crossed by a European. And they have known his terrible tempers, when he had two rebellious captains beheaded and quartered and left other rebels in the desert. Magellan is now carrion, a trophy in the hands of Filipino natives who shot a poisoned arrow into his leg.

Of the 237 sailors and soldiers who left Seville three years ago, 18 have returned. They arrived in one creaky ship with a worm-eaten keel that leaks on all four sides.

The survivors. These men dead of hunger who have just sailed around the world for the first time.

(20 and 78)

1523: Cuzco

Huaina Cápac

Before the rising sun he throws himself down and touches his forehead to the ground. He grasps the first rays in his hands, brings them to his mouth, and drinks the light. Then he rises, stands, and looks straight at the sun, without blinking.

Behind Huaina Cápac his many women wait with bowed heads. Waiting, too, in silence, the many princes. The Inca is looking at the sun, he looks at it equal to equal, and a murmur of scandal grows among the priests.

Many years have passed since the day when Huaina Cápac, son of the resplendent father, came to the throne with the title of young-and-potent-chief-rich-in-virtues. He has extended the empire far beyond the frontiers of his ancestors. Eager for power, Huaina Cápac, discoverer, conqueror, has led his armies from the Amazon jungle to the heights of Quito and from the Chaco to the coasts of Chile. With flying arrow and deadly battle-ax, he has made himself the master of new mountains, plains, and sandy deserts. There is no one who does not dream about him and fear him in this kingdom that is now bigger than Europe. On Huaina Cápac depend pastures, water, and"people. His will has moved mountains and men. In this empire that does not know the wheel, he has had buildings constructed in Quito with stones from Cuzco *so that in the future his greatness may be known and his word believed by men.*

The Inca looks fixedly at the sun. Not defiantly, as the priests fear, but out of pity. Huaina Cápac feels sorry for the sun, because, being his father and father of all the Incas since the most ancient of days, the sun has no right to fatigue or boredom. The sun never rests, plays, or forgets. He may not miss his daily appointment and runs today the same course across the sky as yesterday and tomorrow.

While he contemplates the sun, Huaina Cápac decides: "Soon I'll be dying."

(50 and 76)

1523: Cuauhcapolca

The Chief's Questions

He delivers food and gold and accepts baptism. But he asks Gil González de Avila to explain how Jesus can be man and god; and Mary, virgin and mother. He asks where souls go when they leave the body and whether the holy father in Rome is immune to death.

He asks who elected the king of Castile. Chief Nicaragua was elected by the elders of the communities, assembled at the foot of a ceiba tree. Was the king elected by the elders of his communities?

The chief also asks the conquistador to tell him for what purpose so few men want so much gold. Will their bodies be big enough for so much adornment?

Later he asks if it is true, as a prophet said, that the sun, stars, and moon will lose their light and the sky will fall.

Chief Nicaragua does not ask why no children will be born in these parts. No prophet has told him that within a few years the women will refuse to give birth to slaves.

(81 and 103)

1523: Painala

Malinche

By Cortés she had a child and for Cortés she opened the gates of an empire. She has been his shadow and watchman, interpreter, counselor, go-between, and mistress all through the conquest of Mexico and continues to ride beside him.

She passes through Painala dressed as a Spanish woman, fine woolens, silks, satins, and at first no one recognizes the distinguished lady who comes with the new masters. From the back of a chestnut steed, Malinche surveys the banks of the river, takes a deep breath of the sweet air, and seeks in vain the leafy nooks where she discovered magic and fear more than twenty years ago. She has known many rains and suns and sufferings and sorrows since her mother sold her as a slave and she was dragged from Mexican soil to serve the Maya lords of Yucatán.

When her mother learns who has come to visit her in Painala, she throws herself at her feet and bathes them in tears imploring forgiveness. Malinche restrains her with a gesture, raises her by the shoulders, embraces her, and hangs around her neck the necklaces she is wearing. Then she remounts her horse and continues on her way with the Spaniards.

She does not need to hate her mother. Ever since the lords of Yucatán made a present of her to Hernán Cortés four years before, Malinche has had time to avenge herself. The debt is paid: Mexicans bow and tremble at her approach. One glance from her black eyes is enough for a prince to hang on the gallows. Long after her death, her shadow will hover over the great Tenochtitlán that she did so much to defeat and humiliate, and her ghost with the long loose hair and billowing robe will continue striking fear for ever and ever, from the woods and caves of Chapultepec.

(29 and 62)

1524: Quetzaltenango

The Poet Will Tell Children the Story of This Battle

The poet will speak of Pedro de Alvarado and of those who came with him to teach fear.

He will relate that when the native troops had been destroyed, and when Guatemala was a slaughterhouse, Captain Tecum Umán rose into the air and flew with wings, and feathers sprouted from his body. He flew and fell upon Alvarado and with one fierce blow severed the head of his horse. But Alvarado and the horse divided into two and stayed that way: the conquistador detached himself from the decapitated horse and stood up. Captain Tecum flew off again and rose higher, all aglow. When he dived down from the clouds, Alvarado dodged and ran him through with this lance. The dogs dashed up to tear Tecum Umán apart, and Alvarado's sword held them back. For a long time Alvarado contemplated his beaten enemy, his body slashed open, the quetzal feathers sprouting from his arms and legs, the wings broken, the triple crown of pearls, diamonds, and emeralds. Alvarado called to his soldiers. "Look," he said to them, and made them remove their helmets.

The children, seated in a circle around the poet, will ask: "And all this you saw? You heard?"

"Yes."

"You were here?" the children will ask.

"No. None of our people who were here survived."

The poet will point to the moving clouds and the sway of the treetops.

"See the lances?" he will ask. "See the horses' hooves? The rain of arrows? The smoke? Listen," he will say, and put his ear against the ground, filled with explosions.

And he will teach them to smell history in the wind, to touch it in stones polished by the river, and to recognize its taste by chewing certain herbs, without hurry, as one chews on sadness.

(8 and 107)

1524: Utatlán

The Vengeance of the Vanquished

The Indian chiefs are a handful of bones, black as soot, which lie amid the rubble of the city. Today in the capital of the Quichés there is nothing that does not smell of burning.

Almost a century ago, a prophet had spoken. It was a chief of the Cakchiqueles who said, when the Quichés were about to tear out his heart: *Know that certain men, armed and clothed from head to feet and not naked like us, will destroy these buildings and reduce you to living in the caves of owls and wildcats and all this grandeur will vanish.*

He spoke while they killed him, here, in this city of ravines that Pedro de Alvarado's soldiers have just turned into a bonfire. The vanquished chief cursed the Quichés, and even then it had already been a long time that the Quichés had dominated Guatemala's other peoples.

(8 and 188)

1524: Scorpion Islands

Communion Ceremony

The sea swallowed them, vomited them out, gobbled them up again, and dashed them against the rocks. Dolphins and manatees flew through the air, and the sky was all foam. When the little ship fell to pieces, the men did their best to embrace the crags. All night long the waves fought to tear them off, blow by blow; many were dislodged, smashed against the stones, and devoured.

At dawn the storm let up and the tide receded. Those who were saved left their destination to fate and set themselves adrift in a ramshackle canoe. For five days they drifted among the reefs, finding no drinking water nor any fruit to put in their mouths.

This morning they landed on one of the islets.

They crawl forward on all fours beneath a sun that fries the stones. None has the strength to drag anyone who is left behind. Naked, badly wounded, they curse the captain, lawyer Alonso Zuazo, a good litigant and a bad navigator, and curse the mother who bore him, and the king, the pope, and God.

This little slope is the highest mountain in the world. The men keep climbing and console themselves counting the hours that remain before death.

And suddenly they rub their eyes. They can't believe it. Five giant turtles await them on the beach. Five of those turtles that in the sea look like rocky islands and that make love unperturbed as ships graze against them.

The men rush for them, grab their shells, howling with hunger and fury, and shove until the turtles turn over and lie pawing the air. They stick in their knives, open the turtles' bellies with slashes and fists, and bury their heads in the gushing blood.

And they fall asleep, submerged to their necks in these barrels of good wine, while the sun continues its slow march to the center of the sky.

No one listens to lawyer Alonso Zuazo. His mouth smeared with blood, he kneels in the sand, raises his hands, and offers the turtles to the five wounds of Our Redeemer.

(166)

1525: Tuxkahá

Cuauhtémoc

From the branch of an old ceiba tree, hung by the ankles, swings the body of the last king of the Aztecs.

Cortés has cut off his head.

He had arrived in the world in a cradle surrounded by shields and spears, and these were the first sounds he heard: "*Your real home is elsewhere. You are promised to another land. Your proper place is the battlefield. Your task is to give the blood of your enemy to the sun to drink and the body of your enemy to the earth to eat.*"

Twenty-nine years ago, the soothsayers poured water over his head and pronounced the ritual words: "*Where are you hiding, misfortune? In which limb do you conceal yourself? Away from this child!*"

They called him Cuauhtémoc, *eagle that falls*. His father had extended the empire from sea to sea. When the prince took over the throne, the invaders had already come and conquered. Cuauh-

témoc rose up and resisted. Four years after the defeat of Tenochtitlán, the songs that call for the warrior's return still resound
from the depths of the forest.

Who now rocks his mutilated body? The wind, or the ceiba
tree? Isn't it the ceiba from its enormous crown? Does it not accept
this broken branch as one more arm of the thousand that spring
from its majestic trunk? Will red flowers sprout from it?

Life goes on. Life and death go on.

(212)

1526: Toledo

The American Tiger

Around the Alcázar of Toledo the tamer parades the tiger that the
king has received from the New World. The tamer, a Lombard
with a broad smile and pointed mustachio, leads him by a leash
like a little dog as the jaguar slips over the gravel with padded
steps.

Gonzalo Fernández de Oviedo's blood freezes. From afar he
yells to the keeper not to be so trusting, not to be chummy with
this wild beast, that such animals are not for people.

The tamer laughs, turns the jaguar loose, and strokes its back.
Oviedo hears its deep purr. He well knows that that clenched-
teeth growl means prayer to the devil and threat. One day not far
off, he is sure the tamer will fall into the trap. He will stretch out
his hand to scratch the tiger and be gobbled up after one quick
lash of a paw. Does this poor fellow believe God has given the
jaguar claws and teeth so that a tamer may serve him his meals at
regular hours? None of his lineage has ever sat down to dinner at
the sound of a bell, nor known any manners but devouring. Oviedo
looks at the smiling Lombard and sees a heap of minced meat
between four candles.

"Cut his nails!" he advises, turning away. "Pull his nails out
by the roots, and all his teeth and fangs!"

(166)

1528: Madrid

To Loosen the Purse Strings

The cold filters through the cracks and freezes the ink in the ink-pots.

Charles V owes every saint a candle. With money from the Welsers, the Augsburg bankers, he has bought his imperial crown, paid for his wedding, and financed a good part of the wars that have enabled him to humiliate Rome, suppress the Flemish rebellion, and scatter half of France's warrior nobles on the fields of Pavia.

The emperor's teeth ache as he signs the decree conceding to the Welsers the exploration, exploitation, and government of Venezuela.

For many long years Venezuela will have German governors. The first, Ambrosio Alfinger, will leave no Indian not branded and sold in the markets of Santa Marta, Jamaica, and Santo Domingo and will die with his throat pierced by an arrow.

(41, 103, and 165)

1528: Tumbes

Day of Surprises

The southern sea expedition finally comes upon a coast free of mangrove swamps and mosquitos. Francisco Pizarro, who has word of a village nearby, orders a soldier and an African slave to start walking.

The white and the black reach Tumbes across lands that are planted and well watered by irrigation ditches, sowings such as they had never seen in America; in Tumbes, people who neither go naked nor sleep outdoors surround the newcomers and welcome them with gifts. Alonso de Molina's eyes are not big enough to measure the gold and silver covering the walls of the temple.

The people of Tumbes are dazzled by so many things from another world. They pull Alonso de Molina's beard and touch his clothing and iron ax. They gesture to ask about this captured monster with the red crest that shrieks in a cage: What does it want? Alonso points to it, says "rooster," and they learn their first word in the language of Castile.

The African accompanying the soldier is not doing so well. He defends himself by slapping the Indians, who want to rub his skin with dry corncobs. Water is boiling in a huge pot. They want to put him in it to soak out the color.

(166 and 185)

1528: Bad Luck Island

"People Very Generous with What They Have . . ."

Of the ships that sailed for Florida from Sanlúcar de Barrameda, one was hurled by a storm onto the treetops of Cuba, and the sea devoured the others in successive shipwrecks. No better fate awaited the ships that Narváez's and Cabeza de Vaca's men improvised with shirts for sails and horses' manes for rigging.

The shipwrecked men, naked specters, tremble with cold and weep among the rocks of Mal Hado Island. Some Indians turn up to bring them water and fish and roots and seeing them weep, weep with them. The Indians shed rivers of tears, and the longer the lamentations continue, the sorrier the Spaniards feel for themselves.

The Indians lead them to their village. So that the sailors won't die from the cold, they keep lighting fires at rest stops along the way. Between bonfire and bonfire they carry them on litters, without letting their feet touch ground.

The Spaniards imagine that the Indians will cut them into pieces and throw them in the stewpot, but in the village they continue sharing with them the little food they have. As Álvar Núñez Cabeza de Vaca will tell it, the Indians are horrified and hot with anger when they learn that, while on the beach, five Christians *ate one another until only one remained, who being alone had no one to eat him.*

(39)

1531: *Orinoco River*

Diego de Ordaz

The wind remains recalcitrant, and launches tow the ship upstream. The sun flagellates the water.

The captain's coat of arms features the cone of the volcano Popocatépetl, because he was the first Spaniard to tread the snow of its summit. On that day he was at such an altitude that through the whirlwinds of volcanic ash he saw the backs of eagles as well as the city of Tenochtitlán shimmering in the lake; but he had to make a fast getaway because the volcano thundered with fury and threatened him with a rain of fire and stones and black smoke.

Today Diego de Ordaz, drenched to the bone, wonders if this Orinoco River will lead him to where the gold waits. The Indians of the villages keep gesturing, farther on, farther on, while the captain chases mosquitos and eases the crudely patched hull of the ship creakily forward. The monkeys protest and invisible parrots scream *getoutahere, getoutahere,* and many nameless birds flutter between the shores singing *youwontgetme, youwontgetme, youwontgetme.*

(175)

Piaroa People's Song About the White Man

The water of the river is bad.
The fish take shelter
high in the ravines
red with mud.
The man with the beard passes,
the white man.
The man with the beard passes
in the big canoe
with creaking oars
that the snakes bite.

(17)

1531: Mexico City

The Virgin of Guadelupe

That light, does it rise from the earth or fall from the sky? Is it lightning bug or bright star? It doesn't want to leave the slopes of Tepeyac and in dead of night persists, shining on the stones and entangling itself in the branches. Hallucinating, inspired, the naked Indian Juan Diego sees it: The light of lights opens up for him, breaks into golden and ruby pieces, and in its glowing heart appears that most luminous of Mexican women, she who says to him in the Náhuatl language: "I am the mother of God."

Bishop Zumárraga listens and doubts. The bishop is the Indians' official protector, appointed by the emperor, and also guardian of the branding iron that stamps on the Indians' faces the names of their proprietors. He threw the Aztec codices into the fire, papers painted by the hand of Satan, and destroyed five hundred temples and twenty thousand idols. Bishop Zumárraga well knows that the goddess of earth, Tonantzin, had her sanctuary high on the slopes of Tepeyac and that the Indians used to make pilgrimages there to worship *our mother*, as they called that woman clad in snakes and hearts and hands.

The bishop is doubtful and decides that the Indian Juan Diego has seen the Virgin of Guadelupe. The Virgin born in Estremadura, darkened by the suns of Spain, has come to the valley of the Aztecs to be the mother of the vanquished.

(60 and 79)

1531: Santo Domingo

A Letter

He presses his temples as he follows the words that advance and retreat: *Do not consider my lowly estate and roughness of expression*, he entreats, *but the goodwill that moves me to say it*.

Fray Bartolomé de las Casas is writing to the Council of the Indies. It would have been better for the Indians, he maintains, *to go to hell with their heresies, their procrastination and their isolation*, than to be saved by the Christians. *The cries of so much*

*spilled human blood reach all the way to heaven: those burned
alive, roasted on grills, thrown to wild dogs . . .*

He gets up, walks. His white habit flaps amid clouds of dust.

Later he sits on the edge of the studded chair. He scratches
his nose with the quill pen. The bony hand writes. For the Indians
in America to be saved and for God's law to be fulfilled, Fray
Bartolomé proposes that the cross should rule over the sword. The
garrisons should submit to the bishops; and colonists should be
sent to cultivate the soil under protection of strong fortresses. The
colonists, he says, *could bring black or Moorish or some kind of
slaves to serve them, or live by their own labor or in some other
way not prejudicial to the Indians* . . .

(27)

1531: Serrana Island

The Castaway and the Other

A wind of salt and sun mortifies Pedro Serrano, who wanders naked
along the clifftop. Sea gulls flutter in pursuit of him. Shaded by
an upraised hand, his eyes are fixed on enemy territory.

He descends into the cove and walks on the sand. Reaching
the frontier line, he pees. He does not cross the line but knows
that if the other is watching from some hideaway, he will appear
at one bound to settle accounts for such a provocation.

He pees and waits. The birds scream and fly off. Where has
the man stuck himself? The sky is a dazzling white, a light of lime,
and the island is a burning stone; white rocks, white shadows, foam
over the white sand: a small world of sand and lime. Where can
that bastard be hiding?

Much time has passed since Pedro's ship broke up on that
stormy night, and his hair and beard already reached his chest
when the other appeared, riding a board that the furious tide threw
onto the shore. Pedro wrung the water from his lungs, gave him
food and drink, and taught him how not to die on this desert island,
where only rocks grow. He taught him to turn over turtles and
finish them off with one slash, to cut the meat in strips to dry in
the sun, and to collect rainwater in their shells. He taught him to
pray for rain and to dig for clams under the sand, showed him the
crabs' and shrimps' hideouts and offered him turtle eggs and oysters
that the sea brought in attached to mangrove branches. The other

knew from Pedro that it was necessary to collect everything that the sea delivered to the reefs so that the bonfire would burn night and day, fed by dry algae, seaweed, stray branches, starfish, and fish bones. Pedro helped him put up a roof of turtle shells, a bit of shade against the sun, for lack of trees.

The first war was the water war. Pedro suspected that the other was stealing while he slept, and the other accused him of drinking like a beast. When the water gave out and the last drops disputed with fists were spilt, they had no alternative but to drink their own urine and the blood they got from the only turtle that was to be seen. Then they stretched out to die in the shade and had only enough saliva left for muted insults.

Finally rain saved them. The other thought that Pedro could well reduce by half the roof of his house now that turtle shells were so scarce: "Your house is a turtle-shell palace," he said, "and in mine I spend the day all twisted up."

"I shit on God," said Pedro, "and on the mother that calved you. If you don't like my island, get lost!" And he pointed a finger at the vast sea.

They decided to divide the water. From then on, there was a rain deposit on each end of the island.

The fire war came second. They took turns tending the bonfire, in case some ship passed in the distance. One night, when the other was on guard, the fire went out. Pedro cursed and shook him awake.

"If the island is yours, you do it, you swine," said the other and showed his teeth.

They rolled in the sand. When they tired of hitting each other, they resolved that each would light his own fire. Pedro's knife lashed a stone until it produced a few sparks; and since then there is a bonfire at each end of the island.

The knife war came third. The other had nothing to cut with, and Pedro demanded payment in fresh shrimp each time he lent the knife.

Then the food war and the shell-necklace war broke out.

When the latter war ended in an exchange of stones, they signed an armistice and a border treaty. There was no document, since in this desolation not even a cupay leaf can be found on which to scribble anything, and furthermore neither can sign his name; but they marked off a frontier and swore by God and king to respect it. They tossed a fish into the air. Pedro drew the half of the island that faces Cartagena; the other, the half facing Santiago de Cuba.

Now, standing at the frontier, Pedro bites his nails, looks upward as if seeking rain, and thinks: "He must be hiding in some cranny. I can smell him. Mangy. In midocean and he never bathes. He'd rather fry in his own grease. There he goes, yes, on the dodge as ever."

"Hey, asshole!" he yells.

For answer, the thunder of surf, the racket of gulls, the voices of the wind.

"Ingrate!" he shouts, "Son-of-a-bitch!" and shouts until his throat bursts, and runs from one end of the island to the other, backward and forward, alone and naked on the sand without anybody.

(76)

1532: Cajamarca

Pizarro

A thousand men sweep the path of the Inca into the great square where the Spaniards wait in hiding. The multitude trembles at the passage of the Beloved Father, the One, the Only, lord of labors and fiestas; the singers fall silent, and the dancers freeze up. In the half light, last light of the day, the crowns and vestments of Atahualpa and his cortege of nobles of the realm gleam with gold and silver.

Where are the gods brought by the wind? The Inca reaches the center of the square and gives the order to wait. A few days ago, a spy penetrated the camp of the invaders, tugged at their beards, and returned to report that they were no more than a handful of crooks from the sea. That blasphemy cost his life. Where are the sons of Wirachocha, who wear stars on their heels and send forth thunders that provoke stupor, stampede, and death?

The priest Vicente de Valverde emerges from the shadows and goes to meet Atahualpa. He raises the Bible in one hand and a crucifix in the other, as if exorcising a storm on the high seas, and cries that here is God, the true one, and that all the rest is nonsense. The interpreter translates and Atahualpa, at the head of the throng, asks: "Who told you that?"

"The Bible says it, the sacred book."

"Give it here so it can tell me."

A few paces away, Pizarro unsheathes his sword.

Atahualpa looks at the Bible, turns it over in his hand, shakes it to make it talk, and presses it against his ear: "It says nothing. It's empty."

And he drops it to the ground.

Pizarro has been awaiting this moment ever since the day he knelt before Emperor Charles V, described the empire as big as Europe that he had discovered and proposed to conquer, and promised him the most splendid treasure in human history. And even earlier: since the day when his sword drew a line in the sand and a few soldiers dying of hunger, bent with disease, swore to follow him to the end. And earlier yet, much earlier: Pizarro has awaited this moment since he was dumped at the door of an Estremadura church fifty-four years ago and drank sow's milk for lack of anyone to suckle him.

Pizarro yells and pounces. At the signal, the trap is sprung. From the ambush trumpets blare, arquebuses roar, and the cavalry charges the stunned and unarmed crowd.

(76, 96, and 221)

1533: Cajamarca

The Ransom

To buy the life of Atahualpa, silver and gold pour in. Like a swarm of ants down the empire's four highways come long lines of llamas, and people with shoulders bent under their loads. The most splendid booty comes from Cuzco: an entire garden, trees and flowers of solid gold, and uncut precious stones, and birds and animals of pure silver and turquoise and lapis lazuli.

The oven receives gods and adornments and vomits bars of gold and silver. Officers and soldiers shout to have it divided. For six years they have had no pay.

Of each five ingots, Francisco Pizarro sets one apart for the king. Then he crosses himself. He asks the help of God, who knows all, to see justice done and asks the help of Hernando de Soto, who knows how to read, to keep an eye on the scribe.

He assigns one part to the church and another to the military vicar. He handsomely rewards his brothers and the other captains.

Each soldier of the line gets more than Prince Philip makes in a year, and Pizarro becomes the richest man in the world. The hunter of Atahualpa assigns to himself twice as much as the court of Charles V, with its six hundred servants, spends in a year—without counting the Incas' litter, eighty-three kilos of solid gold, which is his trophy as general.

(76 and 184)

1533: Cajamarca

Atahualpa

A black rainbow crossed the sky. The Inca Atahualpa didn't want to believe it.

In the days of the fiesta of the sun, a condor fell lifeless in the Plaza of Happiness. Atahualpa didn't want to believe it.

He put to death messengers who brought bad news and with one ax blow decapitated the old prophet who announced misfortune. He had the oracle's house burned down and witnesses of the prophecy cut to pieces.

Atahualpa had the eighty sons of his brother Huáscar bound to posts on the roads, and the vultures gorged themselves with that meat. Huáscar's wives tinted the waters of the Adamarca River with blood. Huáscar, Atahualpa's prisoner, ate human shit and sheep's piss and had a dressed-up stone for a wife. Later Huáscar said and was the last to say: *Soon they will kill him as he kills me.* And Atahualpa didn't want to believe it.

When his palace turned into his jail, he didn't want to believe it. Atahualpa, Pizarro's prisoner, said: *I am the greatest of all princes on earth.* The ransom filled one room with gold and two rooms with silver. The invaders melted down even the golden cradle in which Atahualpa heard his first song.

Seated on Atahualpa's throne, Pizarro told him he had decided to confirm his death sentence. Atahualpa replied: *"Don't tell me those jokes."* Nor does he want to believe it now, as step by step he mounts the stairs, dragging his chains, in the milky light of dawn.

Soon the news will be spread among the countless children of the earth who owe obedience and tribute to the son of the sun. In Quito they will mourn the death of the Shadow That Protects:

puzzled, lost, memory denied, alone. In Cuzco there will be joy and drunken sprees.

Atahualpa is bound by the hands, feet, and neck, but still thinks: *What did I do to deserve death?*

At the foot of the gallows, he refuses to believe that he has been defeated by man. Only gods could have done it. His father, the sun, has betrayed him.

Before the iron tourniquet breaks his neck, he weeps, kisses the cross, and accepts baptism with another name. Giving his name as Francisco, which is his conqueror's name, he beats on the doors of the Paradise of the Europeans, where no place is reserved for him.

(57, 76, and 221)

1533: Xaquixaguana

The Secret

Pizarro marches on Cuzco. Now he heads a great army. Manco Cápac, the Incas' new king, has added thousands of Indians to the side of the handful of conquistadors. But Atahualpa's generals harry the advance. In the valley of Xaquixaguana, Pizarro captures a messenger of his enemies.

Fire licks the soles of the prisoner's feet.

"What does this message say?"

The Chasqui is a man experienced in endless trottings through the icy winds of the plain and the scorching heat of the desert. The job has accustomed him to pain and fatigue. He moans but won't talk.

After very long torment his tongue loosens: "That the horses won't be able to climb the mountains."

"What else?"

"That there's nothing to fear. That horses are scary but do no harm."

"And what else?"

They make him tread on the fire.

"And what else?"

He has lost his feet. Before losing his life, he says: "That you people die, too."

(81 and 185)

1533: Cuzco

The Conquerors Enter
the Sacred City

In the noon radiance, the soldiers make their way through the cloud of smoke. A whiff of damp leather mixes with the smell of burning, while the clatter of horses' hooves and cannon wheels is heard.

An altar rises in the plaza. Silk banners embroidered with eagles escort the new god, who has his arms open and wears a beard like his sons. Isn't the new god seeing his sons, battle-axes in hand, pounce upon the gold of the temples and tombs?

Amid the stones of Cuzco, blackened by fire, the old and the paralytic dumbly await the days to come.

(50 and 76)

1533: Riobamba

Alvarado

Half a year before, the ships anchored in Puerto Viejo. Inspired by promises of a virgin kingdom, Pedro de Alvarado had sailed from Guatemala. With him went five hundred Spaniards and two thousand Indian and Negro slaves. Messengers had reported to him: "The power that awaits you makes what you have seem like dirt. To the north of Tumbes you will multiply your fame and wealth. To the south, Pizarro and Almagro have now become the masters, but the fabulous kingdom of Quito belongs to no one."

In the coastal villages they found gold, silver, and emeralds. Loaded with quick fortunes, they set off for the mountains. They faced jungles, swamps, fevers that kill in a day or leave one mad, and terrifying rains of volcanic ash. In the Andean foothills, snowstorms and winds that cut like knives broke the bodies of the slaves, who had never known cold, and many Spaniards left their bones in the mountains. Soldiers dismounting to tighten their horses' girths remained permanently frozen. The booty was thrown to the bottom of ravines: Alvarado offered gold, and the soldiers clamored for food and shelter. His eyes burned by the blinding snow, Alvarado kept charging up the trail to cut off with one sword-blow the heads of slaves who fell and of soldiers who wished they hadn't come.

More dead than alive, with muscles iced and blood frozen, the toughest ones managed to reach the plateau. Finally today they have hit the royal highway of the Incas, the one that leads to Quito, to paradise. No sooner do they arrive than they find in the mud fresh hoofprints. Captain Benalcázar has beaten them to it.

(81 and 97)

1533: Quito

This City Kills Itself

Benalcázar's men break in, unstoppable. Thousands of Indian allies, enemies of the Incas, are spying and fighting for them. After three battles, the die is cast. Already beating a retreat, General Rumiñahui sets fire to Quito. The invaders won't enjoy it alive or find any treasures except those they can dig from graves. The city of Quito, cradle and throne of Atahualpa, is a giant bonfire between two volcanos.

Rumiñahui, who has never been wounded in the back, turns away from the soaring flames. There are tears in his eyes, from the smoke.

(158 and 214)

1533: Barcelona

The Holy Wars

From America come the heralds of good tidings. The emperor closes his eyes and sees sails approaching and savors the smell of tar and salt. The emperor breathes like the ocean, high tide, low tide; and he blows to speed the ships swollen with treasure.

Fate has just awarded him a new kingdom, *where gold and silver abound like iron in Vizcaya.* The astounding booty is on its way. With it he will finally be able to calm down the bankers who are strangling him and pay his soldiers—Swiss pikemen, German mercenaries, Spanish infantry—who never see a coin even in dreams. The Atahualpa ransom will finance the holy wars against the Islamic half moon, which has reached the very gates of Vienna, and against the heretics who follow Luther in Germany. The emperor will fit out a great fleet to sweep Sultan Suliman and the old pirate Redbeard off the Mediterranean.

The mirror reflects the image of the god of war: damascene armor with chiseled insertions at the edge of the gorget and breastplate, feathered helmet, face illumined by the sun of glory—bristling eyebrows over melancholy eyes, bearded chin thrust out. The emperor dreams of Algiers and hears the call of Constantinople. Tunis, fallen into infidel hands, also awaits the general of Jesus Christ.

(41 and 50)

1533: Seville

The Treasure of the Incas

From the first of the ships, gold and silver are tossed onto the docks of Seville. Oxen drag the loaded vats in carts to the Chamber of Commerce. Murmurs of wonder arise from the crowd assembled to witness the unloading. There is talk of mysteries and of the conquered monarch across the ocean.

Two men, two drunks, emerge arm-in-arm from the tavern that faces the docks. They join the crowd and ask shrilly where the notary is. They are not celebrating the treasure of the Incas. They are flushed and glowing from a session of good wine and because they have made a very cordial pact. They have agreed to exchange wives, you take mine, who is a jewel, I take yours, although she isn't worth much, and they are looking for the notary to make it official.

They pay no mind to the gold and silver of Peru; and the dazzled crowd pays none to the castaway who has arrived along with the treasure. The ship, drawn by a bonfire, has rescued him from a Caribbean islet. His name is Pedro Serrano, and nine years before he had swum to safety from a shipwreck. He uses his hair to sit on, his beard as an apron, has leathery skin, and hasn't stopped talking since they took him aboard. Now he keeps on telling his story amid the uproar. No one listens.

(41 and 76)

1534: Riobamba

Inflation

When news of Atahualpa's gold reached Santo Domingo, everyone went looking for a ship. Alonso Hernández, dealer in Indians, was among the first to take off in a hurry. He embarked in Panama and on arrival at Tumbes bought himself a horse. In Tumbes the horse cost seven times more than in Panama and thirty times more than in Santo Domingo.

The climb into the mountains has put Hernández back on foot. To complete the journey to Quito, he buys another horse. He pays ninety times the Santo Domingo price. For 350 pesos he also buys a black slave. In Riobamba a horse costs eight times more than a man.

All is for sale in this realm, even the flags smeared with mud and blood, and everything is priced sky-high. A bar of gold is charged for two sheets of paper.

The merchants, newly arrived, defeat the conquistadors without drawing a sword.

(81, 166, and 184)

1535: Cuzco

The Brass Throne

On the knees of the little king, vassal to another king, lies no gold scepter but a stick shining with bits of colored glass. Manco Inca wears the scarlet tassel on his head, but the triple gold necklace is missing from his breast, where the sun does not gleam, nor do the resplendent discs hang from his ears. The cloak of gold and silver threads and vicuña wool is missing from the back of Atahualpa's brother and enemy and inheritor. From the banners beaten by the wind the falcons have disappeared, replaced by the eagles of the emperor of Europe.

No one kneels at the feet of the Inca crowned by Pizarro.

(57)

1536: *Mexico City*

Motolinía

Fray Toribio de Motolinía walks barefoot up the hill. He carries a heavy sack on his back.

Motolinía is the local word for someone poor and afflicted. He still wears the patched, ragged habit that gave him his name years ago, when he arrived walking barefoot, as now, from the port of Veracruz.

He stops at the top of the slope. At his feet extends the enormous lake and in it gleams the city of Mexico. Motolinía passes a hand over his forehead, breathes deeply, and drives into the ground, one after the other, ten crude crosses, branches tied with rope. As he drives them in, he dedicates them:

"This cross, my God, is for the diseases that were not known here and that rage so terribly among the natives."

"This one is for war, and this for hunger, which have killed as many Indians as there are drops in the sea and grains in the sand."

"This is for the tribute collectors, drones who eat the honey of the Indians; and this one for the tribute, which the Indians must sell their children and their lands to pay."

"This one is for the gold mines, which stink so of death that one can't go within a league of them."

"This is for the great city of Mexico, reared on the ruins of Tenochtitlán, and for those who brought beams and stones on their backs to build it, singing and crying out night and day, until they died of exhaustion or were crushed by landslides."

"This is for the slaves who have been dragged here from all directions like herds of beasts, branded on the face; and this one for those who fall by the wayside carrying the enormous loads to maintain the mines."

"And this one, Lord, for the perpetual conflicts and skirmishes of us Spaniards, which always end with the torture and murder of Indians."

Kneeling before the crosses, Motolinía prays: "Forgive them, Lord. I entreat you to forgive them. I know too well that they continue worshiping bloody idols and that if before they had a hundred gods, with you they have a hundred and one. They can't distinguish the Host from a grain of corn. But if they deserve the punishment of your firm hand, they also deserve the pity of your generous heart."

Then Motolinía crosses himself, shakes his habit, and starts back down the hill. A little before Ave Maria time, he reaches the monastery. Alone in his cell, he stretches out on his pallet and slowly munches a tortilla.

(60 and 213)

1536: Machu Picchu
Manco Inca

Sick of being a king treated like a dog, Manco Inca rises against the men with hairy faces. On the empty throne Pizarro installs Paullo, brother of Manco Inca and of Atahualpa and of Huáscar.

On horseback at the head of a large army, Manco Inca lays siege to Cuzco. Bonfires blaze around the city and arrows of burning tinder fall in a steady rain, but hunger strikes the besiegers harder than the besieged, and Manco Inca's troops withdraw after half a year amid war cries that split the earth.

The Inca crosses the Urubamba River valley and emerges among the high, fogbound peaks. Stone steps lead him to the secret mountaintop hideaway. Protected by parapets and fortified towers, the fortress of Machu Picchu wields supremacy beyond the world.

(57 and 76)

1536: Valley of Ulúa
Gonzalo Guerrero

Victorious, Alonso de Avila's horsemen withdraw. On the battle-field, among the losers, lies an Indian with a beard. His nude body is an arabesque of ink and blood. Golden symbols hang from his nose, lips, and ears. An arquebus shot has split his forehead.

His name was Gonzalo Guerrero. In his first life he had been a sailor from the port of Palos. His second life began a quarter century ago when he was shipwrecked on the Yucatán coast. Since then he has lived among the Indians. He was a chief in peacetime and a captain in war. He had three children by a Maya woman.

In 1519, Hernán Cortés sent for him.

"*No,*" said Gonzalo to the messenger, "*look at my kids, how pretty they are. Just leave me some of those green beads you're carrying. I'll give them to my kids and tell them: 'My brothers sent you these toys, from my country.'*"

Long afterward, Gonzalo Guerrero has fallen defending another country, fighting beside other brothers, the brothers he chose. He is the first conquistador conquered by the Indians.

(62 and 119)

1536: Culiacán

Cabeza de Vaca

Eight years have passed since Cabeza de Vaca was shipwrecked on Mal Hado Island. Of the six hundred men who sailed from Andalusia, a few deserted along the way and the sea swallowed many; others died of hunger, cold, or Indians, and four, just four, now reach Culiacán.

Álvar Núñez Cabeza de Vaca, Alonso del Castillo, Andrés Dorantes, and Estebanico, black Arab, have crossed all America on foot from Florida to the shores of the Pacific. Naked, shedding their skin like snakes, they have eaten wild grasses and roots, worms and lizards, and anything they could find alive until the Indians gave them blankets and prickly pears and ears of corn in exchange for their miracles and cures. Cabeza de Vaca has brought more than one dead Indian back to life with his Paternosters and Ave Marias and healed many sick ones making the sign of the cross and blowing on the place where they hurt. From league to league grew the fame of these miracle workers; multitudes came out to greet them on the roads, and villages sent them on their way with dance and song.

In Sinaloa, as they made their way south, appeared the first traces of Christians. Cabeza de Vaca and his companions found buckles, horseshoe nails, hitching posts. They also found fear: abandoned fields, Indians who had fled into the mountains.

"We're getting warm," said Cabeza de Vaca. "After such a long walk, we're close to our people."

"*They aren't like you,*" the Indians said. "*You come from where*

*the sun rises and they from where it sets. You heal the sick and
they kill the healthy. You go naked and barefoot. You aren't greedy
for anything."*

(39)

The Pope Says They Are Like Us

Pope Paul III stamps his name with the leaden seal, which carries
the likenesses of St. Peter and St. Paul, and ties it to the parchment.
A new bull issues from the Vatican. It is called *Sublimis Deus* and
reveals that Indians are human beings, endowed with soul and
reason.

(103)

The Mirror

The noonday sun makes the stones smoke and metals flash. Uproar
in the port. Galleons have brought heavy artillery from Seville for
the Santo Domingo fortress.

The mayor, Fernández de Oviedo, supervises the transpor-
tation of culverins and cannons. Under the lash, blacks haul the
cargo at top speed. The carts creak under their load of iron and
bronze, and other slaves come and go through the turmoil, throwing buckets of water on the flames that spurt from overheated axles.

Amid the bustle and pandemonium, an Indian girl is searching
for her master. Her skin is covered with blisters, each step a triumph
as her scanty clothing tortures her skin. Throughout the night and
half the day, from one scream to the next, this girl has endured
the burns of acid. She herself roasted the *guao* tree roots and
rubbed them between her hands to make a paste, then anointed
her whole body, from the roots of her hair to the soles of her feet,
because *guao* burns the skin and removes its color, thus turning
Indian and black women into white ladies of Castile.

"Don't you recognize me, sir?"

Oviedo shoves her away; but the girl insists in her thin voice,
sticking to her master like a shadow, as Oviedo runs shouting orders
to the foremen.

"Don't you know who I am?"
The girl falls to the ground and from the ground keeps asking:
"Sir, sir, I bet you don't know who I am?"

(166)

1538: Valley of Bogotá

Blackbeard, Redbeard, Whitebeard

A year ago Gonzalo Jiménez de Quesada, black beard, black eyes, went in search of the springs of gold at the source of the Magdalena River. Half the population of Santa Marta went after him.

They crossed swamps and lands that steamed in the sun. When they reached the banks of the river, not one of the thousands of naked Indians who were brought along to carry the guns and bread and salt remained alive. As there were no longer any slaves to hunt down and catch, they threw the dogs into vats of boiling water. Then the horses, too, were cut into bits. The hunger was worse than the crocodiles, snakes, and mosquitos. They ate roots and leather straps. They quarreled over the flesh of any man who fell, before the priest had even finished giving him passage to Paradise.

They continued up the river, stung by rains and with no wind in the sails, until Quesada decided to change course. El Dorado must be on the other side of the mountains, he had concluded, not at the river's source. So they walked across the mountains.

After much climbing, Quesada now approaches the green valleys of the Chibcha nation. In the presence of seventy scarecrows eaten up with fever, he raises his sword, takes possession, and proclaims that he will never again obey his governor's orders.

Three and a half years ago, Nicolás de Federmann, red beard, blue eyes, left Coro in search of the earth's golden center, on a pilgrimage through mountains and plains. His Indians and blacks were the first to die.

When Federmann reaches the peaks where they tangle with the clouds, he sees the verdant valleys of the Chibcha nation. One hundred and seventy soldiers have survived, ghosts dragging themselves along wrapped in deerskins. Federmann kisses his sword, takes possession, and proclaims that he will never again obey his governor's orders.

Three long years ago Sebastián de Benalcázar, gray eyes, white beard either from age or from road dust, sallied forth in search of the treasures that the city of Quito, emptied and burned, had denied him. Of the multitude that followed him, one hundred and sixty exhausted Europeans and not one Indian remain. Leveler of cities, founder of cities, Benalcázar has left behind him a trail of ashes and blood and new worlds born from the point of his sword: surrounding the gallows, the plaza; around the plaza, church, houses, ramparts.

The conquistador's helmet gleams on the crest of the cordillera. Benalcázar takes possession of the green valleys of the Chibcha nation and proclaims that he will never again obey the orders of his governor.

From the north has come Quesada. From the east, Federmann. From the south, Benalcázar. Cross and arquebus, sky and soil: After so many crazy wanderings, the three rebel captains descend the cordillera slopes and meet on the plain of Bogotá.

Benalcázar knows that the chiefs of this place travel on golden litters. Federmann hears the sweet melodies that breezes play on the sheets of gold hanging from temples and palaces. Quesada kneels at the shore of the lake where native priests covered with gold dust immerse themselves.

Who will end up with El Dorado? Quesada, the Granadan, who says he got here first? Federmann, the German from Ulm, who conquers in the name of the banker Welser? Benalcázar, the Cordoban?

The three armies, ulcerated skin and bones in rags, size up each other and wait.

Then the German bursts out laughing, doubles up with mirth, and the Andalusians catch the contagion until the three captains collapse, floored by laughter and hunger and what brought them all there, that which is without being and arrived without coming: the realization that El Dorado won't be anybody's.

(13)

1538: Masaya Volcano

Vulcan, God of Money

From the mouth of the volcano Masaya came in other times a naked old woman, wise in many secrets, who gave good advice about corn and war. Since the Christians arrived, say the Indians, the old woman refuses to leave the burning mountain.

Many Christians think the Masaya is a mouth of hell and that its flare-ups and everlasting fiery smoke announce eternal chastisements. Others assert that this incandescent smoke cloud, visible for fifty leagues, is produced by gold and silver being melted and purified, seething in the belly of the mountain. The more the fire blazes, the purer they become.

The expedition has been in preparation for a year. Father Blas del Castillo rises very early and hears the confessions of Pedro Ruiz, Benito Dávila, and Juan Sánchez. The four implore forgiveness with tears in their eyes and begin the march at daybreak.

The priest is the first to go down. He climbs into a basket, helmet on head, stole on chest, and cross in hand, and reaches the huge esplanade that surrounds the mouth of fire.

"It isn't hell but paradise!" he proclaims, black with ashes, as he sticks the cross among the stones. Immediately his companions follow him down. From above, the Indians also send down pulley, chains, cauldrons, beams, bolts . . .

They submerge the iron cauldron. From the depths come neither gold nor silver, nothing but sulphur slag. When they dip the cauldron in deeper, the volcano eats it up.

(203)

1541: Santiago de Chile

Inés Suárez

Some months ago Pedro de Valdivia discovered this hill and this valley. The Araucanians, who had discovered the hill thousands of years earlier, called it Huelén, which means *pain*. Valdivia baptized it Santa Lucía.

From the crest of the hill Valdivia saw the green earth between arms of the river and decided that the world contained no better place to dedicate a city to the apostle Santiago, who accompanies the conquistadors and fights for them. He cut the air with his sword to the four cardinal points of the compass and so was born Santiago of the New Frontier. Now it is enjoying its first summer: a few houses of mud and sticks, roofed with straw, a plaza at the center, stockade all around.

A mere fifty men have remained in Santiago. Valdivia stays with them on the banks of the Cachapoal River. At break of day, the sentry sounds the alarm from the top of the stockade. Squadrons of natives are approaching from all four sides. The Spaniards hear the war cries, and immediately a downpour of arrows falls on them.

By noon some houses are nothing but ashes, and the stockade has fallen. They are fighting body to body in the plaza. Then Inés runs to the hut that serves as prison. There, the guard is standing watch over seven Araucanian chiefs whom the Spaniards captured some time ago. She suggests, implores, orders him to cut their heads off.

"What?"

"Their heads!"

"What?"

"Like this!"

Inés seizes his sword, and seven heads fly through the air. Those heads turn the besieged into pursuers. Taking the offensive, the Spaniards invoke not the apostle Santiago but Our Lady of Good Help.

Inés Suárez, the woman from Malaga, had been the first to sign up when Valdivia started recruiting at his house in Cuzco. She came to these southern lands at the head of the invading forces, riding alongside Valdivia, sword of stout steel, coat of fine mail, and ever since she marches, fights, and sleeps with Valdivia. Today she has taken his place.

She is the only woman among the men. They say: "She's *macho*" and compare her with Roldán or El Cid, while she rubs oil on the fingers of Captain Francisco de Aguirre. They have stuck to his sword hilt and cannot be prised off although, for today, the war is over.

(67, 85, and 130)

1541: Rock of Nochistlán

Never

They had seized even his mule. Those who now eat off his silver service and tread his carpets had thrown him out of Mexico with fettered feet.

Ten years later they, the officials, summon the warrior back. Alvarado leaves off governing Guatemala and comes to chastise Indians in these ungrateful lands that he conquered along with Cortés. He wants to push on north to the seven golden cities of

Cíbola, but this morning, at the height of the battle, a horse falls on him and throws him down a cliff.

To Mexico Pedro de Alvarado has returned, and in Mexico he lies. His helmet hangs from a branch, and his sword has fallen among the brambles. *Don't sheath me without honor* can still be read on the steel blade.

(81)

1541: Old Guatemala City

Beatriz

Pedro de Alvarado had married Francisca, but Francisca was struck down by the orange-blossom tea that she drank on the road to Veracruz. Then he married Francisca's sister, Beatriz.

Beatriz was waiting for him in Guatemala when she learned she had been two months widowed. She decked her house in black inside and out and nailed up doors and windows so that she could cry her heart out in private.

She weeps looking in the mirror at her nude body, which has dried up from so much waiting and now has nothing left to wait for, a body that no longer sings, and she weeps through her mouth, which can only sob: "Are you there, my darling?"

She weeps for this house that she hates and this land that is not hers and for the years spent between this house and the church, from Mass to Mess and from baptism to burial, surrounded by drunken soldiers and Indian servants who make her sick. She weeps for the food that upsets her and for him who never came, because there was always some war to fight or land to be conquered. She weeps for all the tears she has shed alone in her bed, when a dog's bark or a rooster's crow made her jump and she learned, all alone, to read the darkness and listen to the silence and make drawings in the air. She weeps and weeps, broken up inside.

When she finally emerges from seclusion, she announces: "I am the governor of Guatemala."

She cannot govern for long.

The volcano vomits a cataract of water and stones that drowns the city and kills whatever it touches. The flood keeps advancing toward Beatriz's house, while she runs to the chapel, goes to the altar, and embraces the Virgin. Her eleven maids embrace her feet and each other while Beatriz cries: "Are you there, my darling?"

The torrent destroys the city that Alvarado founded and, as it roars ever louder, Beatriz keeps crying out: "Are you there?"

(81)

1541: Cabo Frío

At Dawn, the Cricket Sang

It had been silent ever since they took it aboard in the port of Cádiz, two and a half months of silence and sadness in its little cage, until today its cry of joy rang out from bow to stern and woke everybody up.

"A miracle! A miracle!"

There was just time for the ship to alter course. The cricket was celebrating the approach of land. Thanks to its alarm, the sailors were not dashed to pieces against the rocks of the Brazilian coast.

Cabeza de Vaca, chief of this expedition to the River Plate, is very knowing about such matters. They call him Alvar the Miracle Worker since he crossed America from coast to coast reviving the dead in Indian villages.

(39)

1542: Quito

El Dorado

For a long time Gonzalo Pizarro's men have been trekking deep into the jungle, in search of the gold-skinned prince and the groves of cinnamon. They have found snakes and bats, armies of mosquitos, swamps and rains that never stop. Night after night lightning flashed the way for this caravan of naked men huddled together by panic.

Skin and bones and sores, they are arriving this afternoon at the outskirts of Quito. Each one recites his name in order to be recognized. Of the expedition's four thousand Indian slaves, none has returned.

Captain Gonzalo Pizarro kneels and kisses the ground. Last night he dreamed of a dragon that jumped on him, tore him apart, and ate his heart. This keeps him from blinking, now, when they tell him the news:

"Your brother Francisco has been assassinated in Lima."

(97)

1542: Conlapayara

The Amazons

The battle wasn't going badly today, St. John's Day. With bursts of arquebus and crossbow, from their brigantines, Francisco de Orellana's men were emptying the white canoes coming from shore. But witches were on the warpath. The warrior women appeared suddenly, scandalously beautiful and ferocious, and then canoes covered the river, and the ships took flight upstream like scared porcupines, bristling with arrows from stem to stern and even in the mainmasts.

These viragos laughed as they fought. They put themselves in front of the men, females of great attractiveness and charm, and there was no more fear in the village of Conlapayara. They fought laughing and dancing and singing, their breasts quivering in the breeze, until the Spaniards got lost beyond the mouth of the Tapajós River, exhausted from so much effort and astonishment.

They had heard tell of such women, and now they believe it. The women live to the south, in dominions without men, where children born male are drowned. When the body hungers, they make war on the coastal tribes and take prisoners. They return them the next morning. After a night of love, he who went as a boy returns an old man.

Orellana and his soldiers will keep sailing down the world's mightiest river and reach the sea without pilot or compass or chart. They sail in the two brigantines that they improvised with strokes of the ax in midjungle, making nails and hinges out of dead horses' shoes and bellows from old shoe leather. They let themselves drift down the Amazon River, through the jungle, without the energy to row, and mumbling prayers: They pray to God to make the next enemies male, however many they may be.

(45)

1542: Iguazú River

In Broad Daylight

Steamy beneath his iron clothing, tormented by bites and wounds, Álvar Núñez Cabeza de Vaca dismounts from his horse and sees God for the first time.

Huge butterflies flutter around him. Cabeza de Vaca kneels before the Iguazú waterfalls. The roaring, foaming waters plunge from the heavens to wash off the blood of all the fallen and redeem all the deserts, torrents that turn loose vapors and rainbows, that drag jungles from the depths of the dry earth; waters that bellow, God's ejaculation, fertilizing the land, eternal first day of Creation.

To come upon this rain of God, Cabeza de Vaca has walked half the world and sailed the other half. To meet it he has endured shipwrecks and sufferings; to see it he was born with eyes in his face. What remains to him of life will be a gift.

(39)

1543: Cubagua

The Pearl Fishers

The city of New Cádiz has fallen, overwhelmed by seaquake and pirates. Previously the whole island had fallen, this island of Cubagua where forty-five years ago Columbus traded the Indians broken dishes for pearls. After so much fishing, the oysters have given out and the pearl divers lie at the sea bottom.

In these waters, Indian slaves were sent down with stones tied to their backs, to reach where the biggest pearls lay, and from sun to sun they swam without a break, gathering the oysters stuck to the rocks and the bottom.

No slave lasted long. Sooner or later their lungs burst: a stream of blood rose to the surface instead of the diver. The men who had caught or bought them said that the sea turned red because, like women, oysters menstruate.

(102 and 103)

1544: Machu Picchu

The Stone Throne

From here Manco Inca has reigned over the lands of Vilcabamba. From here he has waged a long and hard war, a war of burnings and ambushes. The invaders do not know the labyrinths that lead to the secret citadel. No enemy knows them.

Only Captain Diego Méndez could reach the hideaway. He came in flight. On orders from the son of Almagro, his sword had pierced the throat of Francisco Pizarro. Manco Inca gave him asylum. Afterward Diego Méndez stuck a dagger into Manco Inca's back.

Amid the stones of Machu Picchu, where the bright flowers offer honey to whoever fertilizes them, lies the Inca wrapped in beautiful cloths.

(57)

War Song of the Incas

We will drink from the skull of the traitor
And from his teeth a necklace make.
Of his bones we will make flutes,
Of his skin a drum.
Then we will dance.

(202)

1544: Campeche

Las Casas

For some time he has been waiting, here in the port, alone with the heat and mosquitos. He wanders along the wharves, barefoot, listening to the sea's rise and fall and the tap of his staff on the stones. No one has a word to say to the newly anointed bishop of Chiapas.

This is the most hated man in America, *the Antichrist* of the colonial masters, *the scourge of these lands.* He is responsible for the emperor's promulgation of new laws that deprive the conquistadors' sons of Indian slaves. What will become of them without the hands that sustain them in mines and plantations? The new laws take the food from their mouths.

This is the most beloved man in America. Voice of the voiceless, stubborn defender of *those who get worse treatment than the dung in the plazas,* denouncer of *those who for greed turn Jesus Christ into the cruelest of gods and the king into a wolf ravening for human flesh.*

No sooner had he landed in Campeche than Fray Bartolomé de las Casas announced that no owner of Indians would be absolved in confession. They answered that here his bishop's credentials were worthless, as were the new laws, because they had come printed and not in the royal scribes' handwriting. He threatened excommunication, and they laughed. They roared with laughter, because Fray Bartolomé was well known to be deaf.

This evening the messenger has arrived from the royal city of Chiapas. The town government sends word that there is nothing in its treasury to pay for the bishop's journey to his diocese and sends him a few coins from the burial fund.

(27 and 70)

1544: Lima

Carvajal

The dawn light gives form and face to the shadows that hang from the plaza lanterns. Some early riser recognizes them with a start: Two conquistadors of early vintage, from among those who captured the Inca Atahualpa in Cajamarca, swing with protuding tongues and staring eyes.

Roll of drums, clatter of hooves: The city jumps awake. The town crier shouts at the top of his lungs, and at his side, Francisco Carvajal dictates and listens. The crier announces that all of Lima's principal gentry will be hanged like those two and not a house will be spared from plunder if the council does not accept Gonzalo

Pizarro as governor. General Carvajal, field commander of the rebel troops, gives a noon deadline.

"Carvajal!"

Before the echo dies away, the judges of the royal tribunal and the notables of Lima have flung on some clothes and rushed in disarray to the palace and are signing, without discussion, the decree recognizing Gonzalo Pizarro as sole and absolute authority.

All that is lacking is the signature of lawyer Zárate, who strokes his neck and hesitates while the others wait, dazed, trembling, hearing or thinking they hear the panting of horses and the curses of soldiers who take the field at short rein, eager to attack.

"Get a move on," they implore.

Zárate thinks about the good dowry he is leaving for his unmarried daughter, Teresa, and his generous offerings to the Church that have more than paid for another, serener life than this one.

"What is your honor waiting for?"

"Carvajal's patience is short!"

Carvajal: more than thirty years of wars in Europe, ten in America. He fought at Ravenna and at Pavia. He was in on the sack of Rome. He fought with Cortés in Mexico and with Francisco Pizarro in Peru. Six times he has crossed the cordillera.

"The Devil of the Andes!"

He is a giant who has been known to throw off helmet and cuirass in midbattle and offer his breast. He eats and sleeps on his horse.

"Calm, gentlemen, keep calm!"

"Innocent blood will flow!"

"No time to lose!"

The shadow of the gallows looms over newly purchased titles of nobility.

"Sign, sir! Let us avoid further tragedies for Peru!"

Lawyer Zárate dips the goose-quill pen, draws a cross, and beneath, before signing, writes: *I swear by God and this Cross and by the words of the Evangelist Saints that I sign for three reasons: for fear, for fear, and for fear.*

(167)

1545: Royal City of Chiapas

The Bad News Comes
from Valladolid

The Crown has suspended the most important new laws, which set the Indians free. While they lasted, barely three years, who observed them? In reality, even Indians marked *free* on the arm in vivid red continued to be slaves.

"For this they have told me I was right?"

Fray Bartolomé feels abandoned by God, a leaf without a branch, alone and a nobody.

"They said yes to me so that nothing would change. Now not even paper will protect those who have no more shield than their bowels. Did the monarchs receive the New World from the pope for this? Is God a mere pretext? This hangman's shadow, does it come from my body?"

Wrapped in a blanket, he writes a letter to Prince Philip. He announces that he will visit Valladolid without waiting for a reply or permission.

Then Fray Bartolomé kneels on the mat, facing the night, and recites aloud a prayer invented by himself.

(70)

1546: Potosí

The Silver of Potosí

Fifty Indians killed for refusing to work in the excavations. Less than a year since the first vein appeared, and already the slopes of the mountain have been stained with human blood. And a league from here the rocks of the ravine show the dark green spots of the Devil's blood. The Devil shut tight the ravine that leads to Cuzco and crushed Spaniards who passed that way. An archangel hauled the Devil from his cave and dashed him against the rocks. Now the Potosí silver mines have plenty of labor and an open road.

Before the conquest, in the days of the Inca Huaina Cápac,

when the flint pick bit into the mountain's veins of silver, a frightful roar shook the world. Then the voice of the mountain said to the Indians: *"This wealth has other owners."*

(21)

1547: *Valparaíso*

The Parting

Flies buzz among the remains of the banquet. Neither all that wine nor all this sun puts the guzzlers to sleep. This morning, hearts beat fast. Beneath the arbor, facing the sea, Pedro Valdivia is saying good-bye to those who are about to leave. After so much war and hunger in the wilds of Chile, fifteen of his men are returning to Spain. A tear rolls down Valdivia's cheek as he recalls the shared years, the cities born out of nothing, the Indians subdued by the iron of Spanish lances.

"*My only consolation,*" he says, his speech warming up, "*is the knowledge that you will be resting and enjoying what you so well deserve, and that eases my grief at least a little.*"

Not far from the beach, waves rock the ship that will take them to Peru. From there they will sail for Panama; across Panama to the other sea, and then . . . It will be long, but a stretch of the legs makes one feel that one is already walking the wharves of Seville. The baggage, clothing, and gold has been on board since the night before. The scribe Juan Pinel will be taking three thousand pesos in gold from Chile. With his bundle of papers, quill pen, and inkpot, he has followed Valdivia like a shadow, attesting to his every step and giving his every act the force of law. Many times death has scraped against him. This small fortune will more than even up the score for the teenage daughters who await scribe Pinel in far-off Spain.

The soldiers are dreaming out loud when suddenly someone jumps up and shouts: "Valdivia? Where's Validivia?"

Valdivia is looking smaller by the second. There he goes, rowing the only boat toward the ship loaded with everybody's gold.

On the beach of Valparaíso curses and threats drown out the din of the waves.

The sails swell out and move off in the direction of Peru. Valdivia is off chasing the title of governor of Chile. With the gold that is aboard, and the vigor of his arm, he hopes to convince the top men in Lima.

Sitting on a rock, scribe Juan Pinel clutches his head and cannot stop laughing. His daughters will die as virgins in Spain. Some of the men weep, scarlet with fury; and bugler Alonso de Torres plays an old melody out of tune and then smashes the bugle, which was all he had left.

(67 and 85)

Song of Nostalgia, from the Spanish Songbook

Lonesome I am for thee,
Country that suckled me.

If luckless I should die,
In the mountains bury me high,
So that my body in the grave
Won't miss the land I crave.
Bury me high as you can bear,
To see if I can see from there
The land for which I shed a tear.

(7)

1548: Xaquixaguana

The Battle of Xaquixaguana
Is Over

Gonzalo Pizarro, the best lancer in America, the man who can split a mosquito in flight with an arquebus or a crossbow, yields his sword to Pedro de La Gasca.

Gonzalo slowly removes his armor of Milanese steel. La Gasca came on a mission to clip his wings, and now the chief of the rebels no longer dreams of crowning himself king of Peru. He only dreams of La Gasca sparing his life.

Pedro de Valdivia enters the tent of the victors. The infantry have fought under his orders.

"The king's honor rested in your hands, Governor," says La Gasca.

This is the first time the king's representative calls him governor, governor of Chile. Valdivia thanks him with a nod. He has other things to ask, but hardly does he open his mouth when the soldiers bring in Gonzalo Pizarro's second-in-command. General Carvajal enters wearing his spectacularly plumed helmet. His captors dare not touch him.

Of all Pizarro's officers, Carvajal is the only one who did not change sides when La Gasca offered the king's pardon to repentant rebels. Many soldiers and captains quickly spurred their horses and galloped across the marsh to the other camp. Carvajal stayed put and fought until they unhorsed him.

"Carvajal," says Diego Centeno, commander of the victorious troops, "you have fallen with honor, Carvajal."

The old man does not even look at him.

"Are you pretending not to know me?" says Centeno and puts out a hand to receive his sword.

Carvajal, who has more than once defeated Centeno and has put him to flight and chased him through half of Peru, stares at him and says: "I only knew you from the back."

And he gives his sword to Pedro de Valdivia.

(67 and 85)

1548: Xaquixaguana

The Executioner

Wrapped in ropes and chains, Carvajal arrives inside an enormous basket hauled by mules. Amid clouds of dust and cries of hatred, the old warrior sings. His hoarse voice pierces the clamor of insults, ignoring the kicks and blows of those who yesterday applauded him and today spit in his face.

What a fable!
A child in a cradle,
Old man in a cradle!
What a fable!

he sings from the basket that bumps him along. When the mules reach the block, the soldiers throw Carvajal out at the executioner's feet. The crowd howls as the executioner slowly unsheaths the sword.

"Brother Juan," asks Carvajal, "since we're both in the same trade, treat me like one tailor to another."

Juan Enríquez is the name of this lad with the kind face. He had another name in Seville, when he wandered the wharves dreaming of being the king's executioner in America. They say he loves the job because it instills fear, and there is no important gentleman or great warrior who does not draw aside on passing him in the street. They also say that he is a lucky avenger. They pay him to kill; and his weapon never rusts, nor does his smile vanish.

Poor old grandpa!
Poor old grandpa!

hums Carvajal in a low, sad voice, because he has just thought of his horse Boscanillo, who is also old and defeated, and how well they understood one another.

Juan Enríquez seizes his beard with the left hand and, with the right, slices his neck with one blow.

Beneath the golden sun, applause breaks out.

The executioner holds up the head of Carvajal, who until a moment ago was eighty-four years old and had never forgiven anyone.

(76 and 167)

1548: Xaquixaguana
On Cannibalism in America

Since Francisco Pizarro attended, in mourning dress, the funeral of his victim Atahualpa, several men have succeeded to command and power over the vast kingdom that was the Incas'.

Diego de Almagro, governor of one part of that land, rose against Francisco Pizarro, governor of the other. Both had sworn on the sacred Host that they would share honors, Indians, and lands *without either taking more*, but Pizarro wanted it and won out and Almagro was beheaded.

Almagro's son avenged his father and proclaimed himself governor over the corpse of Pizarro. Then Almagro's son was sent to the scaffold by Cristóbal Vaca de Castro, who passed into history as the only one who escaped gallows, ax, or sword.

Later Gonzalo Pizarro, brother of Francisco, rose in arms against Blasco Núñez Vela, first viceroy of Peru. Núñez Vela fell from his horse badly wounded. His head was cut off and nailed to a pike.

Gonzalo Pizarro was on the point of crowning himself king. Today, Monday, April 9, he ascends the slope that leads to the block. He goes mounted on a mule. They have bound his hands behind his back and thrown over him a black cape, which covers his face and keeps him from seeing the bodiless head of Francisco de Carvajal.

(76 and 81)

1548: Guanajuato

Birth of the Guanajuato Mines

"God's peace be with you, brother."

"So be it, traveler."

Greetings pass between the two muleteers who come from Mexico City and decide to encamp. Night has fallen, and from the shadows those who sleep by day watch them.

"Isn't that the mountain of Cubilete?"

"Of the damned, you might call it."

Maese Pedro and Martín Rodrigo are off to Zacatecas to seek their fortune in its mines, and they bring what they have, a few mules, to sell at a good price. At dawn they will continue on their way.

They lay a few branches on a mattress of dry leaves and encircle it with stones. Flint strikes steel, the spark becomes a flame: facing the fire, the muleteers swap stories, their bad luck, and while they are at it, rags and nostalgia, one of them yells: "They shine!"

"What?"

"The stones!"

Martín Rodrigo leaps into the air, forming a squalid five-pointed star against the moonlit sky, and Maese Pedro breaks his nails on the hot rocks and burns his lips kissing them.

(182)

1549: La Serena

The Return

Pedro de Valdivia has just disembarked at the Quintero anchorage, and soon he runs into the acid smell of carrion.

In Peru, Valdivia has carried more than enough weight to avoid traps and surmount doubts and enemies. The vigor of his arm placed at the king's service plus the glitter of the gold he grabbed from his men on the Valparaíso beach have proved highly eloquent to the top men in Lima. After two years, he returns with his title of governor of Chile well signed and sealed. He also takes back the obligation to return that gold to the last gram as well as another obligation, which gnaws at his heart. Given his brand-new title, he must put an end to his affair with Inés Suárez and bring his legal wife here from Spain.

Chile does not receive him with a smile. In this city of La Serena, which he had baptized with the name of his birthplace, the Spaniards are lying about handless and headless among ruins. His fascinating life stories do not interest the vultures.

(67 and 85)

The Last Time

At dawn an undulating streak opens in the black mist and separates earth from sky.

Inés, who has not slept, detaches herself from Valdivia's embrace and leans on her elbow. She is saturated with him, and every little corner of her body feels fiercely alive; she looks at her hand in the misty first light. Her own fingers scare her: they burn. She feels for the dagger. She raises it. Valdivia is asleep and snoring. The dagger hesitates in midair over the nude body.

Centuries pass.

Finally Inés softly plunges the dagger into the pillow beside his face and moves away on tiptoe over the earth floor, leaving the bed woman-free.

1552: Valladolid

He Who Always Took the Orders Now Gives Them

The woman kisses the bar of silver with her lips, with her forehead, with her breasts, while the priest reads aloud the letter from her husband, Juan Prieto, dated in Potosí. The letter and ingot have taken nearly a year to cross the ocean and reach Valladolid.

Juan Prieto writes that while others spend their time at drinking bouts and bullfights, he doesn't hang out in the taverns or the bullring, that in Potosí men put hand to sword on the slightest provocation, and that there are dust storms that ruin the clothing and madden the spirit. That he thinks of nothing but returning to Spain and now sends this big silver bar for the construction of a garden in which his welcome-home banquet will be held.

The garden must have a double iron gate and a stone arch broad enough for the guests invited to the fiesta to pass through in their carriages. It is to be a walled garden, high walls without any openings, full of trees and flowers and rabbits and doves. In the center there must be a big table with viands for the gentry of Valladolid whom he had served years before as a domestic. A carpet should be laid over the grass next to the head of the table, and on the carpet should sit his wife and his daughter Sabina.

He especially stresses to his wife that she must not take her eyes off Sabina nor let even the sun touch her, that it is to get her a good dowry and good marriage that he has spent all these years in the Indies.

(120)

1553: The Banks of the San Pedro River

Miguel

Plenty of his skin has stuck to the cords of the whip. They accused him of slacking off at work or of losing a tool, and the overseer said, "Let him pay with his body." When they were going to tie him up for some more lashes, Miguel grabbed a sword and lost himself in the woods.

Other slaves from the Buría mines fled behind him. A few Indians joined the black runaways. Thus was born the small army that last year attacked the mines and the newborn city of Barquisimeto.

Afterward the rebels moved farther into the mountains and, far away from everything, founded this free kingdom on the riverbanks. The Jirijara Indians painted themselves black from head to foot and, together with the Africans, proclaimed the Negro Miguel king.

Queen Guiomar strolls magnificently among the palms. Her full skirt of brocade rustles. Two pages raise the tip of her silk train.

From his wooden throne, Miguel orders trenches dug and palisades built, names officials and ministers, and appoints the most learned of his men as bishop. At his feet the heir-apparent plays with little stones.

"My kingdom is round and clear-watered," says Miguel as a courtier straightens his lace ruff and another stretches the sleeves of his soldier's jerkin.

In Tocuyo the troop that will kill Miguel and liquidate his kingdom is being readied under the command of Diego de Losada. The Spaniards will come armed with arquebuses and dogs and crossbows. The blacks and Indians who survive will lose their ears or their testicles or the tendons of their feet as an example for all Venezuela.

(2)

A Dream of Pedro de Valdivia

Light from the torches flutters in the fog. Sound of spurs that strike sparks from the paving on a parade ground that is not of Chile nor of anywhere else. In the gallery, a row of court noblemen; long black capes, swords tight at their waists, plumed hats. As Pedro de Valdivia passes, each of the men bows and doffs his hat. When they remove their hats, they remove their heads.

(67 and 85)

1553: *Tucapel*

Lautaro

The scourge of war has hit every part of Chile.

At the head of the Araucanians waves the red cloak of Caupolicán, the Cyclops who can tear out a tree by the roots.

The Spanish cavalry charges. Caupolicán's army opens up like a fan, lets the cavalry enter, snaps shut, and devours it from the flanks.

Valdivia sends in a second battalion, which shatters against a wall of thousands of men. Then he attacks, followed by his best soldiers. He charges at full speed, shouting, lance in hand, and the Araucanians crumble before his lightning offensive.

Meanwhile, at the head of the Indians who serve the Spanish army, Lautaro waits on a hillside.

"What sort of cowardice is this? What shame for our country?"

Until this moment Lautaro has been Valdivia's page. In a flash of fury the page chooses treason; he chooses loyalty. He blows the horn that hangs on his breast and at full gallop launches the attack. He opens a path with blows to right and left, splitting armor plate and forcing horses to their knees, until he reaches Valdivia, stares him in the face, and brings him down.

He is not yet twenty, this new leader of the Araucanians.

(5)

1553: *Tucapel*

Valdivia

There is a fiesta around the cinnamon tree.

The vanquished, clad in loincloths, are watching the dances of the victors, who wear helmet and armor. Lautaro sports the clothes of Valdivia, the green doublet embroidered with gold and silver, the shiny cuirass and the gold-visored helmet topped with emeralds and elegant plumes.

Valdivia, naked, is bidding farewell to the world.

No one has blundered. This is the land that Valdivia chose to die in thirteen years ago, when he left Cuzco followed by seven Spaniards on horseback and a thousand Indians on foot. No one blundered except Doña Marina, the wife he left behind in Estremadura, who after twenty years has decided to cross the ocean and is now aboard ship, with a retinue worthy of her rank as governor's wife, silver throne, blue velvet bed, carpets, and all her court of relatives and servants.

The Araucanians open Valdivia's mouth and fill it with dirt. They make him swallow dirt, handful after handful. They swell up his body with Chilean soil as they tell him: "*You want gold? Eat gold. Stuff yourself with gold.*"

(5 and 26)

1553: Potosí

Beauty and the Mayor

If Potosí had a hospital and she passed by the door, the sick would be cured. But this city or bunch of houses, born less than six years ago, has no hospital.

The mining camp has grown crazily, now containing twenty thousand souls. Each morning new roofs rear up, raised by adventurers who come from everywhere, elbowing and stabbing each other, in search of an easy fortune. No man takes a chance in its earth streets without a sword and leather doublet, and the women are condemned to live behind shutters. The least ugly run the greatest risk; and among them the Beauty—a spinster on top of everything—has no alternative but to cut herself off from the world. She only emerges at dawn, heavily chaperoned, to attend Mass, because just seeing her makes anyone crave to gobble her up, either in one gulp or in sips, and one-armed people to clap hands.

The lord mayor of the town, Don Diego de Esquivel, has cast an eye upon her. They say that this is why he goes about with a broad grin, and all the world knows that he hasn't smiled since that remote day in his infancy when he hurt his facial muscles trying it.

(167)

To the Strains of the Barrel Organ
a Blind Man Sings to Her
Who Sleeps Alone

Lady,
why do you sleep alone,
When you could sleep with a lad
who has trousers
with polished buttons
and jacket
with silver buttonholes?
Up above
there's a green olive tree.
Down below
there's a green orange tree.
And in between
there's a black bird
that sucks
its lump of sugar.

(196)

1553: Potosí

The Mayor and the Gallant

"Don't sleep alone," says someone, "sleep with that one." And points him out. The girl's favorite is a soldier of fine bearing who has honey in his eyes and voice. Don Diego chews over his despair and decides to await his opportunity.

The opportunity comes one night, in one of Potosí's gambling dens, by the hand of a friar who has gambled away the contents of his begging bowl. A skilled card sharp is picking up the fruits of his efforts when the cleaned-out one lowers an arm, pulls a dagger out from beneath his habit, and nails the man's hand to the table. The gallant, who is there out of pure curiosity, jumps into the fray.

All are taken under arrest.

The mayor, Don Diego, has to decide the matter. He faces the gallant and makes him an offer: "Fine or beating."

"A fine I can't pay. I am poor, but a gentleman of pure blood and honored lineage."

"Twelve lashes for this prince," decides the mayor.

"To a Spanish gentleman!" protests the soldier.

"Tell it to my other ear, this one doesn't believe it," says Don Diego, and sits down to enjoy the beating.

When they unbind him, the beaten lover threatens: "I'll take revenge on those ears of yours, Mr. Mayor. I lend them to you for a year. You can use them for that long, but then they're mine."

(167)

1554: Cuzco

The Mayor and the Ears

Ever since the gallant's threat, Don Diego feels his ears every morning on waking up and measures them in the mirror. He has found that his ears grow when they are happy and that cold and depression make them shrink; that glances and calumnies heat them to bright red and that they flap desperately, like birds in a cage, when they hear the screech of a steel blade being sharpened.

To ensure their safety, Don Diego takes them to Cuzco. Guards and slaves accompany him on the long journey.

One Sunday morning, Don Diego is leaving church after Mass, more parading than walking, followed by the little black boy who carries his velvet hassock. Suddenly a pair of eyes fastens on his ears with sure aim, and a blue cloak flashes through the crowd and disappears, fluttering, in the distance.

His ears feel they have been hurt.

(167)

1554: Lima

The Mayor and the Bill Collector

Before long the cathedral bells will be ringing out midnight. It will mark just a year since that stupid episode that obliged Don Diego to move to Cuzco, and from Cuzco to Lima.

Don Diego confirms for the thousandth time that the doors are bolted and that the people standing guard even on the roof have not fallen asleep. He has personally inspected the house corner by corner, without forgetting even the woodpile in the kitchen. Soon he will throw a party. There will be bullfights and masquerades, joustings and fireworks, fowls roasting on spits, and barrels of wine with open spigots. Don Diego will knock Lima's eye out. At the party he will try out his new damask cloak and his new steed with the black velvet gold-studded saddle, which goes so well with the crimson caparison.

He sits down to await the chimes. He counts them. Takes a deep breath.

A slave raises the candelabrum and lights his carpeted way to the bedroom. Another slave takes off his doublet and shoes, those shoes that look like gloves, and his openwork white hose. The slaves close the door and retire to take up their lookout posts until morning.

Don Diego blows out the candles, buries his head in the big silk pillow and, for the first time in a year, falls into an unperturbed sleep.

Much later, the suit of armor that adorns a corner of the bedroom begins to move. Sword in hand, the armor advances in the darkness, very slowly, toward the bed.

(167)

1554: Mexico City

Sepúlveda

The city council of Mexico, cream of the colonial nobility, resolves to send Juan Ginés de Sepúlveda two hundred pesos in gold in recognition of his services and to encourage him in the future.

Sepúlveda, the humanist, is not only a doctor and archpriest, chronicler and chaplain to Charles V. He also shines in business, as witness his growing fortune; and in the courts, he works as an ardent publicity agent for the owners of America's lands and Indians.

In rebuttal to Bartolomé de las Casas's assertions, Sepúlveda maintains that Indians are serfs by nature, according to God's will, and that the Holy Scriptures contain examples to spare of the punishment of the unjust. When Las Casas proposes that Spaniards learn the Indians' languages and Indians the language of Castile, Sepúlveda replies that the difference between Spaniards and Indians is the same as that between male and female and almost the same as that between man and monkeys. For Sepúlveda, what Las Casas calls abuse and crime is a legitimate system of dominion, and he commends the arts of hunting against those who, born to obey, refuse slavery.

The king, who publishes Las Casas's attacks, places a ban on Sepúlveda's treatise on the just causes of the colonial war. Sepúlveda accepts the censure smiling and without protest. In the last analysis, reality is more potent than bad conscience, and he well knows what those in command all know in their hearts: The desire to make money, not to win souls, is what builds empires.

(90 and 118)

1556: Asunción, Paraguay

Conquistadoras

They carried the firewood and the wounded on their backs. The women treated the men like small children: They gave them fresh water and consolation and cobwebs for their bruises. The words of encouragement and of alarm came from their mouths, and likewise the curses that scourged the cowards and pushed the weaklings. They fired the crossbows and guns while the men lay down seeking a bit of shade in which to die. When the survivors of hunger and arrows reached the brigantines, it was the women who hoisted the sails and set the course upriver, rowing and rowing without complaint. Thus it was in Buenos Aires and on the Paraná River.

After twenty years Governor Irala has distributed Indians and lands in Asunción. Bartolomé García, one of those who arrived in brigantines from the South, mumbles his protests. Irala has given him only sixteen Indians: he who still carries an arrowhead in his arm and who fought body-to-body against the pumas that jumped over the Buenos Aires stockade.

"What about me? If you're beefing, what shall *I* say?" cries Doña Isabel de Guevara.

She also had been there from the outset. She came from Spain to found Buenos Aires together with Mendoza and went with Irala up to Asunción. For being a woman, the governor has given her no Indians at all.

(120)

1556: *Asunción, Paraguay*

"The Paradise of Mahomet"

The dice roll. An Indian woman holds up the candle. Whoever wins her takes her naked, for the one who loses her has wagered her without clothes.

In Paraguay, Indian women are trophies of the wheel, dice, or cards, the booty of expeditions into the jungle, the motives for duels and murders. Although there are many of them, the ugliest is worth as much as a side of bacon or a horse. The conquistadors of Indies and Indians go to Mass followed by flocks of women. In this land sterile of gold and silver, some have eighty or a hundred, who by day grind sugarcane and by night spin thread and let themselves be loved, to provide their masters with honey, clothing, children: They help toward forgetting the dream of wealth that reality denied and the distant girlfriends who grow old waiting in Spain.

"Careful. They go to bed with hatred," warns Domingo Martínez, father of countless mestizos and future monks. He says the Indian women are rancorous and stubborn, always eager to return to the woods where they were captured, and that one can't trust them with even an ounce of cotton because they hide it or burn it or give it away, *that their glory is just to ruin the Christians and destroy whatever there is*. Some have hanged themselves or eaten dirt and there are some who deny the breast to their newly born children. The Indian Juliana killed conquistador Nuño de Cabrera one night and shouted to the others to follow her example.

(73 and 74)

Womanizer Song, from the Spanish Songbook

If the Moors can use
seven women,
Why should Spaniards refuse
to use as many?

Oh, what joy
that Spain is back
on the Moorish track.
To love one is nothing,
To love two is hypocrisy,
To love three and deceive four,
That's the glory that comes from God!

(196)

1556: La Imperial

Mariño de Lobera

The horse, golden of hide and full of dash, decides direction and pace. If he wants to gallop, he gallops; he seeks open country and romps amid tall grasses, approaches the stream, and backs away; respectfully, without haste, he comes and goes along the dirt streets of the brand-new city.

Riding bareback with a free rein, Pedro Mariño de Lobera parades and celebrates. All the wine there was in La Imperial flows through his veins. From time to time he giggles and makes some remark. The horse turns his head, looks, and approves.

It is four years today since Pedro quit the entourage of the viceroy in Lima and took the long road to Chile.

"I'm four years old," says Don Pedro to the horse. "Four little years. You're older and stupider."

During those years he has seen plenty and fought plenty. He says that these Chilean lands sprout joys and gold the way plants grow elsewhere. And when there is war, as there always is, the Virgin throws out a thick fog to blind the Indians, and the apostle Santiago contributes his lance and white horse to the conquering host. Not far from here nor long ago, when the Araucanian squadrons had their backs to the sea, a giant wave knocked them down and swallowed them up.

Don Pedro remembers and comments, and the horse nods.

Suddenly lightning snakes across the sky and thunder shakes the ground.

"It's raining," Don Pedro observes. "It's raining milk!"

The horse raises his head and drinks.

(130)

1558: *Cañete*

The War Goes On

With a hundred arrows in his breast, Caupolicán meets his end. The great one-eyed chief falls, defeated by treachery. The moon used to stop to contemplate his feats, and there was not a man who didn't love him or fear him, but a traitor could do him in.

A year ago treachery also caught Lautaro by surprise.

"And you, what are you doing here?" asked the Spanish leader.

"I come to offer you Lautaro's head," said the traitor.

Lautaro did not enter Santiago as a conqueror at the head of his men. His head was brought in from Mount Chilipirco on the longest lance in the Spanish army.

Treachery is a weapon as devastating as typhus, smallpox, and hunger, all of which plague the Araucanians while the war destroys crops and plantings. Yet the farmers and hunters of these Chilean lands have other weapons. Now they know how to use horses, which previously struck terror into them: they attack on horseback, a whirlwind of mounted men, and protect themselves with rawhide armor. They know how to fire the arquebuses they take on the battlefield, and they tie swords to the tips of their lances. Behind moving tree branches, in the morning mist, they advance unseen. Then they feign retreat, so that the enemy horses will sink into swamps or break their legs in concealed traps. Smoke columns tell them which way the Spanish troops are heading: they bite them and disappear. They return suddenly and hurl themselves on the enemy when the sun burns brightest and the soldiers are frying in their armor plate. Horsemen are brought down with the slipknot lassos invented by Lautaro.

What is more, the Araucanians fly. Before going into battle they rub themselves with feathers of the swiftest birds.

(5 and 66)

Araucanian Song of the
Phantom Horseman

Who is this
riding on the wind,
like the tiger,
with his phantom body?
When the oaks see him,
when people see him,
they say in a whisper
one to the other:
"Look, brother, here comes
the ghost of Caupolicán."

(42)

1558: Michmaloyan

The Tzitzimes

They have caught and are punishing Juan Tetón, Indian preacher
of the village of Michmaloyan in the Valley of Mexico, and also
those who listened and paid heed to him. Juan was going about
announcing the last days of an era and the proximity of a year to
end all years. At that point, he said, total darkness would fall, the
verdure would dry up, and there would be hunger. All who failed
to wash baptism out of their hair would turn into animals. *Tzitzimes*,
terrifying black birds, would descend from the sky and eat everyone
who had not washed off the mark of the priests.

The *tzitzimes* had also been announced by Martín Océlotl,
who was captured and beaten, dispossessed and banished from
Texcoco. He, too, said that there would be no flame at the festival
of new fire and the world would end because of those who had
forgotten the teachings of the fathers and grandfathers and no longer
knew to whom they owed birth and growth. The *tzitzimes* will fall
upon us through the darkness, he said, and devour women and
men. According to Martín Océlotl, the missionary friars are *tzitzimes* in disguise, *enemies of all happiness, who don't know that
we are born to die and that after death we will have neither pleasure
nor joy.*

And the old lords who survive in Tlaxcala also have something to say about the priests: *Poor things,* they say. *Poor things. They must be sick or crazy. At noon, at midnight, and at the dawn hour, when everyone rejoices, they shout and cry. They must have something terribly wrong with them. They are men without any sense. They seek neither pleasure nor happiness, but sadness and loneliness.*

(109)

1558: Yuste

Who Am I? What Have I Been?

Breathing is a violent effort, and his head is on fire. His feet, swollen with gout, will no longer walk. Stretched out on the terrace, he who was monarch of half the world is in flight from his jesters and contemplates the dusk in this Estremaduran valley. The sun is departing beyond the purple mountains, and its last rays redden the shadows over the Jeronomite convent.

He has entered many a city as a conqueror. He has been acclaimed and hated. Many have given their lives for him; the lives of many more have been taken in his name. After forty years of traveling and fighting, the highest prisoner of his own empire wants to rest and be forgotten. Who am I, what have I been? In the mirror he has seen death entering. The deceiver or the deceived?

Between battles, by the light of campfires, he has signed more than four hundred loan agreements with German, Genoese, and Flemish bankers, and the galleons have never brought enough silver and gold from America. He who so loved music has heard more of the thundering of guns and horses than sacred lute melodies; and at the end of so much war his son, Philip, will inherit a bankrupt empire.

Through the fog, from the north, Charles had arrived in Spain when he was seventeen, followed by his entourage of Flemish merchants and German bankers, in an endless caravan of wagons and horses. At the time he could not even say good-morning in the language of Castile. But tomorrow he will choose it to say goodbye.

"*Oh, Jesus!*" will be his last words.

(41 and 116)

1559: Mexico City

The Mourners

The eagle of the Austrias opens his golden wings against the clear sky of the Mexican plateau. On a black cloth, surrounded by flags, glitters the crown. The catafalque renders homage to Charles V and also to death, *which has conquered so invincible a monarch.*

The crown, an exact replica of the one that adorned the emperor in Europe, has toured the streets of Mexico. On a damask cushion it was borne in procession. The multitude prayed and chanted behind it while the bells of all the churches rang out the death toll. The chief nobles paraded on horseback in mourning, black brocades, black velvet cloaks embroidered with gold and silver; and beneath a canopy, the archbishop, the bishops, and their spectacular miters broke through clouds of incense.

For several nights the tailors have not slept. The entire colony is dressed in mourning.

In the slums, the Aztecs are in mourning, too. They have been for months, nearly a year. The plague is exterminating them wholesale. A fever never known before the conquest draws blood from the nose and eyes and kills.

(28)

Advice of the Old Aztec Wise Men

Now that you see with your eyes,
take notice.
See how it is here: there is no joy,
there is no happiness.

Here on earth is the place of many tears,
the place where breath gives up
and where are known so well
depression and bitterness.

An obsidian wind blows and swoops
over us.
The earth is the place of painful joy,
of joy that pricks.

But even though it were thus,
though it were true that suffering is all,
even if things were thus on the earth,
must we always go with fear?
must we forever tremble?
must we live forever weeping?

So that we may not always go with groans,
so that sadness may not ever saturate us,
Our Father has given us
smiles, dreams, food,
our strength,
and finally
the act of love,
which sows people.

(110)

1560: Huexotzingo

The Reward

The native chiefs of Huexotzingo now bear the names of their new lords. They are called Felipe de Mendoza, Hernando de Meneses, Miguel de Alvarado, Diego de Chaves, or Mateo de la Corona. But they write in their own Náhuatl and in that language send a long letter to the king of Spain: *Unfortunates we, your poor vassals of Huexotzingo* . . .

They explain to Philip II that they cannot reach him in any othe · way, because they don't have the price of the journey, and they tell their story by letter. *How shall we speak? Who will speak for us? Unfortunates we.*

They never made war on the Spaniards. They walked twenty leagues to Hernán Cortés and embraced him, fed him, served him, and took charge of his sick soldiers. They gave him men and arms and timber to build the brigantines that assaulted Tenochtitlán.

After the Aztec capital fell, the Huexotzingans fought with Cortés
in the conquest of Michoacán, Jalisco, Colhuacan, Pánuco, Oaxaca,
Tehuantepec, and Guatemala. Many died. And afterward, *when
they told us to break the stones and burn the carvings that we
worshiped, we did it, and destroyed our temples . . . Whatever
they ordered, we obeyed.*
Huexotzingo was an independent kingdom when the Spaniards
came. They had never paid tribute to the Aztecs. *Our fathers,
grandfathers, and ancestors did not know what tribute was and
paid it to no one.*
Now, however, the Spaniards are demanding such high tribute
in money and in corn that *we declare before Your Majesty that
little time will pass before our city of Huexotzingo disappears and
dies.*

(120)

1560: Michoacán

Vasco de Quiroga

Primitive Christianity, primitive communism: the bishop of
Michoacán draws up ordinances for his evangelical communities.
He was inspired in founding them by the *Utopia* of Thomas More,
by the biblical prophets, and by the ancient traditions of America's
Indians.

The communities created by Vasco de Quiroga, where no one
is master of anyone or anything and neither hunger nor money is
known, will not multiply throughout Mexico as he wished. The
Council of the Indies will never take the foolish bishop's projects
seriously nor even glance at the books that he obstinately recom-
mends. But here utopia has returned to America, where it origi-
nated. Thomas More's chimera has been incarnated in the small
communal world of Michoacán; and in times to come the Indians
here will remember Vasco de Quiroga as their own—the dreamer
who riveted his eyes on a hallucination to see beyond the time of
infamy.

(227)

1561: *Villa de los Bergantines*

The First Independence of America

They crowned him yesterday. Curious monkeys trooped up among the trees. Fernando de Guzmán's mouth dripped guanábana juice, and there were suns in his eyes. One after the other, the soldiers knelt down before the throne of sticks and straw, kissed the hand of the elect, and swore fealty. Then they signed the declaration with a name or an X, all who were not women or servants or Indians or blacks. The scribe made it official, and independence was proclaimed.

The seekers of El Dorado, lost in midjungle, now have their own monarch. Nothing binds them to Spain except resentment. They have repudiated vassalage to the king across the sea: "I don't know him!" cried Lope de Aguirre yesterday, all bone and fury, raising his sword covered with mildew. "I don't know him or want to know him, nor to have him nor obey him!"

In the village's biggest hut the court is installed. By the light of candles, Prince Ferdinand eats endless cassava buns spread with honey. He is served by his pages, cup and ewer bearer, and valet; between buns he gives orders to his secretaries, dictates decrees to his scribes, and grants audiences and favors. The royal treasurer, chaplain, chief majordomo, and steward-taster wear tattered doublets and have swollen hands and split lips. The sergeant at arms is swarthy-skinned Lope de Aguirre, lame in one leg, one-eyed, almost a dwarf, who conspires by night and supervises the brigantine construction by day.

Ax- and hammerblows ring out. The Amazon currents have ground their ships to pieces, but ahead two new keels rise on the sand. The jungle offers good timber. They have made bellows out of horses' hides; nails, bolts, and hinges out of horseshoes.

Tortured by mosquitos and gnats, smothered by humid and fever-laden vapors, the men wait for the ships to grow. They eat grass and vulture meat, without salt. No dogs or horses are left, and the fishhooks bring up nothing but mud and decayed algae, but no one in the camp doubts that the hour of revenge has come. They left Peru months ago in search of the lake where according to legend there are solid gold idols as big as boys, and now they want to return to Peru on a war footing. They won't spend another day in pursuit of the promised land, because they realize that they already found it and are sick of cursing their bad luck. They will sail the Amazon, emerge into the ocean, occupy Margarita Island, invade Venezuela and Panama . . .

Those who sleep dream of the silver of Potosí. Aguirre, who never closes his remaining eye, sees it awake.

(123 and 164)

1561: Nueva Valencia del Rey

Aguirre

At center stage, ax in hand, appears Lope de Aguirre surrounded by dozens of mirrors. Outlined on the backdrop, the profile of King Philip II, black, enormous.

Lope de Aguirre *(to the audience)*: On the road of our defeat, passing through death and misadventure, we took more than ten months to reach the mouth of the Amazon, which is a great, fearsome, and ill-starred river. Then we took possession of Margarita Island. There I cashed in twenty-five traitors on gallows or garrote. And then we made our way onto the mainland. King Philip's soldiers are trembling with fright! Soon we'll leave Venezuela . . . Soon we'll be entering the kingdom of Peru in triumph! *(He turns and confronts his own pitiful image in one of the mirrors.)* I crowned Fernando de Guzmán king on the Amazon River! *(Raises his ax and splits the mirror.)* I crowned him king and I killed him! Same with his captain of the guard and the lieutenant general and four captains! *(As he speaks he smashes all the mirrors one after the other.)* Same with his head steward and his chaplain! . . . And with a woman who was in on the plot against me, and that fellow born in Greece who thought himself such a big shot, and an admiral . . . and six more of their allies! . . . And I appointed new captains and a sergeant major! They wanted to kill me and I hanged them! *(Pulverizes the last of the mirrors.)* All of them! All of them! . . . *(He sits, almost suffocating, on the ground covered with glass. The ax held high in his fists, his eyes astray.*

Long silence.) As a lad I crossed the sea to Peru because I was worth more with a lance in my hand . . . A quarter of a century! . . . Mysteries, miseries . . . I dug out whole cemeteries to get silver and gold for others . . . I put up gallows in the middle of unborn cities . . . I hunted down crowds of people on my horse . . . Indians fleeing in terror through the flames . . . Gentlemen with fancy titles and borrowed silk clothes, sons of something or other, sons of nobody, agonizing in the jungle, frothing at the mouth, eating dirt, blood poisoned by arrows . . . Up in the mountains, warriors in steel armor pierced right through by blizzards more violent than any arquebus volley . . . A lot of them found graves in the bellies of vultures . . . A lot ended up as yellow as the gold they were hunting for . . . Yellow skin, yellow eyes . . . And the gold . . . (*Drops his ax. Painfully opens his hands, which are like claws. Shows his palms*.) Vanished . . . Gold turned into shadow or dew . . . (*Looks down incredulously. Long silence. Suddenly he rises. Back to the audience, raises his bony fist toward the huge outline of Philip II, projected with his pointed beard against the backdrop*.) Damn few of you kings go to hell, because there's damn few of you! (*Walks toward backdrop, dragging his lame leg*.) Ungrateful bastard! I lost my body defending you against the rebels in Peru! I gave you a leg and an eye and these hands that aren't much use to me! Now the rebel is me! Rebel till death for your ungratefulness! (*Faces audience, unsheathes his sword*.) Me, prince of the rebels! Lope de Aguirre the Pilgrim, Wrath of God, chief of the cripples! We don't need you, king of Spain! (*Colored lights go on at various points on the stage*.) We mustn't leave any minister of yours alive! (*Sword in hand, lunges at a beam of reddish light*.) Judges, governors, presidents, viceroys! War to the death against all court whores! (*The beam of light stays in place, indifferent to the sword cutting it*.) Usurpers! Thieves! (*The sword wounds the air*.) You have destroyed the Indies! (*Attacks beam of golden light*.) Lawyers, notaries, ink-shitters! How long must we endure your robberies in these lands won by us? (*Sword slashes beam of white light*.) Monks, bishops, archbishops! You won't even bury a poor Indian! For penitence you keep a dozen girls in the kitchen! Traffickers! Traffickers in sacraments! Swindlers! (*The sword's futile assaults on un-*

blinking beams of light, which multiply across the stage, continue. Aguirre begins to lose strength and looks ever more alone and insignificant.)

(123 and 164)

1561: Nueva Valencia del Rey

From Lope de Aguirre's letter to King Philip II

Over here we have got the measure of how cruel you are and how you break your faith and word, so that in this country we give less credit to your promises than to the books of Martin Luther, for your viceroy the Marquis of Cañete hanged Martín de Robles, a man outstandingly dedicated to your service, and the brave conquistador of Piru Tomás Vázquez, and poor Alonso Díaz, who worked harder in the discovery of this land than Moses's scouts in the desert . . .

Listen, listen, Spanish king, stop being cruel and ungrateful to your vassals, because with your father and you comfortably back in Spain away from all worries, your vassals have given you at the cost of their blood and treasure all the many lands and dominions that you have in these parts, and listen, king and sir, you can't call yourself a just king and take any part of these lands for which you ventured nothing without first rewarding those who toiled and sweated . . .

Alas, what a terrible pity that the Imperial Caesar your father should have conquered proud Germany with the forces of Spain, spending so much money brought from these Indies discovered by us, that our old age and exhaustion doesn't pain you enough for you to relieve our hunger even for a day! . . .

(123)

1561: Barquisimeto

Order Restored

Abandoned by his men, who preferred the king's pardon or indulgences, Lope de Aguirre stabs to death his daughter Elvira, *to save her from becoming a mattress for blackguards,* and confronts his executioners. He corrects their aim, not this way, not that way, lousy shot, and falls without commending himself to God.

When Philip reads the letter, seated on his throne a long way from here, Aguirre's head is fixed on a pike as a warning to all the pawns of European development.

(123 and 164)

1562: Maní

The Fire Blunders

Fray Diego de Landa throws into the flames, one after the other, the books of the Mayas.

The inquisitor curses Satan, and the fire crackles and devours. Around the incinerator, heretics howl with their heads down. Hung by the feet, flayed with whips, Indians are doused with boiling wax as the fire flares up and the books snap, as if complaining.

Tonight, eight centuries of Mayan literature turn to ashes. On these long sheets of bark paper, signs and images spoke: They told of work done and days spent, of the dreams and the wars of a people born before Christ. With hog-bristle brushes, the knowers of things had painted these illuminated, illuminating books so that the grandchildren's grandchildren should not be blind, should know how to see themselves and see the history of their folk, so they should know the movements of the stars, the frequency of eclipses and the prophecies of the gods and so they could call for rains and good corn harvests.

In the center, the inquisitor burns the books. Around the huge bonfire, he chastises the readers. Meanwhile, the authors, artist-priests dead years or centuries ago, drink chocolate in the fresh shade of the first tree of the world. They are at peace, because they died knowing that memory cannot be burned. Will not what they painted be sung and danced through the times of the times?

When its little paper houses are burned, memory finds refuge in mouths that sing the glories of men and of gods, *songs that stay on from people to people* and in bodies that dance to the sound of hollow trunks, tortoise shells, and reed flutes.

(205 and 219)

1563: Arauco Fortress

The History That Will Be

The noose tightens and strangles. In this frontier redoubt, twice burned down and rebuilt, water is almost exhausted. Soon they will have to drink their small urinations. So many arrows have fallen inside that the Spaniards use them as firewood for cooking.

The Araucanian chief approaches the foot of the rampart on horseback: "Captain! Do you hear me?"

Lorenzo Bernal leans his head over.

The native chief announces that they will surround the fort with straw and set fire to it. He says that they have not left anyone alive in Concepción.

"Nothing doing!" shouts Bernal.

"Surrender, Captain! You've no way out!"

"Not a chance! Never!"

The horse rears up on two legs.

"Then you'll die!"

"So we die," says Bernal, and yells: "But in the long run we'll win the war! There'll be more and more of us!"

The Indian replies with a chuckle.

"How? With what women?" he asks.

"If there are no Spanish ones, we'll have yours," says the captain slowly, savoring the words, and adds: "*And we'll make children on them who'll be your masters!*"

(130)

1564: Plymouth

Hawkins

The four ships, under command of Captain John Hawkins, await the morning tide. As soon as the water rises they will sail for Africa, to hunt people on the coasts of Guinea. From there they will head for the Antilles to trade slaves for sugar, hides, and pearls.

A couple of years ago, Hawkins made this voyage on his own. In a ship named *Jesus*, he sold three hundred slaves as contraband in Santo Domingo. Queen Elizabeth exploded with fury when she learned of it, but her anger vanished as soon as she saw the balance sheet of the voyage. In no time at all she made herself a business partner of the audacious Devonshire "seadog," and the Earls of Pembroke and Leicester and London's lord mayor bought first shares in the new enterprise.

As the sailors hoist the sails, Captain Hawkins harangues them from the bridge. The British navy will make his orders its own in centuries to come: "*Serve God every day!*" Hawkins orders at the top of his lungs. "*Love one another! Save your provisions! Watch out for fire! Keep good company!*"

(127, 187, and 198)

1564: Bogotá

Vicissitudes of Married Life

"Tell me, do I seem different?"

"Well, a bit."

"A bit what?"

"A bit fat, ma'am, if you'll excuse me."

"See if you can guess. Fat from eating or from laughing?"

"Fat from loving, I'd say, meaning no offense."

"No offense, woman, that's what I called you about . . ."

The lady is very worried. Her body has had little patience, unable to wait for the absent husband; and someone has told her that he's due back in Cartagena. When he sees her tummy, what won't he do, that dour man who cures headaches by cutting off heads?

"That's why I called you, Juana. Help me, you who can fly and can drink wine from an empty cup. Tell me. Is my husband coming in the Cartagena fleet?"

In a silver washbasin the black woman Juana García mixes waters, soils, bloods, weeds. She dips a little green book into the basin and lets it float. Then she buries her nose in it. "No," she says, "he's not coming. And if you want to see your husband, come and take a peek."

The lady bends over the basin. By the light of the candles she sees him. He is seated beside a pretty woman in a place of many silks, while someone cuts a dress of fancy cloth. "Oh, you faker! Tell me, Juana, what place is this?"

"The house of a tailor on the island of Santo Domingo."

In the dense water appears the image of the tailor cutting out a sleeve.

"Shall I stop it?" says the black woman.

"Yes, stop it!"

The hand emerges from the basin with a sleeve of fine cloth dripping between the fingers.

The lady trembles, but with fury.

"He deserves more fat bellies, the lousy pig!"

From a corner, a puppy snores with half-open eyes.

(194)

1565: Road to Lima

The Spy

On Don Antonio Solar's hacienda by the Lurín River, the melons have grown as big as suns. It is the first time that this fruit, brought from Spain, has been planted around here, and the foreman sends the master ten samples for his pleasure and pride. The size of these melons is comparable with that of the Cuzapa Valley radishes, of which they say five horses can be tied to their tops.

Two Indians take the foreman's offering to Lima in two sacks. He has given them a letter to deliver with the melons to Don Antonio Solar. "If you eat any of the melons," he warns them, "this letter will tell him about it."

When they are a couple of leagues from the city of the kings, the Indians sit down to rest in a ravine.

"How would this peculiar fruit taste?"

"Must be marvelous."

"How about trying it? One melon, just one."

"The letter will sing," one of the Indians recalls.

They look at the letter and hate it. They look around for a prison for it. They hide it behind a rock where it can't see anything, and devour a melon in quick bites, sweet juicy pulp, delicious beyond imagining. Then they eat another to even up the sacks. Then they pick up the letter, tuck it in their clothing, throw the sacks over their shoulders, and continue on their way.

(76)

1565: Yauyoa

That Stone Is Me

The king's official is awaiting the witch, skilled in deviltries, who has been summoned to come to explain herself. Face down at his feet lies the stone idol. The witch was caught communing secretly with the idol and will soon pay for her heresy. But before the punishment, the official wants to hear from her own lips her confession of talks with the Devil. While he waits for her to be brought, he amuses himself stomping on the idol and meditating on the fate of these Indians, whom God must be sorry to have made.

The soldiers throw down the witch and leave her trembling on the threshold.

Then the ugly old stone idol greets the ugly old witch in the Quechua language: *"Welcome, princess,"* says the hoarse voice from under the official's foot.

The official is flabbergasted and falls sprawling on the floor.

As she fans him with a hat, the old woman clutches the fainting man's coat and cries: "Don't punish me, sir, don't break it!"

The old woman wants to explain to him that divinities live in the stone and if it were not for the idol, she would not know her name, or who she is, or where she comes from and would be wandering the earth naked and lost.

(221)

Prayer of the Incas, Seeking God

Hear me,
from the sea up there where Thou livest,
from the sea down here where Thou art.
Creator of the world,
potter of man,
Lord of Lords,
to Thee,
with my eyes that despair to see Thee

or just for yearning to know Thee
if I see Thee,
know Thee,
ponder Thee,
understand Thee,
Thou wilt see me and know me.
The sun, the moon,
the day,
the night,
the summer,
the winter,
they don't walk idly,
but in good order,
to the appointed place
and to a good end.
Everywhere Thou carriest with Thee
Thy royal scepter.
Hear me,
listen to me.
Let me not tire out,
let me not die.

(105)

1565: Mexico City

Ceremony

The gilded tunic glints. Forty-five years after his death, Moctezuma heads the procession. The horsemen move at walking pace into the central square of Mexico City. Dancers step out to the thunder of drums and the lament of chirimía pipes. Many Indians, clad in white, hold up flowered branches; others, enormous clay cooking pots. The smoke of incense mingles with the aromas of spicy sauces.

Before Cortés's palace, Moctezuma dismounts.

The door opens. Among his pages, armed with tall, sharpened halberds, appears Cortés.

Moctezuma bows his head, crowned with feathers and gold and precious stones. Kneeling, he offers garlands of flowers. Cortés touches his shoulder. Moctezuma rises. With a slow gesture he tears off his mask and reveals the curly hair and high-pointed mustachio of Alonso de Avila.

Alonso de Avila, lord of gallows and knife, owner of Indians, lands, and mines, enters the palace of Martín Cortés, marquis of the Valley of Oaxaca. The son of a conquistador opens his house to the nephew of another conquistador.

Today the conspiracy against the king of Spain officially commences. In the life of the colony, all is not soirées and tournaments, card and hunting parties.

(28)

1566: Madrid

The Fanatic of Human Dignity

Fray Bartolomé de las Casas is going over the heads of the king and of the Council of the Indies. Will he be punished for his disobedience? At ninety-two, it matters little to him. He has been fighting for half a century. Are not his exploits the key to his tragedy? They have let him win many battles, but the outcome of the war was decided in advance. He has known it for a long time.

His fingers won't obey him anymore. He dictates the letter. Without anybody's permission, he addresses himself directly to the Holy See. He asks Pius V to order the wars against the Indians stopped and to halt the plunder that uses the cross as an excuse. As he dictates he becomes indignant, the blood rises to his head, and the hoarse and feeble voice that remains to him trembles.

Suddenly he falls to the floor.

(70 and 90)

1566: Madrid

Even if You Lose,
It's Still Worthwhile

The lips move, speak soundless words. "Forgivest Thou me, Lord?"

Fray Bartolomé pleads for mercy at the Last Judgment for having believed that black and Moorish slaves would alleviate the fate of the Indians.

He lies stretched out, damp forehead, pallid, and the lips do not stop moving. From far off, a slow thunderclap. Fray Bartolomé, the giver of birth, the doer, closes his eyes. Although always hard of hearing, he hears rain beating on the roof of the Atocha monastery. The rain moistens his face. He smiles.

One of the priests who accompanies him murmurs something about the strange light that has illumined his face. Through the rain, free of doubt and torment, Fray Bartolomé is traveling for the last time to the green worlds where he knew happiness.

"I thank Thee," say his lips in silence while he reads the prayers by the light of fireflies, splashed by the rain that strikes the palm-frond roof.

"I thank Thee," he says as he celebrates Mass in sheds without walls and baptizes naked children in rivers.

The priests cross themselves. The clock's last grains of sand have fallen. Someone turns over the hourglass so that time will not be interrupted.

(27, 70, and 90)

1568: Los Teques

Guaicaipuro

Never again will the river reflect his face, his panache of lofty plumes.

This time the gods did not listen to his wife, Urquía, who pleaded that neither bullets nor disease should touch him and that sleep, the brother of death, should never forget to return him to the world at the end of each night.

The invaders felled Guaicaipuro with bullets.

Since the Indians elected him chief, there was no truce in this valley nor in the Avila Mountains. In the newly born city of Caracas people crossed themselves when in a low voice they spoke his name.

Confronting death and its officials, the last of the free men has fallen shouting, *Kill me, kill me, free yourselves from fear*.

(158)

1568: Mexico City

The Sons of Cortés

Martín was the name of Hernán Cortés's oldest son, his blood son born of the Indian woman Malinche. His father died leaving him a meager annual pension.

Martín is also the name of Hernán Cortés's legitimate son, born of a Spanish woman, a count's daughter and niece of a duke. This Martín has inherited the coat of arms and the fortune: He is marquis of the Valley of Oaxaca, owner of thousands of Indians and leagues of this land that his father had humiliated and loved and chosen to lie in forever.

On a saddle of crimson velvet embroidered with gold, Martín the marquis used to wander the streets of Mexico. Behind him went his red-liveried guards armed with swords. Whoever crossed his path doffed his hat, paid homage, and joined his entourage. The other Martín, the bastard, was one of the retinue.

Martín the marquis wanted to break with Spain and proclaim himself king of Mexico. When the plot failed, he babbled regrets and named names. His life was spared.

Martín the bastard, who has served his brother in the conspiracy and everything else, is now writhing on the rack. At his side, the scribe records: *He was stripped and put in the cincha. On being admonished, he said he owed nothing.* The torturer gives a turn to the wheel. The cords break the flesh and stretch the bones.

The scribe records: *He is again admonished. Says he has no more to say than what he has said.*

Second turn of the wheel. Third, fourth, fifth.

(28)

1569: Havana

St. Simon Against the Ants

Ants harass the city and ruin the crops. They have devoured more than one heavy-sleeping Christian via the navel.

In extraordinary session, Havana's authorities resolve to ask the protection of a patron saint against the bibijaguas and other fierce ants.

Before the Reverend Alonso Álvarez, lots are drawn among the twelve apostles. The winner is St. Simon, whom they take as advocate *so that he may intercede with Our Lord God, that He may remove all ants from this community, the houses and haciendas of this town, and its environs.*

In return, the city will throw an annual party in honor of the blessed St. Simon, with sung vespers, Mass, compulsory-attendance procession, and bullfight.

(161)

1571: Mexico City

Thou Shalt Inform On Thy Neighbor

From the balconies hang coats of arms, gay carpets, velvets, banners. The armor of the knight of the Order of Santiago, who dips his standard before the viceroy, glitters. Pages raise their big axes around the immense cross nailed to the scaffold.

The inquisitor general is arriving from Madrid. Kettledrums and trumpets announce him. He comes on the back of a mule with jeweled trappings, amid countless lighted candles and black capes.

Under his supreme authority heretics will be tortured or burned. Centuries ago Pope Innocent IV ordered assassins of souls and robbers of the faith of Christ to be rewarded with torments; and much later Pope Paul III prohibited the torture to last more than an hour. Since then, inquisitors take a small break from their work every hour. The inquisitor general newly arrived in Mexico will see to it that green wood is never used in the executions, so that the city will not be choked with noxious smoke; and he will order them for clear days so that all may appreciate them. He will not bother with Indians, *since they are new in the faith, feeble folk, and of little substance.*

The inquisitor general takes his seat beside the viceroy. An artillery salvo greets him. The drums roll and the town crier proclaims the general edict of the faith. The edict orders everyone to inform on anyone they know or have seen or heard, not excepting wives, husbands, fathers, or anyone else, no matter how intimate.

All are obliged to denounce live or dead people who have said or believed *heretical, suspicious, erroneous, reckless, offensive, scandalous, or blasphemous words or opinions*.

(115 and 139)

1571: Madrid

Who Is Guilty, Criminal or Witness?

The face itself, or the mirror that reflects it? The king does not think twice about it. By decree he orders the confiscation of all the manuscripts left by Fray Bartolomé de las Casas so that they may not fall into the hands of bad Spaniards and enemies of Spain. Especially worrying to Philip II is the possible publication or circulation in some manner of the extremely voluminous *History of the Indies*, which Las Casas could not finish and which survives, a prisoner under lock and key, in the San Gregorio monastery.

(70 and 90)

1572: Cuzco

Túpac Amaru I

He comes dragging his feet on the cobblestones. On the back of a dwarf donkey, a rope about his neck, Túpac Amaru approaches the scaffold. Ahead of him, the town crier proclaims him tyrant and traitor.

In the main square, the clamor swells up.

"Inca, why do they take you to cut off your head?"

The murmurings of the throng of natives become an uproar. *Let them have us all killed!* shriek the women.

High on the scaffold, Túpac Amaru raises a hand, rests it against his ear and calmly lets it fall back. Then the throng falls silent.

There is nothing but silence when the executioner's sword cleaves the neck of Huaina Cápac's grandson.

With Túpac Amaru, four centuries of the Inca dynasty and nearly forty years of resistance in the Wilcabamba Mountains come to an end. Now the storms of war, the harsh rhythm of the conches, will no longer fall on the valley of Cuzco.

(76)

The Vanquished Believe:

He will come back and move about the earth. The highest mountains know. Being the highest, they see the farthest.

He was the son of the sun and a simple woman.

He took the wind prisoner; and tied up the sun, his father, so that time might endure.

With harness and lash, he brought stones to the heights. With those stones he made temples and fortresses.

Wherever he went, the birds went. The birds greeted him and gladdened his steps. From much journeying his feet spilled blood. When the blood of his feet mixed with the soil, we learned to cultivate. We learned to speak when he told us: "Speak." He was stronger and younger than we.

We have not always had fear in our breasts. Not always bumped along, like the ups and downs of our roads. Our history is long. Our history was born on the day we were hauled from the mouth, the eyes, the armpits, and the vagina of the earth.

Inkarrí's brother Españarrí cut off Inkarrí's head. He has been. The head of Inkarrí turned into money. Gold and silver spurted from his shit-filled entrails.

The highest mountains know. Inkarrí's head is trying to grow toward his feet. The pieces of him will surely come together one day. On that day he will walk the earth followed by the birds.

(15 and 162)

1574: Mexico City

The First *Auto-da-Fé* in Mexico

Ever since the town criers spread the edict of the delations, denunciations have rained down against heretics and bigamists, witches and blasphemers.

The *auto-da-fé* is celebrated on the first Sunday in Lent. From sunrise until dusk the Holy Office of the Inquisition passes sentences on the scarecrows dragged from its cells and torture chambers. High on the sumptuous scaffold, surrounded by lancers and cheering crowds, work the hangmen. *No such multitude can be remembered at a public celebration or at any thing of very great solemnity ever offered on earth*, says the viceroy of New Spain, who attends the spectacle on a velvet throne with a cushion under his feet.

The punishments of *vela*, *soga*, *mordaza*, abjuration *de levi*, and one hundred and two hundred lashes are meted out to a silversmith, a cutler, a goldsmith, a scribe, and a cobbler *for having said that simple fornication is not mortal sin*. Various bigamists suffer similar inflictions, among them the Augustine friar Juan Sarmiento, who with his back one raw wound marches off to row in the galleys for five years.

The Negro Domingo, born in Mexico, and the mestizo Miguel Franco receive a hundred lashes each, the former *for having the custom of denying God*, the latter *because he made his wife confess to him*. A hundred, too, for the Sevillian apothecary Gaspar de los Reyes *for having said it was better to cohabit than to be married and that it was licit for the poor and afflicted to perjure themselves for money*.

To the galleys, *hard prison for the mischievous*, go various Lutherans and Jews, *who sucked their heresy in their mothers' milk*, a few Englishmen of the pirate John Hawkins's fleet, and a Frenchman *who called the pope and the king poltroons*.

An Englishman from the mines of Guanajuato and a French barber from Yucatán end their heretical days in the bonfire.

(139)

1576: Guanajuato

The Monks Say:

She came to Mexico twenty years ago. Two doves guided her to Guanajuato. She arrived without a scratch, although she crossed the sea and the desert, and those who carried her lost their way. The king sent her to us in gratitude for the wealth that never stops spurting from the bowels of these mountains.

For more than eight centuries she had lived in Spain. Hidden from the Moors, she survived in a cave in Granada. When Christians discovered and rescued her, they found no wound on her wooden body. She reached Guanajuato intact. She remains intact, performing miracles. Our Lady of Guanajuato consoles both poor and rich for their poverty; and she shields alike from the cold those who sleep outdoors and in a sheltered palace. In her infinite mercy she does not distinguish between servants and lords. No one invokes her and fails to receive divine favor.

By her grace many Indians of Guanajuato who go to her with repentance and faith are now being saved. She has stayed the sword of the Lord, who with just fury castigates the idolatries and sins of the Indians in Mexico. The afflicted who brought their supplications to her and paid due charity have not been touched by the pestilence.

In other areas, the Indian whom typhus does not kill dies of hunger or hardship. There are corpses in the fields and in the plazas, and there are houses filled with them in which all died and no one remained to tell of it. Throughout Mexico the pestilence is raising such a stink of putrefaction and smoke that we Spaniards have to go about holding our noses.

(79 and 131)

1576: Xochimilco

The Apostle Santiago *versus* the Plague

Here even nursing babies have paid tribute, in money and in corn. If the pestilence goes on, who will pay? Local hands have built the cathedral of Mexico. If the plague does not stop, who will sow these fields? Who will spin and weave in the workshops? Who will build cathedrals and pave streets?

The Franciscans discuss the situation in their monastery. Of the thirty thousand Indians in Xochimilco when the Spaniards came, four thousand are left, and that is an exaggeration. Many died fighting with Hernán Cortés, conquering men and lands for him, and more died working for him and for Pedro de Alvarado, and the epidemic is killing more.

Fray Jerónimo de Mendieta, the monastery guardian, comes up with the inspiration that saves the day.

They prepare to draw lots. An acolyte, blindfolded, stirs slips of paper in the silver dish. On each slip is written the name of a saint of proven prestige at the celestial court. The acolyte chooses one, and Father Mendieta unfolds it and reads: "It's the Apostle Santiago!"

From the balcony it is announced to the Indians of Xochimilco in their language. The apocalyptic monk speaks on his knees, raising his arms. "Santiago will defeat the pestilence!"

He promises him an altar.

(79 and 161)

1577: *Xochimilco*

St. Sebastian *versus* the Plague

During the tough years of the conquest, the clash of arms was heard from the tomb of Santiago on the eve of each battle; and the apostle fought with the invading hosts, lance in hand, on his white horse. Clearly the apostle Santiago has the habit of killing Indians but not of saving them. The plague, which barely scratches the Spaniards, continues massacring Indians in Xochimilco and other parts of Mexico.

From his cell as night falls, Father Mendieta hears shrieks and moans louder than the choruses of angels.

Someone has to intercede with the Lord, since the apostle Santiago is not interested, or Xochimilco will soon be Indianless. The Franciscans talk it over and decide to draw lots again. Fate picks the blessed Sebastian for saint-advocate.

They promise him an altar.

(79 and 161)

1579: *Quito*

Son of Atahualpa

Beto, Indian priest of the Archidona region, saw a vision of the Devil in the shape of a cow, who told him God was very annoyed with the Christians and was not going to defend them. Guami, Indian priest of Tambisa, spent five days in the other world. There he saw marvels and listened to God, and now he has the power of rain and the power of resurrection. Beto and Guami announce that Indians who don't join the rebellion will reap toads and snakes in eternally sterile fields.

The two prophets put themselves at the head of many lances. Southeast of Quito, the Quijo Indians rebel. They attack various towns and vainly await a rising in the mountains. The Inca's son, Francisco Atahualpa, captain of Spanish troops, imprisons the mountain plotters and staves off the insurrection. The Quijo Indians are left all alone.

After some battles comes defeat. The Spaniards oblige all Indians of the Quijo region and the surroundings of Quito to attend the execution of the prophets Beto and Guami. They parade them through the streets of Quito, torture them with hot pincers, hang them, quarter them, and exhibit the pieces. From the royal box, Captain Francisco Atahualpa watches the ceremony.

(156)

1580: Buenos Aires

The Founders

Nearly half a century ago, a Spanish captain sailed from Seville for these unrenowned shores. He sank the whole fortune he had made in the sack of Rome into the expedition. Here he founded a city, a fortress surrounded by huts, and upriver from here he went hunting for the silver mountain and the mysterious lake where the sun sleeps.

Ten years earlier, Sebastian Cabot had sought the treasure of King Solomon sailing up this Plate River—so innocent of its silvery name—which has only mud on one bank and sand on the other and leads to other rivers that lead to jungle.

Pedro de Mendoza's city didn't last long. While his soldiers, maddened by hunger, ate each other, the captain read Virgil and Erasmus and made pronouncements for immortality. In short order, the dream of another Peru having vanished, he wanted to go back to Spain. He didn't get there alive. Afterward came Alonso Cabrera, who set fire to Buenos Aires in the king's name. He could and did return to Spain. There he killed his wife and ended his days in a lunatic asylum.

Comes now Juan de Garay from Asunción. Santa María de los Buenos Aires is born again. With Garay come a bunch of Paraguayans, sons of conquistadors, who have received from their Guaraní mothers their first milk and the native language they speak.

The sword of Garay, stuck into this land, outlines the shadow of the cross. The founders' teeth chatter from cold and fear. The breeze plays rustling music in the treetops, and beyond, on the endless plains, Indians and phantoms silently spy on them.

(74, 97, and 99)

1580: London

Drake

"Three cheers for the gold of the galleons! Hurrah for the silver of Potosí!"

The Dragon is coming! cried the women, and church bells pealed out the alarm. In three years Francis Drake has circumnavigated the world. He has twice crossed the equator and sacked the Spanish Main, stripping ports and ships from Chile to Mexico.

Now he is returning with only one ship and a moribund crew of eighteen, but he brings treasure that multiplies by 120 the capital invested in the expedition. Queen Elizabeth, chief shareholder and author of the plan, converts the pirate into a knight. On the waters of the Thames the ceremony is performed. On the sword that dubs him is engraved this saying of the queen's: *Who strikes you strikes me, Drake*. On his knees, he offers Her Majesty an emerald brooch stolen in the Pacific.

Towering over the fog and soot, Elizabeth is at the summit of a nascent empire. She is the daughter of Henry VIII and Anne Boleyn, who for having produced a daughter lost her head in the Tower of London. The virgin queen devours her lovers, uses her fists on her maids of honor, and spits on her courtiers' clothes.

Francis Bacon will be the philosopher and chancellor of the new empire and William Shakespeare its poet. Francis Drake, captain of its ships. Scorner of storms, master of sails and winds, the pirate Drake moves at court as if climbing masts and rigging. Squat but hefty with fiery beard, he was born by the sea and has been brought up in the fear of God. The sea is his home; and he never launches an attack without a Bible pressing against the chest beneath his clothing.

(149, 187, and 198)

1582: Mexico City

What Color Is a Leper's Skin?

The lamp advances violating the darkness and pulls faces out of the murk, faces of specters, hands of specters, and nails them to the wall.

The official touches nothing, his gloved hands hidden beneath his cape, half closing his eyes as if fearing to infect them. He has come to check the implementation of the new order concerning San Lázaro Hospital. The viceroy has ordered that male patients should not mix. Whites and mestizos have to occupy one room, blacks and mulattoes another, Indians another. The females, however, are to be all together in one room whatever their color or condition.

(148)

1583: Copacabana

God's Aymara Mother

They cross Lake Titicaca in the cattail boat. She travels by his side, dressed for a fiesta. In the city of La Paz her tunic has been gilded. When they land, he puts his cloak over her to shield her from the rain; and with her in his arms, covered up, he enters the village of Copacabana. The rain stings the crowd that has come to receive them.

Francisco Tito Yupanqui enters the sanctuary with her and uncovers her. She is taken up to the altar. From on high, the Virgin of Copacabana embraces them all. She will protect against pestilence and sorrow and the bad weather of February.

The Indian sculptor has modeled her in Potosí. He has worked for nearly two years to give her appropriate beauty. Indians may only paint or carve images that imitate European models, and Francisco Tito Yupanqui did not want to violate the ban. He had intended to make a Virgin identical to Our Lady of Candelaria, but his hands have modeled this Andean body with big lungs hungry for air, large torso, and short legs, and this broad Indian face with fleshy lips and almond eyes that stare sadly at the bruised land.

(47 and 163)

1583: Santiago de Chile

He Was Free for a While

He raises himself on his hands and falls on his face. He tries to lean on an elbow and slips. He manages to bring up one knee and sinks into the mud.

Face down in the mud, beneath the rain, he weeps.

Hernando Maravilla had not wept under the two hundred lashes he received in the streets of Lima on the way to the harbor; and not a tear was seen on his face while he received another two hundred here in Santiago.

Now the rain lashes him, drawing off the dry blood and the mud.

"Wretch! That's how you bite the hand that feeds you!" said his owner, the long-widowed Doña Antonia Nabía, when they brought the fugitive slave back to her.

Hernando Maravilla had escaped because one day he saw a woman who was pretty as a picture and couldn't resist following her. They caught him in Lima, and the Inquisition questioned him. He was sentenced to four hundred lashes *for having said that marriages were made by the Devil and that the bishop was a nothing and that he shat on the bishop.*

He who was born in Africa, grandson of a medicine man, son of a hunter, twists himself around and weeps, his back raw, as the rain falls on Santiago de Chile.

(31 and 138)

1583: Tlatelolco

Sahagún

Lonelyme, lonelyme, sings the ringdove.

A woman offers flowers to a stone that has been smashed to pieces. "Lord," says the woman to the stone, "Lord, how you have suffered."

The old native wise men offer their testimony to Fray Bernardino de Sahagún: "Let us die," they plead, "since our gods have died."

Fray Bernardino de Ribiera, native of Sahagún: son of St. Francis, bare feet, patched cassock, seeker of the plenitude of Paradise, seeker of the memory of these vanquished peoples. For more than forty years Sahagún has been traveling through Mexico, the seigniory of Huexotzingo, Tula of the Toltecs, the Texcoco region, to rescue the images and words of times past. In the twelve books of the *General History of New Spain*, Sahagún and his young assistants have saved and assembled ancient voices, the fiestas of the Indians, their rites, their gods, their way of counting the passage of years and stars, their myths, their poems, their medicines, their tales of remote ages and of the recent European invasion . . . History sings in this first great work of American anthropology.

Six years ago King Philip II had those manuscripts and all the native codices copied and translated by Sahagún seized *so that no original or translation of them should remain*. Where have they ended up, those books suspected of perpetuating and publicizing idolatries? No one knows. The Council of the Indies has not replied to any of the despairing author-copier's pleas. What has the king done with these forty years of Sahagún's life and so many centuries of the life of Mexico? They say in Madrid that the pages have been used as spice wrappings.

Old Sahagún does not give up. At eighty he clutches to his breast a few papers saved from the disaster and dictates to his pupils in Tlatelolco the first lines of a new work, to be called *Divinatory Art*. Later he will go to work on a complete Mexican calendar. When he finishes the calendar, he will begin a Náhuatl-Spanish-Latin dictionary. And after the dictionary . . .

Outside, dogs howl, fearing rain.

(24 and 200)

1583: Ácoma

The Stony Kingdom of Cíbola

Captain Antonio de Espejo, who made a fast fortune on the frontier of Mexico, has responded to the siren call of the seven cities of gold. At the head of a few warrior horsemen he has undertaken the Odyssey to the north; and instead of the fabulous kingdom of Cíbola, he has found an immense desert, very occasionally peppered with villages in the shape of fortresses. No precious stones hang from the trees, because there are no trees except in the rare valleys; and there is no more glitter of gold than what the sun draws from the rocks when it beats down hard on them.

In those villages the Spaniards hoist their flag. The Indians still do not know that they will soon be obliged to change their names and raise temples to worship another god, although the Great Spirit of the Hopis told them some time ago that a new race would arrive, a race of fork-tongued men, bringing greed and boastfulness. The Hopis receive Captain Espejo with offerings of corn tortillas and turkeys and hides; and the Navajos of the high mountains welcome him bringing water and corn.

Beyond, a fortress of rock and mud soars into the purple sky. From the edge of the mesa, the village of the Ácomas dominates the valley, green with cornfields irrigated by canals and dams. The Ácomas, enemies of the Navajos, are famous for their ferocity. Not even Francisco Vázquez de Coronado, who came this way forty years ago, dared go near them.

The Ácomas dance in Captain Espejo's honor and lay at his feet colored cloths, turkeys, ears of corn, and deerskins.

A few years from now they will refuse to pay tribute. The assault will last three days and three nights. Survivors will have one foot chopped off with a single ax blow, and the chiefs will be thrown over the precipice.

(89)

Night Chant, a Navajo Poem

House made of dawn,
House made of evening light,
House made of dark cloud . . .
Dark cloud is at the house's door,
The trail out of it is dark cloud,
The zigzag lightning stands high upon it . . .
Happily may I walk,
Happily, with abundant showers, may I walk.
Happily, with abundant plants, may I walk.
Happily, on the trail of pollen, may I walk.
Happily may I walk.
May it be beautiful before me.

May it be beautiful behind me.
May it be beautiful below me.
May it be beautiful above me.
May it be beautiful all around me.
In beauty it is finished.

(42)

1586: Cauri

The Pestilence

Influenza does not shine like the steel sword, but no Indian can dodge it. Tetanus and typhus kill more people than a thousand greyhounds with fiery eyes and foaming jaws. The smallpox attacks in secret and the gun with a loud bang, amid clouds of sparks and sulfurous smoke, but smallpox annihilates more Indians than all the guns.

The winds of pestilence are devastating these regions. Anyone they strike, they blow down: they devour the body, eat the eyes, close the throat. All smells of decay.

Meanwhile, a mysterious voice ranges over Peru. It treads on the heels of the pestilence and penetrates the litanies of the dying, this voice that whispers, from one ear to another: "Whoever throws the crucifix out of his house will return from the dead."

(221)

1588: Quito

Grandson of Atahualpa

The golden columns, arabesques, and ornamentations sweat gold; the saints and adored virgins in their gilded robes, and the chorus of angels with little golden wings, pray gold: This is one of the houses that Quito offers to him who centuries ago was born in Bethlehem in manger straw and died naked.

The family of the Inca Atahualpa has an altar in this church of St. Francis, in the place of honor in the great transept beside the evangel. At the foot of the altar rest the dead. The son of Atahualpa, who was named Francisco like his father and his father's assassin, occupies the main tomb. God must have reserved glory for Captain Francisco Atahualpa if God listens, as they say, to the views of those in command with more attention than He pays to the screams of the commanded. The Inca's son knew how to suppress the native risings in the South. He brought as prisoners to Quito the rebel chiefs of Cañaribamba and Cuyes and was rewarded with the office of this city's director of public works.

Francisco's daughters and nieces have come to install the image of St. Catherine that a sculptor of Toledo, Juan Bautista Vázquez, has carved for a spot high on the Atahualpas' altar. Alonso, Francisco's son, sent the image from Spain; and the family is still unaware that Alonso died in Madrid while St. Catherine was crossing the ocean to this church.

Alonso Atahualpa, grandson of the Inca, died in prison. He could play the harp, the violin, and the clavichord. He wore only Spanish dress, cut by the best tailors, and for a long time had not paid the rent for his house. Gentlemen are not imprisoned for debt, but Alonso went to jail denounced by Madrid's most important tailors, jewelers, hatters, and glovemakers. Nor had he paid for the carving that his family now places, amid golden garlands, on the gilded altar.

(155 and 215)

1588: Havana

St. Martial *versus* the Ants

Rapacious ants continue to mortify people and undermine walls. They fell trees, devastate farmlands, and gobble fruit and corn and the flesh of the absentminded.

In view of patron St. Simon's inefficacy, the town council unanimously elects another protector.

The city promises to celebrate his day every year. St. Martial is the new shield of Havana against the assaults of bibijagua ants. St. Martial, who three centuries ago was bishop of Limoges, is known as a specialist and is said to have great influence with the Lord.

(161)

1589: Cuzco

He Says He Had the Sun

Rigid beneath the sheets, Mancio Serra de Leguízamo unburdens his conscience. Before a notary he dictates and swears: *"That we discovered these realms in such condition that there was not in all of them one thief, one vicious man, nor idler, nor was there an adulterous or bad woman . . ."*

Pizarro's old captain does not want to depart this world without saying for the first time: *"That the lands and mountains and mines and pastures and hunting grounds and woods and all manner of resources were governed or divided in such a way that everyone knew and had his property, without anyone else occupying or taking it . . ."*

Don Mancio is the last survivor of the army that conquered Peru. Over half a century ago he was one of those who invaded this sacred city of Cuzco, pillaged the treasures of its tombs and houses, and axed down the walls of the Temple of the Sun so clotted with gold that their resplendence made anyone who entered look like a corpse. He says he received the best part of the booty: the immense golden face of the sun, with its fiery rays and flames, which had dominated the city and blinded the people of Cuzco at the hour of dawn.

Don Mancio wagered the sun at cards and lost it in a night.

(118)

1592: Lima

An *Auto-da-Fé* in Lima

The wind carries off the ashes of three Lutheran Englishmen, captured on the island of Puná. One of them, Henry Oxley, was burned alive because he would not renounce his faith.

Smoke curls upward from the center of a circle of tall lances as the crowd grows delirious and the Tribunal of the Holy Office pronounces sentences of lashes and other pains and humiliations.

Several suffer punishment *for marrying twice or for simple fornication and other crimes of the sin of the flesh. For soliciting nuns* a Dominican friar, a Franciscan, an Augustinian, and a Jesuit are condemned. Juan de la Portilla, soldier, *for swearing by the ears of God.* Isabel de Angulo, soldier's wife, *because so that men would desire her she recited the words of the Consecration in a low voice.* Bartolomé de Lagares, sailor, *for affirming that, being a bachelor and paying for it, no sin was committed.* Lorenzo de la Peña, barber, *that because his wife's pew in church was taken, he said if that was the way of it, there was no God.*

The Sevillian Pedro Luis Enríquez goes off to ten years in prison *for having affirmed that by taking a rooster to a field where there was no sound of dogs, and cutting its head off at midnight, one would find a small stone like a hazelnut, rubbing one's lips with which would make the first pretty woman encountered die of love for the one doing this, and that killing a cat in January and inserting a bean into each of its joints and burying it, the beans growing from it, if bitten while looking at oneself in the mirror, would have the virtue of making one invisible; and because he said he was a tough fellow and a healer, in token of which he had a cross on his breast and another on the roof of his mouth, and claimed that in prison he saw splendors and smelled the sweetest of fragrances.*

(137)

1593: Guarapari

Anchieta

Ignacio de Loyola pointed to the horizon and ordered: *"Go, and set fire to the world!"*

José de Anchieta was the youngest of all the apostles who brought the message of Christ, the good news, to the jungles of Brazil. Forty years later, the Indians call him *Caraibebé,* man with wings, and they say that by making the sign of the cross Anchieta wards off storms and turns a fish into a ham and a dying man into an athlete. Choirs of angels descend from the sky to announce to him the arrival of galleons or the attacks of enemies, and God raises him from the earth when he kneels to say his prayers. His skinny body, burned by his hair shirt, sends off rays of light when he flagellates himself, sharing the torments of God's only son.

Brazil will be grateful to him for other miracles. From the hand of this tattered saint have come the first poems written in this land, the first Tupí-Guaraní grammar, and the first theatrical works, sacramental mystery plays in the indigenous language, which transmit the Gospel mixing native personages with Roman emperors and Christian saints. Anchieta has been Brazil's first schoolmaster and physician and the discoverer and chronicler of this land's animals and plants in a book that tells how the *guarás* change the color of their plumage, how the *peixe-boi* lays its eggs in the eastern rivers, and how the porcupine lives.

At sixty he continues founding cities and building churches and hospitals; on his bony shoulders he carries heavy beams along with the Indians. As if inspired by his clean and humble luminosity, the birds seek him out and people seek him out. He walks many leagues without complaining or letting them carry him in nets, through these regions where all has the color of heat and all is born and decays in an instant to be born again, fruit that becomes honey, water, death, seed of new fruits: the land boils, the sea boils with slow fire, and Anchieta writes on the sand, with a stick, his verses of praise to the Creator of everlasting life.

(10 and 38)

1596: London

Raleigh

Choreographer of tobacco, swaggering military artificer, Sir Walter Raleigh emits snakes of smoke from his nose and rings and spirals of it from his mouth as he says: "If they cut my head off, it will fall happily with my pipe between my teeth."

"You stink," comments his friend.

There is no one else in the tavern except a small black slave who waits patiently in the corner. Raleigh is telling how he discovered Earthly Paradise in Guyana the previous year, over there where El Dorado lies hidden. He licks his lips recalling the flavor of iguana eggs and closes his eyes describing the fruits and the leaves that never fall from the treetops.

"Listen, brother," he says. "This play of yours about the young lovers . . . Yes, that one, set in those forest glades, just marvelous. Set it in Verona and it smells of the cage. You got the wrong background, my dear man. That air over there . . ."

Raleigh's friend, a baldhead with mischievous eyes, knows that this Guyana is a swamp where the sky is always black with mosquitos, but he listens in silence and nods his head because he also knows that Raleigh isn't lying.

(198)

1597: Seville

A Scene in Jail

He was wounded and mutilated by Turks. He was attacked by pirates and scourged by Moors. He was excommunicated by the priests. He was in prison in Algiers and in Castro del Río. Now he is a prisoner in Seville. Seated on the floor beside the stone pallet, he dips his pen in the inkpot and wonders, eyes fixed on the candle flame, his good hand poised in the air.

Is it worthwhile to insist? King Philip's reply still hurts, when for the second time he asked for a job in America: *Seek what befits you over here.* If things have changed since then, they have changed for the worse. Before, he had at least the hope of a response. Since that time the black-clad king, detached from the world, is not talking to anyone except his own phantoms within the walls of the Escorial.

Miguel de Cervantes, alone in his cell, does not write to the king. He does not ask for any vacant office in the Indies. On a blank sheet he begins to relate the misadventures of a poet-errant, *one of those knights whose lance is on the rack, shield rusting, steed skin-and-bone, hound run away.*

Melancholy sounds ring through the prison. He does not hear them.

(46 and 195)

1598: Potosí

History of Floriana Rosales,
Virtuous Woman of Potosí
(Abbreviated Version of the
Chronicle by
Bartolomé Arzáns de Orsúa y Vela)

Because of her great beauty ever since the cradle, like a delicate pretty flower, and because her mother's name was Ana, they baptized her Floriana.

Schooled in virtue in the seclusion of the house, the dazzling young lady always avoided seeing and being seen, but this in itself set on fire the desires of suitors who surrounded her since she was twelve. Among them, those who most successfully pursued their suit were Don Julio Sánchez Farfán, mine owner, Captain Rodrigo de Albuquerque, and the governor of Tucumán, who passed this way en route to Lima and lingered in Potosí after spotting Floriana in church.

Out of pure spite, seeing himself rejected, the governor of Tucumán challenged Floriana's father to a duel, and they drew swords by a spring and cut each other about until some ladies, not without courage, interposed themselves.

Floriana burned with fury to see her father wounded and determined to avenge it with her own hand. She sent word to the governor that on the next night she would await him in a certain shop, where she wished to speak to him without witnesses.

The governor donned his best clothes—a department in which he was excessively vain, that abominable vice in men who have studied in the school of Heliogabalus, of whom Herodiano said that he despised Roman and Greek woolen clothing and wore gold and purple with precious stones in the Persian style, as Lampridio records. The governor arrived punctually, exquisitely arrayed, and at the designated hour Floriana appeared bringing amid the lovely flowers of her face the poisonous asp of her anger. Taking a broad and well-sharpened razor out of her sleeve, she rushed at him like a lioness to cut his face, hurling many an insult at him. The governor fended off the blade with his hand and produced a dagger.

Alert to the danger, Floriana threw over his face a bundle of cloth, behind which she was able to seize in both hands a stout stick which there and then sealed his fate. She gave the governor of Tucumán such a whack that he fell flat.

Heavyhearted and scared, Floriana's parents tried to hide her in their house, but it was not possible. The magistrate, the highest justice and police authority, came running and Floriana had no alternative to going up to her room and throwing herself out of the window into the street. God willed her skirt to catch on a projection from the window frame and she hung from it head downward.

A servant who knew Don Julio Sánchez Farfán and knew he loved her mistress told him to go to the alley behind the houses and see if Floriana was there, because she had just thrown herself from the window. But as Captain Rodrigo de Albuquerque saw Don Julio secretly talking to the servant, he followed him to the alley.

Don Julio arrived just when the afflicted Floriana, who had been suspended for some time, was pleading in mortal fear for help, saying that she was choking. Her knightly lover approached and, stretching out his arms, took her by the shoulders and gave her a hard pull, tumbling with her to the ground.

At that moment Captain Rodrigo turned up and with amorous words covered Floriana with his cape and raised her up. Seeing this, Don Julio, aflame with jealousy, got to his feet and taking out a dagger plunged it into the captain, calling him a scurvy traitor. With a mortal wound in his chest, the captain fell to the ground imploring for confession, hearing which Floriana cursed her fate and the ordeals of her honor and departed at full speed.

Floriana put on Indian clothing to escape from this town of Potosí, but when she was about to get on a mule somebody tipped off the magistrate, who came to the spot to put her in prison. When the magistrate saw Floriana, the blind child known as Cupid pierced his heart through with a terrible arrow. Panting, he took her by the hands and carried her off to the palace.

At ten o'clock that night, the hour when she had to go to the magistrate's bedroom, Floriana tied a rope to the balcony and let herself down into the hands of Don Julio, who awaited her below. The damsel told Don Julio that before moving a single step he must swear the security of her person and purity.

Seeing the danger they ran, for the flight had already been discovered, Don Julio took Floriana on his shoulders and ran, carrying her to the far-off Plaza del Gato. He flew over stones and mud, in a bath of sweat, and when he could finally sit down to rest and lowered Floriana from his back, he suddenly collapsed.

Thinking that he had just fainted, she put Don Julio's head in her lap. But noticing that he was dead, she sprang up with a start and fled to the barrios of San Lorenzo, in the month of March of that year 1598.

There she remained in concealment, resolved to maintain perpetual chastity and to continue till the end of her days being an obedient servant of the Lord.

(21)

Spanish Couplets to Be Sung and Danced

I have seen a man survive
with a hundred wounds from a lance
and later saw him die
from just a single glance.

Down in the sea a whale
sighed and sighed again
and his sighings told this tale:
"He who has love, has pain."

Today I want to sing
now that I have no sorrow,
in case the fates should bring
tears to my eyes tomorrow.

(196)

1598: *Panama City*

Times of Sleep and Fate

Simón de Torres, apothecary of Panama, would like to sleep but cannot take his eyes off the hole in the roof. Each time his lids close, his eyes open by themselves and fasten on the hole. Simón lights and puts out his pipe and lights it again, trying to discourage the mosquitos with the smoke and with his hand. He twists and turns, soaking and boiling in the bed that was left crooked by the shock it received the other day. The stars wink at him through the hole and he would like to stop thinking. So the hours pass until the rooster crows, either announcing the day or calling the hens.

A week ago a woman tumbled through the roof and fell on Simón.

"Who, who, who are you?" the apothecary stammered.

"We don't have much time," said she as she tore off her clothes.

In the morning she got up, shining, delicious, and dressed herself in no time flat.

"Where are you going?"

"To Nombre de Dios. I left the bread in the oven there."

"But that's twenty leagues away!" cried the apothecary.

"Only eighteen," she corrected him. And as she disappeared, she said: "Take care of yourself. Whoever enters me loses his memory."

(157)

1599: *Quito*

The Afro-Indians of Esmeraldas

They keep on the alert. They don't bat an eyelash. They are full of suspicion. That brush that robs them of their image, won't it rob them of their souls? The brush is magic like the mirror. Like the mirror, it takes possession of people.

From time to time, the horrible cold of Quito makes them sneeze, and the artist growls at them. Uncomfortable, half strangled by the ruffs, they resume the poses, rigid until the next sneeze. They have been in this city a few days and they still can't grasp why such powerful people have come to live in such a cold place, nor why the houses have doors, nor why the doors have locks, bolts, and padlocks.

Half a century ago a storm dashed a slave ship against the coastal reefs, near the mouth of the Esmeraldas River. The ship contained slaves from Guinea to be sold in Lima. The blacks took off and lost themselves in the woods. They founded villages and had children with native women, and those children multiplied, too. Of the three whose portrait Andrés Sánchez Gallque is now painting, two were born of that mixture of Africans and Ecuadorean women. The other, Francisco de Arobe, came from Guinea. He was ten at the time of the shipwreck.

They have been rigged out as distinguished gentlemen, tunics and cloaks, lace cuffs, hats, so as not to make a bad impression on the king when he receives, in Madrid, this portrait of his new subjects, *these barbarians who have been invincible up to now*. They also have lances in their hands, necklaces of teeth, and sea-shells over their Spanish dress; and on their faces are gold ornaments that pierce their ears, their nostrils, and their lips.

(176)

1599: Chagres River

The Wise Don't Talk

This is the shiniest road on earth. From sea to sea winds the long, silver trail. Countless strings of mules cross the jungle, weighed down by the metals of Potosí, en route to the galleons waiting in Portobello.

Little monkeys accompany the silver across Panama. Screaming without letup, they jeer at the muleteers and pelt them with guavas.

On the banks of the Chagres River, Fray Diego de Ocaña watches them admiringly. To cross the river, the monkeys form a chain from the crown of a tree, clutching each other by the tails: the chain swings and gathers speed until a strong shove hurls it to the highest branches on the other bank.

The Peruvian Indian carrying Ocaña's baggage comes up to

him and says: "Father, these are people. They don't talk so that the Spaniards won't notice it. If they see that they're people, they'll send them to work in the mines."

(157)

1599: La Imperial

Flaming Arrows

Rebellion breaks out on the Pacific coasts, and the repercussions shake the Andes cordillera.

Martín García Óñez de Loyola, nephew of St. Ignatius, came here from Peru with the fame of a tireless hunter and crack killer. There he captured Túpac Amaru, last of the Incas. Then they sent him as governor to Chile to tame the Araucanians. Here he killed Indians, stole sheep, and burned crops without leaving a grain. Now the Araucanians are parading his head on the point of a lance.

The Indians use Christians' bones as trumpets to sound the call to battle. War masks, armor of leather: The Araucanian cavalry devastates the South. Seven towns fall, one after the other, under a rain of fiery arrows. The hunted become the hunters. The Araucanians lay siege to La Imperial. To deny it water, they alter the course of the river.

Half of the realm of Chile, everything south of the Bío-Bío, becomes Araucanian again.

The Indians say, pointing at the lance: *This is my master. This won't be ordering me to dig gold, nor to bring herbs or firewood, nor to mind the cattle, nor to sow or reap. I want to stay with this master.*

(66 and 94)

1599: Santa Marta

They Make War to Make Love

Rebellion breaks out on the Caribbean coasts, and its repercussions shake the Sierra Nevada. The Indians are rising for the freedom to love.

At the fiesta of the full moon, the gods dance in the body of Chief Cuchacique and lend magic to his arms. From the villages

of Jeriboca and Bonda, the voices of war awaken the whole land
of the Tairona Indians and shake Masinga and Masinguilla, Zaca
and Mamazaca, Mendiguaca and Torama, Buritaca and Tairama,
Maroma, Taironaca, Guachaca, Chonea, Cinto and Nahuanje, Mamatoco, Ciénaga, Dursino and Gairaca, Origua and Durama, Dibocaca, Daona, Chengue and Masaca, Daodama, Sacasa, Cominca,
Guarinea, Mauracataca, Choquenca and Masanga.

Chief Cuchacique wears a jaguar skin. Arrows that whistle,
arrows that burn, arrows that poison: The Taironas burn chapels,
break crosses, and kill friars, fighting against the enemy god who
prohibits their customs.

Since time immemorial in these lands, anyone got a divorce
who wanted one, and siblings made love if they felt like it, and
women with men or men with men or women with women. Thus
it was in these lands until the men in black and the men in iron
came, they who throw to their dogs anyone loving as his ancestors
loved.

The Taironas celebrate their first victories. In their temples,
which the enemy calls houses of the Devil, they play the flute on
bones of the vanquished, drink corn wine, and dance to the lilt of
drums and shell trumpets. The warriors have closed all passes and
roads to Santa Marta and are preparing the final assault.

(189)

1600: Santa Marta

They Had a Country

The fire takes time to catch. How slowly it burns.

Grindings of metal, armored men in motion. The assault on
Santa Marta has failed and the governor has passed a sentence of
annihilation. Weapons and soldiers have arrived from Cartagena
in the nick of time and the Taironas, bled white by so many years
of tribute and slavery, scatter in defeat.

Extermination by fire. Burning villages and plantations, cornfields and cottonfields, cassava and potato crops, fruit orchards.
The irrigated plantings that delighted the eye and gave food, the
farmlands where the Taironas made love in full daylight, because
children made in the dark are born blind—everything burns.

How many worlds do these fires illuminate? The one that was and was seen, the one that was and was not seen . . .

Exiled at the end of seventy-five years of rebellions, the Taironas flee into the mountains, the most arid and remote places, where there is no fish and no corn. Far up there the invaders have expelled them, seizing their lands and uprooting their memory, so that in their remote isolation oblivion may descend upon the songs they sang when they lived together, a federation of free peoples, and were strong and wore robes of multicolored cotton and necklaces of gold and flashing stones: so that they should never again remember that their grandparents were jaguars.

Behind them they leave ruins and graves.

The wind whispers, souls in travail whisper, and fire dances in the distance.

(189)

Techniques of Hunting and Fishing

Deep in the Amazon jungle a fisherman of the Desana tribe sits on a high rock and contemplates the river. The waters slide down, carry fish, polish stones—waters gilded by the first light of day. The fisherman looks and looks, and feels that the old river turns into the flow of blood through his veins. The fisherman will not fish until he has won the hearts of the fishes' wives.

Nearby, in the village, the hunter gets ready. He has already vomited, and later bathed in the river, and is clean inside and out. Now he drinks infusions of plants that have the color of deer, so that their aromas may impregnate his body, and paints on his face the mask that the deer like best. After blowing tobacco smoke on his weapons, he walks softly to the spring where the deer drink. There he drops juice of the pineapple, which is the milk of the daughter of the sun.

The hunter has slept alone these last nights. He has not been with women nor dreamed of them, so that the animal he will hunt and pierce with lance or arrows should not be jealous.

(189)

1600: Potosí

The Eighth Wonder of the World

Caravans of llamas and mules carry to the port of Arica the silver that the Potosí mountain bleeds from each of its mouths. At the end of a long voyage the ingots arrive in Europe to finance war, peace, and progress there.

In exchange, from Seville or by contraband, Potosí receives the wines of Spain, the hats and silks of France, the lace, mirrors, and tapestry of Flanders, German swords, Genoese paper, Neapolitan stockings, Venetian glass, Cypriot wax, Ceylonese diamonds, East Indian marbles, the perfumes of Arabia, Malacca, and Goa, Persian carpets and Chinese porcelain, black slaves from Cape Verde and Angola, and dashing steeds from Chile.

Everything is very dear in this city, the dearest in the world. Only *chicha* corn liquor and coca leaves are cheap. The Indians, forcibly seized from the communities of all Peru, spend Sundays in the corrals dancing to their drums and drinking *chicha* till they roll on the ground. On Monday mornings they are herded into the mountain and, chewing coca and beaten with iron bars, they pursue the veins of silver, greenish-white serpents that appear and take flight through the entrails of this immense paunch, no light, no air. There the Indians toil all week, prisoners, breathing dust that kills the lungs, and chewing coca that deceives hunger and masks exhaustion, never knowing when night falls or day breaks, until Saturday ends and the bell rings for prayer and release. Then they move forward, holding lighted candles, to emerge on Sunday at dawn, so deep are the diggings and the infinite tunnels and galleries.

A priest newly come to Potosí sees them arriving in the city's suburbs, a long procession of squalid ghosts, their backs scarred by the lash, and remarks: "I don't want to see this portrait of hell."

"So shut your eyes," someone suggests.

"I can't," he says. "With my eyes shut I see more."

(21 and 157)

Prophecies

Last night they were married, before the fire as tradition demands, and heard the sacred words:

To her: *"When he ignites with the fire of love, do not be icy."*

And to him: *"When she ignites with the fire of love, do not be icy."*

By the glow of the fire they awaken, embrace, congratulate themselves with their eyes, and tell their dreams.

During sleep the soul travels outside the body and gets to know, in an eternity or the blink of an eye, what is going to happen. Beautiful dreams are to be shared; and to share them, couples awaken very early. Bad dreams, however, are to be thrown to the dogs.

Bad dreams, nightmares about abysses or vultures or monsters, may portend the worst. And the worst, here, is being forced to go to the Huancavélica mercury mines or to the far-off silver mountain of Potosí.

(150 and 151)

Ballad of Cuzco

A llama wished
to have golden hair,
brilliant as the sun,
strong as love
and soft as the mist
that the dawn dissolves,
to weave a braid
on which to mark,
knot by knot,
the moons that pass,
the flowers that die.

(202)

1600: Mexico City

Carriages

Carriages have returned to the broad streets of Mexico. More than twenty years ago the ascetic Philip II banned them. The decree said that use of a carriage turns men into idlers and accustoms them to a pampered and lazy life; and that this costs them muscle for the arts of war.

Now that Philip II is dead, carriages reign again in this city. Inside them, silks and mirrors; outside, gold and tortoise shell and coats of arms on the door. They exude an aroma of fine woods, roll smoothly as a gondola, rock like a cradle; behind the curtains the colonial nobility wave and smile. On his lofty perch, amid silken fringes and tassels, sits the disdainful coachman, almost like a king; and the horses are shod with silver.

Carriages are still banned for Indians, prostitutes, and those punished by the Inquisition.

(213)

1601: Valladolid

Quevedo

For twenty years Spain has reigned over Portugal and all its colonies, so that a Spaniard can walk the earth without treading on foreign soil. But Spain is the most expensive country in Europe: It produces ever fewer things and ever more coins. Of the thirty-five million escudos born six years ago, not even a shadow remains. The data recently published here by Don Martín González de Cellorigo in his *Treatise on Necessary Policy* are not encouraging: by virtue of chance and inheritance, every Spaniard who works maintains thirty more. For those with incomes, work is a sin. The gentry have the bedroom as a battlefield; and in Spain fewer trees grow than monks and beggars.

Galleys laden with the gold of America sail for Genoa. The metals arriving from Mexico and Peru do not even leave a smell in Spain. The feat of the conquest seems to have been achieved by German, Genoese, French, and Flemish merchants and bankers.

In Valladolid lives a crippled and myopic youth of pure blood, with a sharp sword and tongue. In the evenings, while his page removes his boots, he dreams up couplets. In the morning his snakes slither under the doors of the royal palace.

Head buried in his pillow, young Francisco de Quevedo y Villegas personifies in his head the force that turns a coward into a warrior and that softens up the most severe judge; and cursing this trade of poet, he rubs his eyes, draws up the lamp, and with one tug hauls from inside his head the verses that won't let him sleep. The verses tell of Don Doubloon, who

> *is honorably born in the Indies,*
> *where the world accompanies him,*
> *comes to die in Spain*
> *and is buried in Genoa.*

(64, 183, and 218)

1602: Recife

First Expedition Against Palmares

In the mills that press and squeeze sugarcane and men, each slave's work is measured as the weight of the cane and the pressure of the crusher and the heat of the oven are measured. The strength of a slave is exhausted in five years, but in only one year the owner will recover the price paid for him. When slaves cease to be useful hands and become useless mouths, they receive the gift of freedom.

In the mountains of northeastern Brazil hide the slaves who win freedom before sudden old age or early death topples them. The sanctuaries where the fugitives take refuge, in the groves of lofty palms in Alagoas, are called Palmares.

The governor general of Brazil sends out the first expedition against Palmares. It consists of a few poor whites and mestizos anxious to capture and sell blacks; a few Indians who have been promised combs, knives, and little mirrors; and many mulattoes.

Returning from the Itapicurú River, the commander of the expedition, Bartolomeu Bezerra, announces in Recife: *The core of the rebellion has been destroyed.* And they believe him.

(32 and 69)

1603: Rome

The Four Parts of the World

An illustrated and enlarged edition of Cesare Ripa's *Iconology* is published in Rome. This dictionary of symbolic images shows the world as it looks from the north shore of the Mediterranean.

On top appears Europe, the queen, with her emblems of power. Horses and lances support her. With one hand she holds up the columns of the temple, with the other she holds a scepter. She has a crown on her head and other crowns lie at her feet, amid miters and books and paintbrushes, zithers, and harps. Next to the horn of plenty lie compass and ruler.

Beneath, to the right, Asia. She offers coffee, pepper, incense. Garlands of flowers and fruit adorn her. A kneeling camel awaits her.

At one side, Africa, a dusky Moorish woman topped by an elephant's head. On her breast, a necklace of coral. Around her the lion, the snake, the scorpion, and ears of grain.

Beneath everything America, *a woman with face fearsome to look upon.* She wears feathers over her naked olive skin. At her feet she has a newly severed human head and a lizard. She is armed with bow and arrows.

(125)

1603: Santiago de Chile

The Pack

Santiago's town council has purchased a new branding iron—of silver—to brand Indian slaves on the face. The governor, Alonso de Ribera, orders that a fifth part of the value of each Araucanian sold at the ports of Valdivia and Arica should go to the costs of war and maintenance of the soldiery.

One hunting expedition follows another. The soldiers cross the Bío-Bío and do their lashing out at night. They burn and butcher and return with men, women, and children roped around the neck. Once branded, they are sold to Peru.

The governor raises the spouted wine pitcher and toasts the

battles won. He toasts in the Flemish style, like Pedro de Valdivia. First, swig after swig to the gentlemen and ladies who come to his mind. When he finishes with people, he toasts saints and angels; and he never forgets to thank them for the pretext.

(94)

1605: Lima

The Night of the Last Judgment

Right after Christmas, nature's heavy artillery blew up the city of Arequipa. The cordillera exploded and the earth vomited the foundations of houses. People were left in fragments under the wreckage, crops burned under the cinders. The sea rose up, meanwhile, and smothered the port of Arica.

Yesterday, at dusk, a barefooted friar assembled a throng in Lima's plaza. He announced that this libertine city would collapse in the next few hours, and with it all its surroundings as far as the eye could see.

"No one will get away!" he howled. "Not the fastest horse nor the swiftest ship will be able to escape!"

At sunset, the streets are already filled with penitents scourging themselves by torchlight. Sinners proclaim their sins on the corners, and from the balconies rich folk throw silverware and party dresses down into the street. Hair-raising secrets are revealed out loud. Unfaithful wives tear up pavingstones and use them to beat their breasts. Thieves and seducers kneel before their victims, masters kiss the feet of their slaves, and beggars have not hands enough for so much charity. The Church receives more money than in all the Lents in its history. If not seeking a priest to confess to, people seek one to marry them. The churches are crammed with folk who want to nestle within their protection.

Then the dawn.

The sun shines on Lima as never before. Penitents look for ointments for their flayed backs, and masters pursue their slaves. Newlyweds inquire for their just-acquired husbands whom daylight has evaporated; people who repented of their sins wander the streets in search of new ones to commit. Sobs and curses are heard behind every door. There is no beggar who hasn't dropped from sight. The priests have also hidden themselves, to count the mountains of coins that God accepted last night. With the leftover cash, Lima's churches will buy in Spain the authentic feathers of the archangel Gabriel.

(157)

The Strawberry

Captain Alonso González de Nájera, who has lived six years in Chile, remembers and relates.

He speaks of those who are born amid trumpets and drums, the noble host who wear coats of mail from the cradle and make a wall of their bodies against attacks by the Indians. He insists that rain pulls grains of gold out of the Chilean soil and that the Indians pay tribute with gold they take from the bellies of lizards.

He also tells of a rare fruit, with the color and form of the heart, which explodes with sweet juices at the touch of the teeth. For vividness, flavor, and scent it could well compete with the most delectable fruits of Spain, *although over there in Chile they insult it by calling it a strawberry*.

(66)

1608: Puerto Príncipe
Silvestre de Balboa

In the mud and palm-frond house of Silvestre de Balboa, clerk of the Puerto Príncipe town council, the first epic poem in Cuba's history is born. The author dedicates his royal stanzas to Bishop Altamirano, who four years ago was kidnaped by the French pirate Gilbert Giron in the port of Manzanillo.

From the kingdom of Neptune rose seals and sea nymphs to the pirate's ship, sympathizing with the bishop, who would accept nothing in his defense. The people of Manzanillo managed to raise two hundred ducats, a thousand hides, and other provisions, and finally the Lutheran pirate freed his prisoner. To welcome the rescued bishop satyrs, fauns, and centaurs came down to the beach from the woods bringing guanábanas and other delicacies. From the meadows came nymphs loaded with mameys, prickly pears,

pineapples, avocados, and tobacco, and petticoat-clad dryads descended from trees with arms full of wild pitahayas and fruit of the
birijí and the tall jagua tree. The bishop also received guabinas,
dajaos, and other river fish from naiads; and fountain and pond
nymphs brought some tasty hicatee turtles from Masabo. When
the pirates were ready to collect the ransom, a few lads, the flower
of Manzanillo youth, fell on them and valiantly gave them what
they deserved. It was a black slave named Salvador who pierced
pirate Gilbert Giron's breast with his lance:

Oh Creole Salvador, honorable slave!
May your fame go soaring without end;
for in praise of soldier so brave
never should weary the tongue or the pen.

Filled with admiration and awe, Silvestre de Balboa invokes
Troy and compares the Manzanillans with Achilles and Ulysses,
after mixing them up with nymphs, fauns and centaurs. But amid
all the portentous deities, the people of this village have been
humbly immortalized—a black slave who behaved like a hero, and
many of this island's fruits, herbs, and animals that the author calls
and loves by their names.

(23)

1608: Seville

Mateo Alemán

Mateo Alemán boards the ship that is sailing for Mexico. To travel
to the Indies he has bribed the king's secretary and demonstrated
purity of blood.
    Jewish on both father's and mother's sides, with one relative
burned by the Inquisition, Mateo Alemán has invented for himself
a super-Christian lineage and an imposing coat of arms and inci-
dentally changed his mistress Francisca de Calderón into his eldest
daughter.
    The novelist knew how to learn the arts of his character Guz-
mán de Alfarache, *skilled in the business of flamboyant roguery,*
who changes dress, name, and city to wipe away disgraces and

escape from poverty. *I must dance to the same tune as all the others, as long as it may last*, explains Guzmán de Alfarache in the novel that all Spain is reading.

(6 and 147)

1608: Córdoba

The Inca Garcilaso

At sixty he leans over the table, wets the pen in the horn inkpot, and writes apologetically. He writes a meticulous and handsome prose. He praises the invader in the invader's tongue, which he has made his own. With one hand he salutes the conquest as the work of Divine Providence: the conquistadors, arms of God, have evangelized the New World, and tragedy has paid the price of salvation. With the other hand, he bids farewell to the kingdom of the Incas, *destroyed before it was known*, and invokes it with a nostalgia for paradise. One hand belongs to his father, a captain of Pizarro's. The other to his mother, Atahualpa's cousin, whom that captain humiliated and threw into the arms of a soldier.

Like America, the Inca Garcilaso de la Vega has been born of a rape. Like America, he lives torn to pieces.

Although he has been in Europe for half a century, he still listens, as if they were something recent, to the voices of his childhood in Cuzco, *things received in the mantillas and the milk:* in that devastated city he came into the world eight years after the Spaniards arrived, and in that city he drank from his mother's lips the stories that come down from that distant day when the sun dropped over Lake Titicaca the prince and princess born of his loves with the moon.

(76)

1609: Santiago de Chile

How to Behave at the Table

They told him of it this morning when they brought the steaming, aromatic chocolate. At one bound, the governor detached himself from the Holland sheets: The king of Spain has decided to legalize the enslavement of Indians captured in war.

The news took almost a year to cross the ocean and the cordillera. For some time now Araucanians have been sold in the presence of a public notary, and any who try to escape have their tendons cut; but the king's approval will shut the mouths of a few grumblers.

"God bless this bread . . ."

The governor offers a supper to the people-tamers of these unfriendly lands. The guests drink wine of the country from oxhorns and eat corn bread wrapped in corn leaves, the savory humita favored by the Indians. As indicated by Alfonso the Wise, they pick up with three fingers the strips of chili-peppered meat; and as Erasmus of Rotterdam recommended, they do not gnaw bones or throw fruit peelings under the table. After taking the hot quelén-quelén drink, they use a toothpick without either leaving it between the lips or parking it behind the ear.

(94 and 172)

1611: Yarutini

The Idol-Exterminator

They are smashing Cápac Huanca with pickaxes. The priest Francisco de Avila shouts to the Indians to get a move on. Many idols still remain to be discovered and broken to pieces in these lands of Peru, where he knows no one who refrains from the sin of idolatry. The divine anger never rests. Avila, scourge of sorcerers, never sits down.

But his slaves, who know, are hurt by each blow. This big rock is a man chosen and saved by the god Pariacaca. Cápac Huanca alone shared with him his corn *chicha* and his coca leaves when Pariacaca disguised himself in rags and came to Yarutini and begged for something to drink and chew. This big rock is a generous man. Pariacaca froze him and turned him into stone so that the punitory hurricane that blew everyone else away would not take him.

Avila has the pieces thrown down the cliff. In place of Cápac Huanca he puts up a cross. Afterward he asks the Indians for Cápac Huanca's history, and he writes it.

(14)

1612: San Pedro de Omapacha

The Beaten Beats

The symbol of authority, plaited rawhide tipped with cord, whistles through the air and bites. It tears off the skin in strips and splits the flesh.

Naked, bound to the punishment block, Cristóbal de León Mullohuamani, chief of the Omapacha community, endures the torment. His moans keep time with the whip.

From cell to stocks, from stocks to lash, the chief lives in agony. He dared to protest to the viceroy in Lima and has not delivered his quota of Indians. He was responsible for the lack of hands to bring wine from the plains to Cuzco and to spin and weave clothing as the magistrate ordered.

The executioner, a black slave, wields the lash with pleasure. This back is no better or worse than any other.

(179)

1613: London

Shakespeare

The Virginia Company is meeting great disappointment on the coast of North America, which lacks gold or silver; nonetheless, propaganda pamphlets circulate all over England claiming that the English are trading the Indians in Virginia *pearls of Heaven for pearls of earth.*

Not long ago, John Donne was exploring his mistress's body in a poem as one discovering America; and Virginia, the gold of Virginia, is the central theme of the celebrations of Princess Elizabeth's wedding. In honor of the king's daughter a masquerade by George Chapman is performed, which revolves around a great rock of gold, symbol of Virginia or of the illusions of its shareholders: gold, key to all powers, secret of life pursued by the alchemists, son of the sun as silver is daughter of the moon and copper is born of Venus. There is gold in the warm zones of the world, where the sun generously sows its rays.

In the wedding celebrations for the princess, a work by William Shakespeare is also staged, *The Tempest*, inspired by the wreck of a Virginia Company ship in the Bermudas. The great creator of souls and marvels locates his drama this time on an island in the Mediterranean that more resembles the Caribbean. There Duke Prospero meets Caliban, son of the witch Sycorax, worshiper of the god of the Patagonian Indians. Caliban is a *savage*, an Indian of the type Shakespeare has seen in some exhibition in London: *a thing of darkness*, more beast than man, who only learns to curse and has no capacity for judgment nor sense of responsibility. Only as a slave, or tied up like a monkey, could he find a place in human society; that is, European society, which he has absolutely no interest in joining.

(207)

1614: Lima

Minutes of the Lima Town Council: Theater Censorship Is Born

In this council it has been stated that, for lack of examination of the comedies presented in this city, there have been said many things injurious to parties and against the authorities and the honesty that is owing to this republic. In order that said improprieties may cease in the future, it behooves us to provide a remedy. And the question having been posed and discussed, it was agreed and so ordered that present and future authors of comedies be notified not to present or have presented in any form any comedy without its first being seen and examined and approved by the person duly named by this council, under pain of two hundred pesos . . .

(122)

1614: Lima

Indian Dances Banned in Peru

Wings of condor, head of parrot, skins of jaguar: the Peruvian Indians dance their ancestral Raymi on Corpus Christi day. In the Quechuan language they perform their invocations to the sun at the time of sowing, or pay the sun homage when there is a birth or at the harvest season.

To the end that with Our Lord's help occasions for falling into idolatry may be suppressed, and the devil may not continue exercising his deceits, the archibishop of Lima decides that *neither in the local dialect nor in the general tongue may dances, songs, or taquies be performed.* The archbishop announces terrible punishments and orders all native musical instruments to be burned, including the dulcet reed flute, the messenger of love:

> *By the shore you shall sleep,*
> *At midnight I will come . . .*

(21)

1615: Lima

Guamán Poma

At seventy, he leans over the table, wets the pen in the horn inkpot, and writes and draws defiantly. He is a man of hasty and broken prose. He curses the invader in the invader's tongue and makes it explode. The language of Castile keeps tripping over Quechua and Aymara words, but after all, Castile is Castile for the Indians, and *without the Indians Your Majesty isn't worth a thing.*

Today Guamán Poma de Ayala finishes his letter to the king of Spain. At the start it was addressed to Philip II, who died while Guamán was writing it. Now he wants it delivered into Philip III's own hand. The pilgrim has trekked from village to village, *the author walking over mountains with much snow,* eating if he could and always carrying on his back his growing manuscript of sketches and words. *The author has returned from the world . . . He went through the world weeping the whole way* and has finally reached Lima. From here he proposes to travel to Spain. How he will manage that, he doesn't know. What does it matter? No one knows Guamán, no one listens to him, and the monarch is very remote and very high up; but Guamán, pen in hand, treats him as an equal, addresses him familiarly, and explains to him what he should do.

Exiled from his province, naked, treated as a nothing, Guamán does not hesitate to proclaim himself inheritor of the royal dynasties of the Yarovilcas and Incas and calls himself king's counselor, first Indian chronicler, prince of the realm, and second-in-command. He has written this long letter out of pride: His lineage stems from the ancient lords of Huánuco, and he has incorporated in the name he gives himself the falcon and puma of his ancestors' coat of arms, they who ruled the lands of northern Peru before Incas and Spaniards. *To write this letter is to weep. Words, images, tears of rage. The Indians are the natural owners of this realm and the Spaniards, natives of Spain, are strangers here in this realm.* The apostle Santiago, in military uniform, tramples on a fallen native. At banquets, the plates are heaped with miniature women. The muleteer carries a basket filled with the mestizo children of the priest. *Also it is God's punishment that many Indians die in mercury and silver mines. In all Peru, where there were a hundred not ten remain.* "Do you eat this gold?" asks the Inca, and the conquistador replies: "This gold we eat."

Today, Guamán finishes his letter. He has lived for it. It has taken him half a century to write and draw. It runs to nearly twelve hundred pages. Today, Guamán finishes his letter and dies.

Neither Philip III nor any other king will ever see it. For three centuries it will roam the earth, lost.

(124, 125, and 179)

1616: Madrid

Cervantes

"What news do you bring of our father?"

"He lies, sir, amid tears and prayers. All swelled up he is, and the color of ashes. He's already put his soul to rest with the notary and with the priest. The mourners are waiting."

"If only I had the balsam of Fierabrás . . . Two swallows of that and he'd get well right away!"

"And him going on seventy, and dying? With six teeth in his mouth and only one hand that works? With the scars from all them battles, and insults, and jailings? That balls stuff wouldn't do nothing for him, sir."

"I don't say two swallows. Two drops."

"It'd be too late."

"He's dead, you say?"

"Dying, sir."

"Take off your hat, Sancho. And you, Rocinante, lower your head. Ah, prince of arms! King of letters!"

"What'll we do without him, sir?"

"Nothing that doesn't do him homage."

"Where'll we be putting ourselves, so all alone?"

"We'll go where he wanted to go but couldn't."

"Where's that, sir?"

"To set right whatever is crooked on the shores of Cartagena, in the ravines of La Paz and the woods of Soconusco."

"Nice places to get your bones ground up."

"You must know, Sancho, my brother of so many roads and rides, that in the Indies glory awaits the knight-errant thirsting for justice and fame . . ."

"Well, it's been a while since we got beaten up . . ."

" . . . and their squires are rewarded with huge, never-explored kingdoms."

"Wouldn't there be some a bit closer?"

"And you, Rocinante, in the Indies horses are shod with silver and champ on gold bits. They're regarded as gods!"

"A thousand beatings ain't enough for him. He wants a thousand and one!"

"Shut up, Sancho."

"Didn't our father say that America is a refuge for scoundrels and a sanctuary for whores?"

"Shut up, I tell you!"

"Whoever embarks for the Indies, he said, leaves his conscience on the pier."

"So we'll go there to clean off the honor of him who fathered us as free men in prison!"

"Can't we just mourn him here?"

"Do you call such treachery homage? Ah, villain! We'll take to the road again. If he made us to sojourn in the world, we'll take him through the world. Reach me my helmet! Shield on arm, Sancho! My lance!"

(46)

1616: Potosí

Portraits of a Procession

Magic mountain of Potosí: On these high and hostile plains that offered only solitude and cold, the world's most populated city has been made to bloom.

Lofty silver crosses head the procession, which advances between two lines of banners and swords. On silver streets ring out the silver hooves of horses decked with velvets and pearl-studded bridles. For confirmation of those who rule and consolation of those who serve, silver passes in parade, gleaming, confident, strutting, sure that there is no space on earth or in heaven it cannot buy.

The city is dressed up for a fiesta; balconies display hangings and heraldries; from a sea of rustling silks, foam of lace, and cataracts of pearls, the ladies watch and admire the cavalcade that moves with a din of trumpets, shawms, and harsh drums. A few gentlemen have a black patch over an eye and lumps and wounds on their foreheads, which are signs not of war but of syphilis. Kisses and flirtations keep flying from balconies to street, from street to balconies.

Masked figures of Selfishness and Greed appear. Greed, from behind a mask of snakes, sings as his horse performs caprioles:

Root of all evils
They call me, and I never tire
Not to satisfy desire.

Selfishness, black breeches, black gold-embroidered doublet, black mask beneath black, many-plumed cap, answers:

If I have conquered love
And love conquers death, all agree
Nothing is stronger than me.

The bishop heads a long, slow army of priests and hooded penitents armed with tall candles and silver candelabra; then the heralds' trumpets impose themselves on the peal of church bells announcing the Virgin of Guadelupe, Light of the patient, Mirror of justice, Refuge of sinners, Consolation of the afflicted, green Palm, flowered Staff, luminous Rock. She appears on waves of gold and mother-of-pearl, in the arms of fifty Indians; stifled by so much jewelry, she observes with astonished eyes the turmoil of silver-winged cherubs and the spectacular display of her worshipers. On a white steed comes the Knight of the Burning Sword, followed by a battalion of pages and lackeys in white liveries. The knight hurls his hat into the distance and sings to the Virgin:

Brown as is my lady fair,
so much beauty she betrays
heaven and earth stand in a daze.

Lackeys and pages in purple livery run behind the Knight of Divine Love, who comes mounted at a trot, Roman-style horseman, purple silk coattails flying in the wind: he falls to his knees before the Virgin and lowers his laurel-crowned head, but when he puffs out his chest to sing his couplets, a volley of sulphur smoke erupts. The devils' float has invaded the street, and no one pays the smallest attention to the Knight of Divine Love.

Prince Tartar, worshiper of Mohammed, opens his bat wings, and Princess Proserpine, hair and trains of snakes, hurls from on high blasphemies that the retinue of devils applaud. Somewhere the name of Jesus Christ is pronounced, and the Inferno float blows up with a big bang. Prince Tartar and Princess Proserpine jump through the smoke and flames and fall as prisoners at the Mother of God's feet.

The street is covered with small angels, halos, and wings of sparkling silver, and violins and guitars, zithers and shawms sweeten the air. Musicians dressed as damsels celebrate the arrival of Mercy, Justice, Peace, and Truth, four elegant daughters of Potosí raised on litters of silver and velvet. The horses pulling their float have Indian heads and breasts.

Then comes the Serpent, coiling and weaving. On a thousand Indian legs the enormous reptile slithers along, now to the light of flaming torches, instilling fear and fire into the festivities and showing defiance and combat at the feet of the Virgin. When soldiers cut off his head with axes and swords, from the Serpent's entrails emerges the Inca with his pride smashed to pieces. Dragging his fantastic robes, the son of the Sun falls to his knees before the Divine Light. The Virgin sports a robe of gold, rubies, and pearls the size of chickpeas, and the gold cross on her imperial crown shines brighter than ever over her astonished eyes.

Then the multitude. Artisans of every trade, and rogues and beggars who could draw a tear from a glass eye: the mestizos, children of violence, neither slaves nor masters, go on foot. The law prohibits them from having horses or weapons, as it prohibits mulattos from using parasols, so that no one can conceal the stigma that stains the blood to the sixth generation. With the mestizos and mulattos come the quadroons and the half-black, half-Indian zambos and the rest of the mixtures produced by the hunter and his prey.

Bringing up the rear, a mass of Indians loaded with fruits and flowers and dishes of steaming food. They implore the Virgin for forgiveness and solace.

Beyond, some blacks sweep up the litter left by all the others.

(21 and 157)

1616: Santiago Papasquiaro

Is the Masters' God the Slaves' God?

An old Indian prophet spoke of the free life. Clad in traditional raiment, he went through these deserts and mountains raising dust and singing, to the sad beat of a hollow tree trunk, about the ancestors' feats and the liberty lost. The old man preached war against those who had seized the Indians' lands and gods and made the Indians themselves burst their lungs in the Zacatecas' mines. Those who died in the necessary war would revive, he announced, and old people who died fighting would be reborn young and swift.

The Tepehuanes stole muskets and fashioned and hid bows and arrows, because they are bowmen as skilled as the Morning Star, the divine archer. They stole and killed horses to eat their agility, and mules to eat their strength.

The rebellion broke out in Santiago Papasquiaro, in the North of Durango. The Tepehuanes, the region's most Christian Indians, the first converts, trampled on the Host; and when Father Bernardo Cisneros pleaded for mercy, they answered *Dominus vobiscum.* To the south, in the Mezquital, they smashed the Virgin's face with machetes and swigged wine from the chalices. In the village of Zape, Indians clad in Jesuit surplices and bonnets chased fugitive Spaniards through the woods. In Santa Catarina, they used their clubs on Father Hernando del Tovar while saying to him: *Let's see if God saves you.* Father Juan del Valle ended up stretched on the ground naked, with his sign-of-the-cross hand up in the air, the other hand covering his never-used sex.

But the insurrection didn't last long. On the plains of Cacaria, colonial troops struck the Indians down. A red rain falls on the dead. The rain falls through air thick with powder and riddles the dead with bullets of red mud.

In Zacatecas the bells ring out, summoning to celebratory banquets. The owners of mines sigh with relief. There will be no shortage of hands for the diggings. Nothing will interrupt the prosperity of the realm. They will be able to continue urinating tranquilly into tooled silver chamberpots, and nobody will prevent their ladies from attending Mass accompanied by a hundred maids and twenty damsels.

(30)

1617: London

Whiffs of Virginia in the London Fog

Dramatis personae:

The King (James I of England, VI of Scotland). He has written: *Tobacco makes a kitchen of man's interior parts, dirtying them and infecting them with a sort of oily and greasy soot.* He has also written that anyone who smokes imitates *the barbarous and beastly manners of the wilde, godlesse, and slavish Indians . . .*

John Rolfe. English colonist in Virginia. One of the most distinguished members of that *peculiar people marked and chosen by the finger of God . . . for undoubtedly He is with us*—as Rolfe himself defines his countrymen. With seeds brought to Virginia from Trinidad, he has produced good mixtures of tobacco on his plantations. Three years ago he sent to London in the hold of the *Elizabeth* four casks full of leaves, which have launched the recent but already very fruitful tobacco trade with England. It can well be said that John Rolfe has put tobacco on the throne of Virginia, as a queen plant with absolute power. Last year he came to London with Governor Dale, seeking new colonists and new investments for the Virginia Company and promising fabulous profits for its shareholders; for tobacco will be to Virginia what silver is to Peru.

He also came to present to King James his wife, the Indian princess Pocahontas, baptized Rebecca.

Sir Thomas Dale.   Governor of Virginia until last year. Authorized the marriage of John Rolfe and Princess Pocahontas, first Anglo-Indian marriage in Virginia's history, on the understanding that it was an act of high political convenience that would contribute to the peaceful supply of grains and hands by the native population. However, in his request for permission, John Rolfe did not mention this aspect of the affair; nor did he make any mention of love, although he did take pains to deny emphatically any *unbridled desire* toward his handsome eighteen-year-old fiancée. Rolfe said he wished to wed this pagan *whose education hath been rude, her manners barbarous, her generation accursed, . . . for the good of this plantation, for the honour of our countrie, for the glory of God, for my own salvation, and for the converting to the true knowledge of God and Jesus Christ, an unbeleeving creature . . ."*

Pocahontas.   Also known as Matoaka when she lived with the Indians. Favorite daughter of the great chief Powhatan. After marrying Rolfe, renounced idolatry, changed her name to Rebecca, and covered her nudity with English clothes. Wearing crown hats and high lace collars at the neck, she came to London and was received at court. She spoke like an Englishwoman and thought like an Englishwoman; she devoutly shared her husband's Calvinist faith, and Virginia tobacco found in her the most able and exotic promoter it needed to plant itself in London. She died of an English disease. Sailing down the Thames en route to Virginia, while the ship awaited favorable winds, Pocahontas breathed her last in the arms of John Rolfe at Gravesend in March of this year 1617. She was not yet twenty-one.

Opechancanough.   Uncle of Pocahontas, elder brother of the great chief Powhatan. He gave the bride away in the Protestant church at Jamestown, a bare wooden church, three years ago. Spoke not a word before, during, or after the ceremony, but Pocahontas told Rolfe the story of her uncle. Opechancanough had once lived in Spain and in Mexico; he was then a Christian known as Luis de Velasco, but no sooner was he back in his country than he threw his crucifix, cape, and stole in the fire, cut the throats of the priests who accompanied him, and took back his name of Opechancanough, which in the Algonquin language means *he who has a clean soul*.

Some Globe Theatre actor has put this story together and now asks himself, confronting a mug of beer, what he will do with it. Write a love tragedy or a moral play about tobacco and its evil powers? Or perhaps a masquerade with the conquest of America as its theme? The play would have a sure success, because all London is talking about Princess Pocahontas and her fleeting visit here. That woman . . . a harem all by herself. All London dreams of her nude among the trees, with aromatic flowers in her hair. What avenging angel ran her through with his invisible sword? Did she expiate the sins of her pagan people, or was her death God's warning to her husband? Tobacco, illegitimate son of Proserpine and Bacchus . . . Does not Satan protect the mysterious pact between that weed and fire? Smoke that makes the virtuous giddy, isn't it the breath of Satan? And the hidden lechery of John Rolfe . . . And the past of Opechancanough, formerly known as Luis de Velasco, traitor or avenger . . . Opechancanough entering the church with the princess on his arm . . . Tall, erect, silent . . .

"No, no," concludes the indiscreet hunter of histories as he pays for his beers and walks out into the street, "This story is too good to write. As the gentle Silva, poet of the Indies, used to say: 'If I write it, what do I have left to tell my friends?' "

(36, 159, and 207)

1618: Lima

Small World

The owner of Fabiana Criolla has died. In his will he has lowered the price of her freedom from 200 to 150 pesos.

Fabiana has spent the night without sleeping, wondering how much her guaiacum-wood box full of powdered cinnamon would be worth. She does not know how to add, so she cannot calculate the freedoms she has bought with her work through the half century that she has been in the world, nor the price of the children who have been made on her and taken from her.

With the first light of dawn, the bird comes and taps its beak on the window. Every day the same bird announces that it is time to wake up and get going.

Fabiana yawns, sits up on the mat, and inspects her worn-down feet.

(31)

1618: Luanda

Embarcation

They have been caught in the hunters' nets and are marching to the coast, tied to each other at the neck, as drums of pain resound in the villages.

On the African coast, a slave is worth forty glass necklaces or a whistle with a chain or two pistols or a handful of bullets. Muskets and machetes, rum, Chinese silks, or Indian calicoes are paid for with human flesh.

A monk inspects the column of captives in the main square of the port of Luanda. Each slave receives a pinch of salt on the tongue, a splash of holy water on the head, and a Christian name. Interpreters translate the sermon: *Now you are children of God* . . . The priest instructs them not to think about the lands they are leaving and not to eat dog, rat, or horse meat. He reminds them of St. Paul's epistle to the Ephesians (*Slaves, serve your masters!*) and Noah's curse upon the children of Ham, who remained black through centuries of centuries.

They see the ocean for the first time, and the enormous, roaring beast terrifies them. They think the whites are taking them to some remote slaughterhouse to eat them and make oil and fat from them. Hippopotamus-hide whips drive them onto enormous canoes that cross the breakers. In the ships they face fore-and-aft guns with lighted fuses. The fetters and chains keep them from throwing themselves into the sea.

Many will die on the voyage. The survivors will be sold in the markets of America and again branded with hot irons.

They will never forget their gods. Oxalá, at once man and woman, will be disguised as St. Jerónimo and St. Barbara. Obatalá will be Jesus Christ; and Oshún, spirit of sensuality and fresh waters, will turn into the Virgins of Candelaria, the Conception, Charity, and Pleasures and will be St. Anne in Trinidad. Behind

St. George, St. Anthony, and St. Michael will lurk the lances of Ogum, god of war; and inside St. Lazarus, Babalú will sing. The thunders and fires of fearsome Shangó will transfigure St. John the Baptist and St. Barbara. In Cuba, Elegguá will continue having two faces, life and death, and in southern Brazil, Exú will have two heads, God and the Devil, to offer the faithful Solace and vengeance.

(68, 127, 129, and 160)

1618: Lima

Too Dark

The friends toss back their tattered capes and sweep the ground with their hats. Their respects duly paid, they exchange compliments: "That stump of yours, a bloody marvel!"

"Your chancre—what a masterpiece!"

Pursued by flies, they cross the empty lot.

They talk as they pee, backs to the wind.

"Long time no see."

"I been on the run like a fly. Suffering, suffering."

"Ay."

Lizard takes a crust from his pocket, breathes on it, polishes it, and invites Breadbeggar to be his guest. Seated on a rock, they contemplate the flowers on the thistles.

Breadbeggar takes a bite with his three teeth and reports: "Up at the courthouse, good handouts . . . Best damn place in Lima. But the porter threw me out. Kicked me out, he did."

"You don't mean Juan Ochoa?"

"Satan, more likely name for him. God knows I didn't do nothing to him."

"Juan Ochoa ain't there no more."

"That right?"

"They chucked him out like a dog. Now he ain't porter at the courthouse, nor nothing."

Breadbeggar, feeling avenged, smiles. He stretches his bare toes.

"Must've been because of his misdeeds."

"It wasn't that."

"Because he was too stupid, then?"
"No, no. Because he's the son of a mulatto and grandson of a
nigger. Too bloody dark."

(31)

1620: Madrid

The Devil's Dances Come
from America

Thanks to the corpse of St. Isidro, which slept beside him for the
past few nights, King Philip III feels better. This noon he ate and
drank without choking. His favorite dishes lit up his eyes, and he
emptied the wineglass at a gulp.

Now he moistens his fingers in the bowl offered by a kneeling
page. The pantryman reaches out the napkin to the majordomo of
the week. The majordomo of the week passes it to the chief majordomo. The chief majordomo bows to the duke of Uceda. The
duke takes the napkin. Bowing his head, he holds it out to the
king. While the king dries his hands, the trencherman brushes
crumbs from his clothes, and the priest offers God a prayer of
thanks.

Philip yawns, loosens his high lace collar, asks what is the
news.

The duke reports that the Hospital Board people have come
to the palace. They complain that the public refuses to go to the
theater since the king banned dances; and the hospitals live from
the takings of the comedies. "Sir," the board people have told the
duke, "since there have been no dances there have been no takings.
The sick are dying. We have nothing to pay for bandages and
doctors." Actors recite verses by Lope de Vega extolling the American Indian:

Taquitán mitanacuní,
Spaniard from here to there.
. . . In Spain there is no love
so it seems to me:
there selfishness is king
here love's the thing.

But what the public wants from America are the kind of salty songs and dances that set the most respectable folk on fire. No use for the actors to make the stones weep and the dead laugh, nor for proscenium arts to draw lightning out of cardboard clouds. "If the theaters stay empty," say the board people, groaning, "the hospitals will have to close."

"I told them," says the duke, "Your Highness would decide."

Philip scratches his chin, investigates his nails.

"If Your Majesty has not changed his mind . . . What is banned is banned and well banned."

The saraband and chaconne dances make sex shine in the dark. Father Mariana has denounced these dances, *inventions of negroes and American savages, infernal in words and in movements.* Even in processions their couplets eulogizing sin are heard; and when their lascivious tambourine and castanet rhythms burst forth, the very nuns in the convents can no longer control their feet and the Devil's ticklings galvanize their hips and bellies.

The king's eyes are following the flight of a big, lazy fly among the remains of the banquet. "You—what do you think?" the king asks the fly.

The duke thinks he is being addressed: "These clownish dances are music for a witches' sabbath, as Your Majesty has well said, and the place for witches is in the bonfires in the central plaza."

The goodies have disappeared from the table, but the smell sticks in the air.

Babbling, the king orders the fly: "You decide."

"Your Majesty's worst enemy couldn't accuse you of intolerance," insists the duke. "Your Majesty has been indulgent. In the time of the king your father, whom God keeps in glory . . ."

"Aren't you the one in command?" babbles Philip.

". . . anyone who dared to dance the saraband got a different reward. Two hundred lashes and a dose of the galleys!"

"You, I say," whispers the king and closes his eyes.

"You"—and a gob of foam, saliva that his mouth always produces to excess, appears on his lips.

The duke smells a protest and immediately shuts up and withdraws on tiptoe.

Drowsiness overtakes Philip, heavy eyelids, and he dreams of a plump, nude woman who devours playing cards.

(186)

1622: Seville

Rats

Father Antonio Vázquez de Espinosa, newly arrived from America, is the guest of honor.

While the servants serve slices of turkey with sauce, foamy waves break in the air; a high, white sea maddened by storm; and when the stuffed chickens come on, tropical rains explode over the table. Father Antonio relates that on the Caribbean coast it rains so hard that women become pregnant and their children are born waiting for it to stop; by the time it clears, they are already grown up.

The other guests, captives of the story and the banquet, eat and are silent; the priest has his mouth full of words and forgets the dishes. From the floor, seated on hassocks, children and women listen as if at Mass.

The crossing from the Honduran port of Trujillo to Sanlúcar de Barrameda has been quite a feat. The ships proceeded bump by bump, tormented by squalls; several ships were swallowed by the angry sea, and many sailors by sharks. But nothing was worse, and Father Antonio's voice lowers, nothing was worse than the rats.

In punishment for the many sins committed in America, and because no one bothers with confession and Communion as they should before going aboard, God filled the ships with rats. He put them in the storage holds among the victuals, and beneath the quarterdeck; in the stern saloon, in the cabins, and even on the pilot's seat; so many rats, and such big ones, that they aroused fear and admiration. Four quintals of bread the rats stole from the cabin where the priest slept, plus the biscuits that were under the hatchway. They wolfed the hams and the sides of bacon in the stern storechest. When thirsty passengers went looking for water, they found drowned rats floating in the containers. When hungry ones went to the hen coop, all they found were bones and feathers and perhaps one sprawling chicken with its feet gnawed off. Not even the parrots in their cages escaped. Sailors kept watch over the remaining water and food night and day, armed with clubs and knives, and the rats attacked them and bit their hands and ate each other.

Between olive and fruit courses, the rats have arrived. The desserts are intact. No one touches a drop of wine.

"Would you like to hear the new prayers I composed? Since old ones just didn't placate the wrath of the Lord . . ."

No one answers.

The men cough, raising napkins to mouths. The women who were on their feet giving orders to the servants have all disappeared. Those listening from the floor are cross-eyed and open-mouthed. The children see Father Antonio with long snout, enormous teeth, and mustachio and twist their necks looking for his tail under the table.

(201)

1624: Lima

People for Sale

"Walk!"

"Run!"

"Sing!"

"What blemishes does he have?"

"Open that mouth!"

"Is he drunk, or just cantankerous?"

"How much do you offer, sir?"

"And diseases?"

"He's worth twice that!"

"Run!"

"Better not cheat me, or I'll bring him back."

"Jump, you dog!"

"You don't get goods like that for nothing."

"Make him lift up his arms!"

"Make him sing good and loud!"

"This woman, with kids or without?"

"Let's see her teeth!"

They pull them by one ear. The buyer's name will be marked on the cheeks or forehead, and they will be work tools on the plantations, fisheries, and mines, or weapons of war on the battle-fields. They will be midwives and wet nurses, giving life, and executioners and gravediggers taking it. They will be minstrels and bed-flesh.

The slave corral is right in the center of Lima, but the town council has just voted to move it. The blacks on offer will be lodged in a barracoon the other side of the Rímac River, beside the San Lázaro slaughterhouse. There they will be far enough from the city for the winds to carry off their rotten and contagious vapors.

(31 and 160)

1624: Lima

Black Flogs Black

Three African slaves have paraded the streets of Lima with bound hands and a rope around their necks. The executioners, also black, walked behind. At every few steps, a stroke of the lash, up to a total of a hundred; and when they fell down, extra lashes as a dividend.

The mayor gave the order. The slaves had brought playing cards into the cathedral cemetery, turning it into a gambling den, using gravestones as tables; and the mayor well knew that the lesson would not be lost on the blacks in general who have become so insolent and so numerous, and so addicted to making trouble.

Now the three lie in the patio of their master's house. Their backs are raw flesh. They howl as their wounds are washed with urine and rum.

Their master curses the mayor, shakes his fist, vows vengeance. One just doesn't play such games with other people's property.

(31)

1624: Lima

The Devil at Work

The moon shines bright as the church bells announce one o'clock. Don Juan de Mogrovejo de la Cerda leaves the tavern and starts walking through the orange-blossom-scented Lima night.

At the Bargain Street intersection he hears strange voices or echoes; he stops and cups his ear.

A certain Asmodeo is saying that he has moved several times since his ship sailed from Seville. On arriving at Portobello he

inhabited the bodies of various merchants *who call dirty tricks*
"deals" and robbery "business," and a picklock a measuring stick;
and in Panama he lived in a phony gentleman with a false name,
who knew by heart how to act like a duke, the routine of a marquis,
and the litanies of a count . . .

    "Tell me, Asmodeo. Did this character observe the rules of
modern gentry?"

    "All of them, Amonio. He lied and never paid debts nor both-
ered himself with the Sixth Commandment; he always got up late,
talked during Mass, and felt cold the whole time, which is said to
be in the best of taste. Just think how hard it is to feel cold in
Panama, which makes a good try at being our hell. In Panama the
stones sweat and people say: 'Hurry up with the soup, it'll get
hot.' "

    The indiscreet Don Juan de Mogrovejo de la Cerda cannot
see either Asmodeo or Amonio, who are talking at some distance,
but he knows that such names do not occur in the *Lives of the*
Saints, and the unmistakable smell of sulphur in the air is enough
to get the drift of this eloquent conversation. Don Juan flattens his
back against the tall cross at the Bargain Street intersection, whose
shadow falls across the street to keep Amonio and Asmodeo at a
distance; he crosses himself and invokes a whole squadron of saints
to protect and save him. But pray he cannot, for he wants to listen.
He is not going to lose a word of this.

    Asmodeo says that he left the body of that gentleman to enter
a renegade clergyman and then, en route to Peru, found a home
in the entrails of a devout lady who specialized in selling girls.

    "So I got to Lima, and your advice about operating in its
labyrinths would be most helpful. Tell me what goes on in these
provincial wilds. . . . Are the fortunes here honestly won?"

    "If they were, it would be less crowded in hell."

    "What's the best way of tempting the businessmen?"

    "Just put them in business and leave them to it."

    "Do people here feel love or respect for their superiors?"

    "Fear."

    "So what do they have to do to get ahead?"

    "Not deserve to."

    Don Juan invokes the Virgin of Atocha, searches for the rosary
he has forgotten, and clutches the handle of his sword as the ques-
tioning and Amonio's quick answers proceed.

"*About the ones who presume to be the best people, tell me, do they dress well?*"

"*They could, considering how busy they keep the tailors all year round.*"

"*Do they grumble a lot?*"

"*In Lima it's always time for beefing.*"

"*Now tell me, why do they call all the Franciscos Panchos, all the Luises Luchos, and all the Isabelas Chabelas?*"

"*First to avoid telling the truth, and second so as not to name saints.*"

An inopportune fit of coughing attacks Don Juan at that moment. He hears shouts of "Let's go! Let's be off!" and after a long silence he detaches himself from the protecting cross. Shaking at the knees, he moves on toward Merchant Street and the Provincia gates. Of the garrulous pair, not a puff of smoke remains.

(57)

1624: Seville

Last Chapter of the "Life of the Scoundrel"

The river reflects the man who interrogates it.

"So what do I do with my crook? Do I kill him off?"

From the stone wharf his ill-fitting boots go into a dance on the Guadalquivir. This guy has the habit of shaking his feet when he is thinking.

"I have to decide. I was the one who created him the son of a barber and a witch and nephew of a hangman. I crowned him prince of the underworld of lice, beggars, and gallows-fodder."

His spectacles shine in the greenish waters, fixed on the depths as he fires his questions: "What do I do? I taught him to steal chickens and implore alms for the sake of the wounds of Christ. From me he learned his trickery at dice and cards and fencing. With my arts he became a nuns' Don Juan and a notorious clown."

Francisco de Quevedo wrinkles his nose to keep his spectacles up. "It's my decision, and I must make it. There never was a novel in all literature that didn't have a last chapter."

He cranes his neck toward the galleons that lower their sails as they approach the docks.

"Nobody has suffered with him more than I have. Didn't I make his hunger my own when his belly groaned and not even explorers could find any eyes in his head? If Don Pablos has to die, I ought to kill him. Like me, he is a cinder left over from the flames."

From far off, a ragged lad stares at the gentleman who is scratching his head and leaning over the river. "Some old hag," the boy thinks. "Some crazy old hag trying to fish without a hook."

And Quevedo thinks: "Kill him? Doesn't everyone know it's bad luck to break mirrors? Kill him. Suppose I make the crime a just punishment for his evil life? A small dividend for the inquisitors and censors! Just thinking about their pleasure turns my stomach."

A flight of sea gulls explodes. A ship from America is weighing anchor. With a jump, Quevedo starts walking. The lad follows him, imitating his bowlegged gait.

The writer's face glows. He has found on the decks the appropriate fate for his character. He will send Don Pablos, the scoundrel, to the Indies. Where but in America could his days end? His novel has a dénouement, and Quevedo plunges abstractedly into this city of Seville, where men dream of voyages and women of homecomings.

(183)

1624: Mexico City

A River of Anger

The multitude, covering all of the central plaza and neighboring streets, hurls curses and rocks at the viceroy's palace. Paving stones and yells of *Traitor! Thief! Dog! Judas!* break against tightly closed shutters and portals. Insults to the viceroy mix with cheers for the archbishop, who has excommunicated him for speculating with the bread of this city. For some time the viceroy has been hoarding all the corn and wheat in his private granaries, and playing with prices at his whim. The crowd is steaming. *Hang him! Beat him up! Beat him to death!* Some demand the head of the officer who has profaned the Church by dragging out the archbishop; others want to lynch Mejía, who fronts for the viceroy's business deals; and everybody wants to fry the hoarding viceroy in oil.

Pikes, sticks, and halberds rise above heads; pistol and musket shots ring out. Invisible hands hoist the king's pennon on the roof of the palace, and trumpets wail for help; but no one comes to defend the cornered viceroy. The realm's top people have shut themselves in their palaces, and the judges and officials have slipped away through crannies. No soldier is obeying orders.

The walls of the prison on the corner do not resist the attack. The inmates join the furious tide. The palace portals fall, fire consumes the doors, and the mob invades the rooms, a hurricane that pulls draperies off the walls, breaks open chests, and devours whatever it meets.

The viceroy, disguised as a monk, has fled through a secret tunnel to the San Francisco monastery.

(72)

1625: Mexico City

How Do You Like Our City?

Father Thomas Gage, newly arrived, amuses himself on the Alameda promenade. With hungry eyes he watches the ladies float along beneath the tunnel of tall trees. None wears her fichu or mantilla below the waist, the better to show off swaying hips and a pretty walk; and behind each lady comes a retinue of flashy black and mulatto women, their breasts peeping from their décolletage. Fire and fun, they wear roses on their extra-high-heeled shoes, and amorous words are embroidered on the silk bands around their foreheads.

On an Indian's back the priest arrives at the palace.

The viceroy offers him pineapple preserve and hot chocolate and asks how he likes the city.

In the middle of Father Gage's eulogy of Mexico, its women, carriages, and avenues, the host interrupts: "Do you know that I saved my life by a hair? And a baldpate's hair at that . . ."

From the viceroy's mouth bursts a torrential account of last year's uprising.

After much smoke and blood and two helpings of chocolate drained sip by sip, Father Gage learns that the viceroy has spent a year in the San Francisco monastery and still cannot put his nose outside the palace without risking a hail of stones. However, the rebellious archbishop is suffering the punishment of exile in remote, miserable Zamora, a few priests have been sent to row in the galleys, and the hanging of three or four agitators sufficed to crush the insolence of the hoi polloi.

"If it were up to me, I'd hang the lot," says the viceroy. He rises from his chair, proclaims: "Yes, the lot! The whole of this damned city!" and sits down again. "These are lands always ready for rebellion," he breathes. "I have cleaned the bandits off the roads of Mexico!"

Confidentially, stretching his neck, he adds: "D'you know something? The children of Spaniards, the ones born here . . . Who was at the head of the mob? It was them! The Creoles! They think the country belongs to them, they want to rule . . ."

Father Gage stares with the eyes of a mystic at the heavy crystal candelabrum that threatens his head and says: "They give grave offense to God. A second Sodom . . . I saw it with my own eyes this evening. Worldly delights . . ."

The viceroy nods confirmation.

"For they shall soon be cut down like the grass." The priest passes sentence. "They shall wither as the green herb."

He takes the last sip of chocolate.

"Psalm Thirty-seven," he adds, gently resting the little cup on his plate.

(72)

1625: Samayac

Indian Dances Banned
in Guatemala

The monks proclaim that no memory or trace remains of the rites and ancient customs of the Verapaz region, but the town criers grow hoarse proclaiming the succession of edicts of prohibition.

Juan Maldonado, judge of the Royal Audiencia, now issues in the town of Samayac new ordinances *against dances injurious to the Indians' consciences and to the keeping of the Christian law they profess*, because such dances *bring to mind ancient sacrifices and rites and are an offense to Our Lord*. The Indians squander money on feathers, dresses, and masks and *lose much time in rehearsals and drinking bouts, which keep them from reporting*

*for work at the haciendas, paying their tribute, and maintaining
their households.*

Anyone dancing the *tun* will get a hundred lashes. In the *tun*,
the Indians have a *pact with demons.* The *tun*, or Rabinal Achí, is
a fertility dance dramatized with words and masks, and the *tun* is
also the hollow log whose beat is accompanied by long, resonant
trumpets as the drama of the son of the Quichés, prisoner of the
Rabinals, proceeds: The victors sing and dance in homage to the
greatness of the vanquished, who says a dignified farewell to his
land and mounts to the stake at which he will be sacrificed.

(3)

1626: Potosí

A Wrathful God

The lake stampedes, smashes the dike, and invades the city. Many
are ground to pieces by the flood. Mules drag bits of people out
of the mud. A mixture of Spaniards, Creoles, mestizos, and Indians
ends up in common graves. Potosí's houses look like broken corpses.

The fury of Lake Caricari does not abate until priests parade
the Christ of the True Cross through the streets. When they see
the procession approaching, the waters halt.

From the pulpits of all Peru the same sermons are heard in
these days: "Sinners! How long will you play games with the mercy
of the Lord? God has infinite patience. How long, sinners? Have
not the warnings and punishments been enough?"

In these broad and opulent realms, the bursting of Potosí's
lake is nothing new. Forty-five years ago a huge rock plunged
suddenly onto a community of Indian sorcerers in Achocalla, a few
leagues from the city of La Paz. The only survivor was the chief,
who was struck dumb and told the story by signs. Another immense
rock buried a community of heretical Indians shortly afterward in
Yanaoca, near Cuzco. In the following year, the earth opened and
swallowed men and houses in Arequipa; and as the city had not
learned the lesson, the earth showed its fangs a little later and left
nothing standing except the San Francisco monastery. In 1586, the
ocean overwhelmed the city of San Marcos de Arica and all its
harbors and beaches.

When the new century began, the Ubinas volcano blew up.

Its anger was such that the ashes crossed the cordillera by land and reached the coasts of Nicaragua by sea.

Two warning stars appeared in this sky in 1617. They would not go away. Finally they moved into the distance thanks to the sacrifices and promises of the faithful all over Peru, who prayed five novenas without a stop.

(142)

1628: Chiapas
Chocolate and the Bishop

He doesn't put in black pepper, as do those who suffer from chills on the liver. He doesn't add corn, because it bloats. He generously sprinkles cinnamon, which empties the bladder, improves the sight, and strengthens the heart; nor does he spare the hot, well-ground-up chilis. He adds orange-blossom water, white sugar, and achiote spice to give color, and never forgets the handful of anise, two of vanilla, and the powdered Alexandria rose.

Father Thomas Gage adores well-prepared foamy chocolate. If not dunked in chocolate, sweets and marzipans have no flavor. He needs a cup of chocolate at midmorning to keep going, another after dinner to get up from the table, and another to stretch out the night and keep drowsiness at bay.

Since he arrived in Chiapas, however, he hasn't touched it. His belly protests; but Father Thomas prefers living badly between dizziness and faintings if it avoids the fate that killed Bishop Bernardo de Salazar.

Until recently, the ladies of this city would go to Mass with a retinue of pages and maids who, in addition to carrying the velvet hassock, brought along a brazier, boiler, and cup to prepare chocolate. Having delicate stomachs, the ladies couldn't endure the ordeal of a prayer service without the hot elixir, still less a High Mass. So it was, until Bishop Bernardo de Salazar decided to ban the custom because of all the confusion and hubbub it caused it in the church.

The ladies took revenge. One morning the bishop turned up dead in his office. At his feet, broken in pieces, the cup of chocolate that someone had served him.

(72)

1628: Madrid

Blue Blood for Sale

Off the coast of Matanzas, in Cuba, the Spanish fleet has fallen into the hands of the pirate Piet Heyn. All the silver coming from Mexico and Peru will end up in Holland. In Amsterdam, Heyn gets promoted to grand admiral, and a national hero's welcome is prepared for him. From now on, Dutch children will sing:

Piet Heyn, Piet Heyn
Short is your name
but long is your fame.

In Madrid, heads are clutched. Of the royal treasure, only a hole remains.

The king decides, among other emergency measures, to put new noble titles on the market. Nobility is granted *for distinguished deeds.* And what deed more distinguished than having the money to pay for it? For four thousand ducats, any plebeian can wake up a noble of ancient lineage; and he who last night was the son of a Jew or grandson of a Muslim can start the day with pure blood.

But secondhand titles can be had cheaper. Castile has plenty of nobles who would go around with their arses in the air if their capes didn't cover them, gentlemen of illusory grandeur who live brushing invisible crumbs from their jerkins and mustaches: they are offering to the highest bidder the right to use the *Don,* which is all they have left.

Those who have come down in the world have in common with those who ride in silver carriages only a sense of honor and nostalgia for glory, a horror of work—begging is less unworthy— and a disgust for bathing, which is a custom of Moors, foreign to the Catholic religion, and frowned on by the Inquisition.

(64 and 218)

Song About the Indies Hand,
Sung in Spain

To Ronda one goes for pears,
for apples to Argonales,
to the Indies for money
and to the Sierra for follies.

My husband went to the Indies
his poverty to end:
came back with a lot to tell me,
but precious little to spend.

My husband went to the Indies
and brought me back a dirk
with an inscription on it that tells you:
"If you want to eat, work."

The men go off to the Indies,
to the Indies for a golden lark.
Right here they have the Indies,
if they only wanted to work!

(19)

1629: Las Cangrejeras
Bascuñán

His head creaks and hurts. Stretched out in the mud amid the pile of dead, Francisco Núñez de Pineda y Bascuñán opens his eyes. The world is a mess of blood and mud, riddled with rain, which whirls and bounces and splashes and whirls.

Indians throw themselves on him. They tear off his armor and his iron helmet, dented by the blow that knocked him out, and jerkily strip him naked. Francisco manages to cross himself before they tie him to a tree.

The storm lashes his face. The world stops spinning. A voice from inside tells him through the yells of the Araucanians: "You are in a swamp in the Chillán region in your land of Chile. This rain is what dampened your powder. This wind is what blew out your fuses. You lost. Listen to the Indians who are arguing about your death."

Francisco mutters a last prayer.

Suddenly a gust of colored feathers bursts through the rain. The Araucanians make way for the white horse that charges up spurting fire from its nostrils and foam from its mouth. The rider, masked by a helmet, sharply reins in his horse. The horse rears up on two legs before Maulicán, winner of the battle. Everyone falls silent.

"It's the executioner," thinks Francisco. "Now it's all over."

The feathered horseman leans down and says something to Maulicán. Francisco hears only the voices of rain and wind. But when the horseman wheels around and disappears, Maulicán unties the prisoner, takes off his cape, and covers him with it.

Then the horses gallop southward.

(26)

1629: Banks of the Bío-Bío River

Putapichun

Soon they see a throng approaching from the far-off cordillera. Maulicán spurs his horse and advances to meet Chief Putapichun.

The group from the cordillera also has a prisoner, who stumbles along between the horses with a rope around his neck.

On a flat hillock, Putapichun sticks his three-pointed lance into the ground. He has the prisoner unbound and throws a branch at his feet.

"Name the three bravest captains of your army."

"I don't know," babbles the soldier.

"Name one," orders Putapichun.

"Don't remember."

"Name one."

He names Francisco's father.

"Another."

He names another. With each name he is told to break the branch. Francisco watches the scene with clenched teeth. The soldier names twelve captains. He has twelve sticks in his hand.

"Now dig a hole."

The prisoner throws the sticks into the hole, one by one, repeating the names.

"Throw dirt in. Cover them up."

Then Putapichun passes sentence. "Now the twelve brave captains are buried."

And the executioner brings down on the prisoner the club bristling with nails.

They tear out his heart. They invite Maulicán to take the first sip of blood. Tobacco smoke floats in the air as the heart passes from hand to hand.

Then Putapichun, swift in war and slow in word, says to Maulicán: "We came to buy the captain you have there. We know he is the son of Alvaro, the big chief who has caused our land to tremble."

He offers him one of his daughters, a hundred Castilian sheep, five llamas, three horses with tooled saddles, and several necklaces of precious stones. "All that would pay for ten Spaniards and leave something over."

Francisco swallows saliva. Maulicán stares at the ground. After a while he says:

"First I must take him for my father and the other chiefs of my Repocura region to see. I want to show them this trophy of my valor."

"We'll wait," Putapichun says calmly.

"My life is just one death after another," thinks Francisco. His ears hum.

(26)

1629: Banks of River Imperial

Maulicán

"You bathed in the river? Come up to the fire. You're shivering. Sit down and drink. Come, Captain, are you dumb? And you talking our language like one of us . . . Eat, drink. We have a long journey ahead. Don't you like our chicha? You don't like our unsalted meat? Our drums don't make your feet dance. You're in luck, Captain boy. You people burn the faces of captives with the iron that doesn't rub out. You're out of luck, Captain boy. Now your freedom is mine. I'm sorry for you. Drink, drink, tear that fear from your heart. I'll hide you. I'll never sell you. Your fate is in the hands of the Lord of the world and of man. He is just. So. Drink. More? Before the sun arrives we'll be off to Repocura. I want to see my father and celebrate. My father is very old. Soon his spirit will go to eat black potatoes over beyond the snow peaks. Hear the footsteps of the night walking? Our bodies are clean and vigorous to start the trip. The horses are waiting for us. My heart beats fast, Captain boy. Hear the drums of my heart? Hear the music of my happiness?"

(26)

1629: Repocura Region

To Say Good-Bye

Moon by moon, time has passed. Francisco has heard and learned much in these months of captivity. He has learned, and someday will write, the other side of this long Chile war, this *just war that the Indians made against those who deceived and wronged them and took them as slaves, and even worse.*

In the forest, kneeling before a cross of *arrayán* branches, Francisco says prayers of gratitude. Tonight he will be hitting the trail for Nacimiento fort. There he will be exchanged for three captive Araucanian chiefs. He will make the journey protected by a hundred lances.

Now he walks toward the settlement. Beneath a brush arbor a circle of threadbare ponchos and muddy faces awaits him. The strawberry or apple chicha passes from mouth to mouth.

The venerable Tereupillán receives the cinnamon-tree branch, which is the word, and raising it, he makes a long speech of praise for each of the chiefs present. Then he eulogizes Maulicán, the brave warrior, who won such a valuable prisoner in battle and knew how to take him alive.

"*It is not for generous hearts,*" says Tereupillán, "*to take life in cold blood. When we took up arms against the Spanish tyrants who held us under persecution and humiliation, only in battle I felt no compassion for them. But afterward, when I saw them as captives, it gave me great sadness and pain, and it hurt my soul to perceive that truly we did not hate them as persons. Their greed, yes. Their cruelties, their arrogance, yes.*"

Turning to Francisco, he says: *"And you, Captain, friend and comrade, who are going away and leaving us hurt, sad, and without consolation, do not forget us."*

Tereupillán drops the cinnamon branch in the center of the circle and the Araucanians shake the ground awake, stamping their feet.

(26)

1630: Motocintle

They Won't Betray Their Dead

For nearly two years Fray Francisco Bravo had been preaching in this village of Motocintle. One day he told the Indians he had been called back to Spain. He wanted to return to Guatemala, he said, and stay here forever with his beloved flock, but his superiors over there in Spain would not let him.

"Only gold could convince them," said Fray Francisco.

"Gold we don't have," said the Indians.

"Yes, you do," corrected the priest. "I know there's a seam of it hidden in Motocintle."

"That gold doesn't belong to us," they explained. "That gold belongs to our ancestors. We're just looking after it. If any were missing, what would we say to them when they return to the world?"

"I only know what my superiors in Spain will say. They'll say: 'If the Indians of that village where you want to stay love you so much, how come you're so poor?' "

The Indians got together to discuss the matter.

One Sunday after Mass, they blindfolded Fray Francisco and made him turn around until he was dizzy. Everybody went along behind him, from the oldest to children at the breast. When they reached the back of a cave, they took off the blindfold. The priest blinked, his eyes hurting from the glitter of gold, more gold than all the treasures of the Thousand and One Nights, and his trembling hands did not know where to start. He made a bag of his cassock and loaded up what he could. Afterward he swore by God and the holy gospels that he would never reveal the secret, and he received a mule and tortillas for his journey.

In the course of time the royal audiencia of Guatemala received a letter from Fray Francisco Bravo from the port of Veracruz. With great pain to his soul the priest was fulfilling his duty, *as an act of service to the king in an important and outstanding matter of business.* He described the possible location of the gold: "I think I went only a short distance from the village. There was a stream running to the left . . ." He enclosed some sample nuggets and promised to use the rest for devotions to a saint in Malaga.

Now mounted judge and soldiers descend upon Motocintle. Dressed in red tunic and with a white wand hanging from his breast, Judge Juan Maldonado exhorts the Indians to surrender the gold.

He promises and guarantees them good treatment.

He threatens them with severities and punishments.

He puts a few in prison.

Others he puts in the stocks and tortures.

Others he forces up the steps of the scaffold.

And nothing.

(71)

1630: Lima

María, Queen of the Boards

"Every day more problems and less husband!" says María del Castillo with a sigh. At her feet, the stagehand, the prompter, and the star actress offer consolation and breezes from their fans.

In the heavy dusk, the guards of the Inquisition took Juan from María's arms and threw him in jail because poisoned tongues said that he said, while listening to the Gospel: *"Hey! All there is is living and dying!"*

A few hours earlier, in the central plaza and along the four streets giving onto the merchants' corner, the Negro Lázaro had announced the viceroy's new orders concerning comedy playhouses.

The viceroy, Count Chinchón, orders that an adobe wall must separate women from men in the theater, under pain of imprisonment and fine for anyone invading the territory of the other sex. Also that comedies must ring down the curtain earlier, when the bells toll for prayers, and that men and women must leave by different doors so that the grave offenses being committed against God Our Father should not continue in the darkness of the alleyways. And as if that were not enough, the viceroy has decided that the price of tickets must come down.

"He'll never have me!" cries María. "No matter how much he lays siege to me, he'll never have me!"

María del Castillo, great chief of Lima's comedy stage, has kept intact the poise and beauty that made her famous, and after sixty long years she still laughs at the *covered ones* who wear their shawls over one eye; since both of hers are handsome, she looks, seduces, and frightens with open face. She was almost a child when she chose this magical profession, and she has been bewitching people from the Lima stage for half a century. Even if she wanted to, she explains, she could not now change theater for convent, for God would not want her for wife after three such thoroughly enjoyed marriages.

Although the inquisitors have left her husbandless and the government's decrees seek to scare the public, María swears she won't get into bed with the viceroy.

"Never, never!"

Against hell and high water, alone and by herself, she will continue presenting cape-and-sword works in her comedy playhouse behind the San Augustín monastery. Shortly she will be reviving *The Nun Lieutenant* by the well-known Spanish wit Juan Pérez de Montalbán and will produce two new and very salty plays so that everyone may dance and sing and thrill with emotion in this city where nothing ever happens, so boring that two aunts can die on you in the time it takes to yawn.

(122)

1631: Old Guatemala

A Musical Evening at the Concepción Convent

In the convent garden Juana sings and plays the lute. Green light, green trees, green breeze: The air was dead until she touched it with her words and music.

Juana is the daughter of Judge Maldonado, who apportions Indians in Guatemala among farms, mines, and workshops. The dowry for her marriage to Jesus was a thousand ducats, and six black slaves serve her in the convent. While Juana sings her own or others' words, the slaves, standing at a distance, listen and wait.

The bishop, seated before the nun, cannot keep his face under control. He looks at Juana's head bent over the neck of the lute, throat bare, mouth glowingly open, and orders himself to calm down. He is famous for never changing his expression when bestowing a kiss or a condolence, but now this immutable face wears a frown: His mouth twists and his eyelids flutter. His normally firm pulse seems foreign to this hand that tremblingly holds a wineglass.

The melodies, praises of God or profane plaints, rise into the foliage. Beyond stands the green-water volcano. The bishop would like to concentrate on the cornfields and wheatfields and springs that shine on its slope.

That volcano holds the water captive. Anyone approaching it hears seethings as in a stewpot. The last time it vomited, less than a century ago, it drowned the city that Pedro de Alvarado founded at its foot. Here the earth trembles every summer, promising furies; and the city lives on tenterhooks, between two volcanos that cut off its breath. One threatens flood, the other inferno.

Behind the bishop, facing the water volcano, is the fire volcano. By the flames coming from its mouth a letter can be read at midnight a league away. From time to time is heard a thunder as of many guns, and the volcano bombards the world with stones: It shoots out rocks so large that twenty mules could not move them, and it fills the sky with ash and the air with the stink of sulphur.

The girl's voice soars.

The bishop looks at the ground, wanting to count ants, but his eyes slip over to the feet of Juana, which her shoes hide and yet reveal, and his glance roves over that well-made body that palpitates beneath the white habit, while his memory suddenly awakes and takes him back to childhood. The bishop recalls those uncontrollable urges he used to feel to bite the Host in the middle of Mass, and his panic that it would bleed; then he takes off on a sea of unspoken words and unwritten letters and dreams never told.

After a while, silence has a sound. The bishop notices with a start that for some time Juana has not been singing and playing. The lute rests on her knees and she looks at the bishop, smiling broadly, with those eyes that not even she deserves. A green aura floats around her.

The bishop suffers an attack of coughing. The anise falls to the ground and he blisters his hands with applause.

"I'll make you a mother superior!" he cries, "I'll make you an abbess!"

(72)

Popular Couplets of the Bashful Lover

I want to say and I don't,
I'm speaking without any word.
I want to love and I don't
And I'm loving without being heard.

I've a pain from I don't know where,
That comes from I don't know what.
I'll be cured I don't know when
By someone whose name I forgot.

Each time you look at me
And I at you
With my eyes I say
What I don't say.
As I don't find you
I look, to remind you.

(196)

1633: Pinola

Gloria in Excelsis Deo

The chigger is smaller than a flea and fiercer than a tiger. It enters by the feet and knocks you out if you scratch. It does not attack Indians but has no mercy on foreigners.

Father Thomas Gage has been at war for two months, and as he celebrates his victory against the chigger he balances up his stay in Guatemala. If it were not for the chigger, he would have no complaint. The villages welcome him with trumpets beneath canopies of branches and flowers. He has the servants he wants, and a groom leads his horse by the bridle.

He collects his salary on the dot, in silver, wheat, corn, cacao, and chickens. The Masses he says here in Pinola and in Mixco are paid for separately, as well as baptisms, weddings, and burials, and the prayers he offers upon request against locusts, pests, or earthquakes. Counting in the offerings to the many saints in his charge and those at Christmas and Easter, Father Gage takes in more than two thousand escudos a year, free of dust and straw, in addition to wine and cassock free of cost.

The priest's salary comes from the tribute that the Indians pay to Don Juan de Guzmán, owner of these men and these lands. As only the married ones pay tribute and the Indians are quick to nose out and spread scandal, the officials force children of twelve and thirteen into matrimony, and the priest marries them while their bodies are still growing.

(72 and 135)

1634: Madrid

Who Was Hiding Under
Your Wife's Cradle?

The Supreme Council of the Holy Office of the Inquisition, watching over purity of blood, decides that in the future there will be an exhaustive investigation before its officials get married.

All who work for the Inquisition, porter and prosecutor, torturer and executioner, doctor and scullion, must state the two-century genealogy of the chosen woman *to obviate marriage with infected persons.*

Infected persons, that is: with liters or drops of Indian or black blood, or with great-great-grandfathers of the Jewish faith or Islamic culture or adherence to any heresy.

(115)

1636: Quito

The Third Half

For twenty long years he has been the big shot of the realm of Quito, president of the government and king of love, card table, and Mass. Everyone else walks or runs at the pace of his mount.

In Madrid, the Council of the Indies has found him guilty of fifty-six misdemeanors, but the bad news has not yet crossed the sea. He will have to pay a fine for the shop he has operated for twenty years in the royal audiencia, selling the silks and Chinese taffetas he has smuggled in, and for countless scandals involving married women, widows, and virgins; and also for the casino he installed in the embroidery room of his house beside the private chapel where he received communion every day. The turn of the cards has netted Don Antonio de Morga two hundred thousand pesos just in admissions collected, not counting the feats of his own deft, fleecing fingers. (For debts of ten pesos, Don Antonio has sentenced many Indians to spend the rest of their lives chained to looms in the mills.)

But the Council of the Indies' resolution has not yet reached Quito. That is not what worries Don Antonio.

He stands in his room naked before the tooled gold mirror and sees someone else. He looks for his bull's body and does not find it. Beneath the flaccid belly and between the skinny legs hangs mute the key that has known the combination to so many female locks.

He looks for his soul, but the mirror does not have it. Who has stolen the pious half of the man who preached sermons to friars and was more devout than the bishop? And the shine of his mystic's eyes? Only darkness and wrinkles above the white beard.

Don Antonio de Morga moves forward till he touches the mirror, and he asks for his third half. There must be a region where the dreams he once dreamed and has forgotten have taken refuge. There has to be: a place where the eyes, spent from so much looking, will have retained the colors of the world; and the ears, now almost deaf, its melodies. He searches for some taste that has not been broken, some smell that has not vanished, some warmth that the hand can yet feel.

He finds nothing that has been saved and was worth saving. The mirror gives back only an empty old man who will die tonight.

(176)

1637: Mouth of the River Sucre

Dieguillo

A few days ago Father Thomas Gage learned to escape from crocodiles. If you zigzag away from them, the crocodiles get confused. They can run only in a straight line.

On the other hand, no one has taught him how to escape from pirates. But does anyone really know how you flee from those stout Dutch ships in a slow, gunless frigate?

Fresh out of the Caribbean Sea, the frigate lowers its sails and surrenders. More deflated than the sails, the soul of Father Gage lies prone. Aboard with him is all the money he has collected in the twelve years he has spent in America warding off sacrilege and pulling the dead out of hell.

The skiffs come and go. The pirates take the bacon, the flour, the honey, the chickens, the fats, and the hides. Also nearly all of the fortune the priest was carrying in pearls and gold. Not all, because they have respected his bed, and he has sewn a good part of his belongings into the mattress.

The pirate captain, a hefty mulatto, receives him in his cabin. He does not offer his hand but a seat and a mug of spiced rum. A cold sweat breaks out on the priest's neck and runs down his back. He takes a quick drink. He has heard about this Captain Diego Guillo. He knows that he used to do his pirating under orders of the fearsome Pegleg, and is now on his own with a corsair's license from the Dutch. They say that Dieguillo kills so as not to lose his aim.

The priest implores, babbles that they have left him nothing but the cassock he has on. Refilling his mug, the pirate, deaf and without blinking an eye, tells of the mistreatment he suffered when he was a slave of the governor of Campeche.

"My mother is still a slave in Havana. You don't know my mother? Such a good heart, poor woman, that it puts you to shame."

"I am not a Spaniard," whines the priest. "I'm English." He

repeats it in vain. "My country is not an enemy of yours. Aren't England and Holland good friends?"

"Win today, lose tomorrow," says the pirate. He holds a swig of rum in his mouth, sends it slowly down his throat.

"Look," he orders, and tears off his jacket. He displays his back, the weals left by the lash.

Noises from the deck. The priest is thankful, for they muffle the wild beatings of his heart.

"I am English . . ."

A vein beats desperately in Father Gage's forehead. The saliva refuses to go down his throat.

"Take me to Holland. I beseech you, sir, take me to Holland. Please! A generous man cannot leave me this way, naked and without . . ."

With one jerk the pirate frees his arm from the thousand hands of the priest. He strikes the floor with a cane, and two men come in. "Take him out of here!"

He turns his back in farewell, looking at himself in the mirror. "If you hit Havana anytime," he says, "don't fail to look up my mother. Remember me to her. Tell her . . . Tell her I'm doing fine."

As he returns to his frigate, Father Gage feels cramps in his stomach. The waves are acting up, and the priest curses whoever it was who said, back there in Jerez de la Frontera, twelve years ago, that America was paved with gold and silver and you had to walk carefully not to trip over the diamonds.

(72)

1637: Massachusetts Bay

"God is an Englishman,"

said the pious John Aylmer, shepherd of souls, some years ago. And John Winthrop, founder of the Massachusetts Bay Colony, says that the English can take over the Indians' lands as legitimately as Abraham among the Sodomites: *That which is common to all is proper to none. This savage people ruleth over many lands without title or property.* Winthrop is the chief of the Puritans who arrived in the *Arbella* four years ago. He came with his seven sons. Reverend John Cotton said good-bye to the pilgrims on Southampton's docks, assuring them that God would fly overhead like an eagle leading them from old England, land of iniquities, to the promised land.

To build the new Jerusalem on a hilltop came the Puritans. Ten years before the *Arbella*, the *Mayflower* arrived at Plymouth, at a time when other Englishmen hungry for gold had already reached the Virginia coasts to the south. The Puritan families are fleeing from the king and his bishops. They leave behind them taxes and wars, hunger and diseases. They are also fleeing from threats of change in the old order. As Winthrop, Cambridge lawyer born into a noble cradle, says, *God Almightie in his most holy and wise providence hath soe disposed of the Condition of mankinde, as in all times some must be rich some poore, some highe and eminent in power and dignitie; others meane and in subjection.*

For the first time, the Indians saw a floating island. The mast was a tree, the sails white clouds. When the island stopped, the Indians put out in their canoes to pick strawberries. Instead of strawberries they found smallpox.

The smallpox devastated Indian communities and cleared the ground for God's messengers, God's chosen, people of Israel on the sands of Canaan. Those who had lived here for more than three thousand years died like flies. Smallpox, says Winthrop, was sent by God to oblige the English colonists to occupy lands depopulated by the disease.

(35, 153, and 204)

1637: Mystic Fort

From the Will of John Underhill, Puritan of Connecticut, Concerning a Massacre of Pequot Indians

They knew nothing of our coming. Drawing near to the fort, we yielded up ourselves to God and entreated His assistance in so weighty an enterprise . . .

We could not but admire at the providence of God in it, that

*soldiers so unexpert in the use of their arms, should give so complete
a volley, as though the finger of God had touched both match and
flint. Which volley being given at break of day, and themselves
fast asleep for the most part, bred in them such a terror, that they
brake forth into a most doleful cry; so as if God had not fitted the
hearts of men for the service, it would have bred in them a com-
miseration towards them. But every man being bereaved of pity,
fell upon the work without compassion, considering the blood they
had shed of our native countrymen, and how barbarously they had
`dealt with them, and slain, first and last, about thirty persons . . .
Having our swords in our right hand, our carbines or muskets in
our left hand, we approached the fort . . .*

*Many were burnt in the fort . . . Others forced out . . . which
our soldiers received and entertained with the point of the sword.
Down fell men, women, and children; those that scaped us, fell
into the hands of the Indians that were in the rear of us. It is
reported by themselves, that there were about four hundred souls
in this fort, and not above five of them scaped out of our hands.
Great and doleful was the bloody sight to the view of young soldiers
that never had been in war, to see so many souls lie gasping on
the ground, so thick, in some places, that you could hardly pass
along. It may be demanded, Why should you be so furious (as some
have said)? Should not Christians have more mercy and compassion? But I would refer you to David's war. When a people is
grown to such a height of blood, and sin against God and man,
and all confederates in the action, there he hath no respect to
persons, but harrows them, and saws them, and puts them to the
sword, and the most terriblest death that may be. Sometimes the
Scripture declareth women and children must perish with their
parents. Sometimes the case alters; but we will not dispute it now.
We have sufficient light from the Word of God for our proceedings.*

(204)

1639: Lima

Martín de Porres

The bells of Santo Domingo church ring out the death toll. By the
candles' light, bathed in icy sweat, Martín de Porres has delivered
up his soul after much fighting against the Devil with the aid of

Most Holy Mary and of St. Catherine, virgin and martyr. He died in his bed, with a stone for pillow and a skull at his side, while the viceroy of Lima knelt and kissed his hand and implored his intercession for a small place for him up in Heaven.

Martín de Porres was the offspring of a black slave and her master, a gentleman of pure Spanish lineage, who did not impregnate her by way of using her as an object but rather to apply the Christian principle that in bed all are equal before God.

At fifteen, Martín was given to a monastery of Dominican friars. Here he performed his works and miracles. Being a mulatto, he was never ordained as a priest; but embracing the broom with love, he swept out each day the rooms, cloisters, infirmary, and church. Razor in hand, he shaved the monastery's two hundred priests; he nursed the sick and distributed clean clothes smelling of rosemary.

When he learned that the monastery was hard up for money, he went to see the prior: *"Ave María."*

"Gratia plena."

"Your Grace should sell this mulatto dog," he offered.

He put in his bed ulcerated beggars from the street, and prayed on his knees all night long. A supernatural light made him white as snow; white flames escaped from his face when he crossed the cloister at midnight, flying like a divine meteor, heading for the solitude of his cell. He walked through padlocked doors and sometimes prayed kneeling in the air, far off the ground; angels accompanied him to the choir holding lights in their hands. Without leaving Lima he consoled captives in Algiers and saved souls in the Philippines, China, and Japan; without budging from his cell he pealed the Angelus. He cured the dying with clothes dipped in black roosters' blood and powdered toad and with exorcisms learned from his mother. With the touch of a finger he stopped toothaches and turned open wounds into scars; he made brown sugar white and put out fires with a glance. The bishop had to forbid him to perform so many miracles without permission.

After matins he would strip and scourge his back with a whip of ox sinews tied in thick knots and cry as he drew blood: *"Vile mulatto dog! How long is your sinful life to last?"*

With imploring, tearful eyes always begging pardon, the first dark-skinned addition to the Catholic Church's lily-white sanctoral calendar has passed through the world.

(216)

From a Denunciation of the Bishop of Tucumán,
Sent to the Inquisition Tribunal in Lima

With the sincerity and truth with which so sacred a tribunal should be addressed, I denounce the person of the Reverend Bishop of Tucumán, Don Fr. Melchor Maldonado de Saavedra, of whom I have heard things most gravely suspicious in our holy Catholic faith, which are of general currency through this whole bishopric. That in Salta, celebrating confirmations, a comely young girl came and he said to her: "Your Grace is better taken than confirmed"; and in Córdoba this last year of 1638 another came in the presence of many people and lifting his cassock he said: "Get out! I shouldn't be confirming you from below but from on top"; and with the first one he notoriously cohabited . . .

(140)

1639: Potosí

Testament of a Businessman

Through the curtains pokes the nose of the notary. The bedroom smells of wax and of death. By the light of the one candle the skull can be seen beneath the dying man's skin.

"What are you waiting for, you vulture?"

The businessman does not open his eyes but his voice sounds firm.

"My shadow and I have discussed and decided," he says. And sighs. And orders the notary: "You are not to add or subtract anything. Hear me? I'll pay you two hundred pesos in birds, so that with their feathers, and the ones you use to write, you can fly to hell. Are you listening? Ay! Each day I live is borrowed time. Every day it costs me more. Write, get going! Hurry up, man. I order that with a fourth part of the silver I leave, there should be built in the small square of the bridge a great latrine so that nobles and plebeians of Potosí may pay homage there every day to my memory. Another fourth part of my bullion and coins to be buried in the yard of this my house, and at the entrance to be kept four of the fiercest dogs, tied with chains and with plenty of food, to guard this interment.

His tongue does not tangle up and he continues, without taking a breath: "And with another fourth part of my wealth, that the most exquisite dishes be cooked and placed in my silver service and inserted in a deep ditch, with everything that remains in my larders, because I want the worms to gorge themselves sick as they will do with me. And I order . . ."

He wags his index finger, projecting a clublike shadow on the white wall: "And I order . . . that nobody whatever should attend my funeral, that my body be accompanied by all the asses that there are in Potosí, decked with the richest vestments and the best jewels, to be provided from the rest of my fortune."

(21)

The Indians Say:

The land has an owner? How's that? How is it to be sold? How is it to be bought? If it does not belong to us, well, what? We are of it. We are its children. So it is always, always. The land is alive. As it nurtures the worms, so it nurtures us. It has bones and blood. It has milk and gives us suck. It has hair, grass, straw, trees. It knows how to give birth to potatoes. It brings to birth houses. It brings to birth people. It looks after us and we look after it. It drinks chicha, accepts our invitation. We are its children. How is it to be sold? How bought?

(15 and 84)

1640: São Salvador de Bahia
Vieira

The mouth sparkles as it fires words lethal like gunfire. The most dangerous orator in Brazil is a Portuguese priest raised in Bahia, a Bahian to the soul.

The Dutch have invaded these lands, and the Jesuit Antonio Vieira asks the colonial gentry *if we are not just as dark-colored to the Dutch as the Indians are to us.*

From the pulpit the lord of the word rebukes the lords of the land and of the people: *"Does it make me a lord that I was born farther away from the sun, and others, slaves, that they were born closer? There can be no greater departure from understanding, no greater error of judgment among men!"*

In the little Ayuda church, oldest in Brazil, Antonio Vieira also accuses God, who is guilty of helping the Dutch invaders: *"Although we are the sinners, my God, today it is you who must repent!"*

(33, 171, and 226)

1641: Lima

Avila

He has interrogated thousands and thousands of Indians without finding one who is not a heretic. He has demolished idols and temples, has burned mummies; has shaved heads and skinned backs with the lash. At his passage, the wind of Christian faith has purified Peru.

The priest Francisco de Avila has reached seventy-five to find that his strength is failing him. He is half deaf and even his clothes hurt; and he decides not to leave the world without obtaining what he has wanted since he was a boy. So he applies to enter the Company of Jesus.

"No," says the rector of the Jesuits, Antonio Vázquez.

"No," because *although he claims to be a learned man and great linguist, Francisco de Avila cannot conceal his condition of mestizo.*

(14)

1641: Mbororé

The Missions

The *mamelukes* are coming from the region of San Pablo. Hunters of Indians, devourers of lands, they advance to the beat of a drum, raised flag and military order, thunder of war, wind of war, across

Paraguay. They carry long ropes with collars for the Indians they will catch and sell as slaves in the plantations of Brazil.

The *mamelukes* or *bandeirantes* have for years been devastating the missions of the Jesuits. Of the thirteen missions in the Guayrá, nothing is left but stones and charcoal. New evangelical communities have arisen from the exodus, downstream on the Paraná; but the attacks are incessant. In the missions the snake finds the birds all together and fattened up, thousands of Indians trained for work and innocence, without weapons, easy to pick off. Under the priests' tutorship the Guaranís share a regimented life, without private property or money or death penalty, without luxury or scarcity, and march to work singing to the music of flutes. Their sugarcane arrows are futile against the arquebuses of the *mamelukes*, who test the blades of their swords by splitting children in half and carry off shredded cassocks and caravans of slaves as trophies.

But this time, a surprise awaits the invaders. The king of Spain, scared by the fragility of these frontiers, has ordered firearms issued to the Guaranís. The *mamelukes* flee in disorder.

From the houses rise plumes of smoke and songs of praise to God. The smoke, which is not from arson but from chimneys, celebrates victory.

(143)

1641: Madrid

Eternity Against History

The count-duke of Olivares gnaws his fists and mutters curses. He commands much, after twenty years of doings and undoings at court, but God has a stronger tread.

The Board of Theologians has just turned down his project of channeling the Tagus and Manzanares rivers, which would be so welcomed by the plains of Castile. The rivers will remain as God made them, and the plans of engineers Carducci and Martelli will end up in the files.

In France, it is announced that the great Languedoc canal will soon be opened, to join the Mediterranean with the Garonne Valley. Meanwhile, in this Spain that has conquered America, the Board of Theologians decides that *he sins against Divine Providence who tries to improve what she, for inscrutable motives, has wished to be imperfect.* If God had desired that the rivers should be navigable, he would have made them navigable.

(128)

1644: Jamestown

Opechancanough

Before an English soldier shoots him in the back, Chief Opechancanough asks himself: "Where is the invisible guardian of my footsteps? Who has stolen my shadow?"

At the age of one hundred, he has been defeated. He had come to the battlefield on a litter.

Over eighty years ago, Admiral Pedro Menéndez de Avilés took him to Cádiz. He presented him at the court of Philip II: *Here is a fine Indian prince of Florida.* They dressed him in breeches, doublet, and ruff. In a Dominican monastery in Seville they taught him the language and religion of Castile. Then in Mexico, the viceroy gave him his name, and Opechancanough became Luis de Velasco. Later he returned to the land of his fathers as interpreter and guide to the Jesuits. His people thought he was returning from the dead. He preached Christianity and then took off their clothes and cut the Jesuits' throats and went back to his old name.

Since then he has killed many and seen much. He has seen villages and fields devoured by flames and his brothers sold to the highest bidder, in this region that the English baptized Virginia in memory of a spiritually virginal queen. He has seen men swallowed up by smallpox and lands devoured by enslaving tobacco. He has seen seventeen of the twenty-eight communities that were here wiped off the map and the others given a choice between diaspora and war. Thirty thousand Indians welcomed the English navigators who arrived at Chesapeake Bay one fresh morning in 1607. Three thousand survive.

(36 and 207)

1645: Quito

Mariana de Jesús

Year of catastrophes for the city. A black bow hangs on every door. The invisible armies of measles and diphtheria have invaded and are destroying. Night has closed in right after dawn and the volcano Pichincha, king of snow, has exploded: a great vomit of lava and fire has fallen on the fields, and a hurricane of ash has swept the city.

"Sinners, sinners!"

Like the volcano, Father Alonso de Rojas hurls flame from his mouth. In the gleaming pulpit of the church of the Jesuits, a church of gold, Father Alonso beats his breast, which echoes as he weeps, cries, clamors: "Accept, O Lord, the sacrifice of the humblest of Your servants! Let my blood and my flesh expiate the sins of Quito!"

Then a young woman rises at the foot of the pulpit and says serenely: "I."

Before the people who overflow the church, Mariana announces that she is the chosen one. She will calm the wrath of God. She will take all the castigations that her city deserves.

Mariana has never played at being happy, nor dreamed that she was, nor ever slept for more than four hours. The only time a man ever brushed her hand, she was ill with a fever for a week after. As a child she decided to be the bride of God and gave Him her love, not in the convent but in the streets and fields: not embroidering or making sweets and jellies in the peace of the cloisters, but praying with her knees on thorns and stones and seeking bread for the poor, remedy for the sick, and light for those in the darkness of ignorance of divine law.

Sometimes Mariana feels called by the patter of rain or the crackle of fire, but always the thunder of God sounds louder: that God of anger with beard of serpents and eyes of lightning, who appears nude in her dreams to test her.

Mariana returns home, stretches out on her bed, and readies herself to die in place of all. She pays for God's forgiveness. She offers her body for Him to eat and her blood and her tears for Him to drink until he gets dizzy and forgets.

That way the plague will cease, the volcano will calm down, and the earth will stop trembling.

(176)

1645: Potosí

Story of Estefanía, Sinful Woman of Potosí (Abbreviation of Chronicle by Bartolomé Arzáns de Orsúa y Vela)

Estefanía was born in this imperial Town and grew up in beauty beyond the power of nature to enhance.

At fourteen, the lovely damsel left home, advised by other lost women; and her mother, seeing the abominable determination with which this daughter broke away, gave up the ghost within a few days.

This did not cause the daughter to mend her ways. Having already lost the priceless treasure of virginity, she dressed profanely and became a public and scandalous sinner.

Seeing so much discredit and ill fame, her brother called her to his house and said: "Hurt you as it may, you must hear me. While you continue in mortal sin you are an enemy of God and a slave of the Devil, and furthermore you debase your nobility and dishonor all your lineage. Consider, sister, what you are doing, get out of that muck, fear God, and do penance." To which Estefanía replied: "What do you want of me, you bloody hypocrite?" And while the brother reproved her, she seized in a flash the dagger that hung on the wall and set on him with diabolical ferocity, saying: "This is the only answer your arguments deserve." She left him dead in a lake of blood and afterward disguised that misdeed by a pretense of sentiment, dressing herself in mourning and making much of her grief.

Also her aged father, sorrowing for the death of the good son and the scandal of the bad daughter, succeeded in confronting her with good arguments, to which the heartless girl listened against her will. Instead of mending her ways, she ended up loathing the venerable gentleman and at midnight she set fire to the roof of his house. The anguished old man sprang from his bed shouting at the top of his voice: "Fire, fire!" But the beams supporting the roof collapsed, and there and then the terrible element consumed him.

Seeing herself free, Estefanía gave herself with more wantonness to greater vices and sins.

In those days there came to Potosí a man of the realms of Spain, one of the most opulent merchants who came in those galleons to Peru, and the beauty and grace of that public sinner came to his attention. He solicited her, and when they were most enjoying their obscenities a former lover of the lady, armed with every weapon and with two thirsty pistols, turned up determined to avenge the affront.

The former lover found the woman alone, but she restrained his angry spirit with deceitful words, and when she had mitigated his fury she took a knife from her sleeve with great promptness and the wretch fell to the ground dead.

Estefanía mentioned the event to the rich merchant. After some months, being much tormented by jealousy, he threatened to bring her to justice for the homicide. In those days they went together to bathe in Tarapaya Lake. She threw off her rich clothing, revealing the snow of her body dotted with loveliest crimson, and threw herself naked into the water. The carefree merchant followed her, and when they were together in the middle of the lake, she pushed the luckless man's head into the water with all the strength of her arms.

Let it not be thought that her abominations stopped there. With one blow of a sword she ended the life of a gentleman of illustrious blood; and she killed two others with poison she inserted in a lunch. Her intrigues ended the days of others with swordthrusts in the breast, while Estefanía remained full of joy that blood should be shed on her account.

So it went up to the year 1645, when the sinful woman heard a sermon by Father Francisco Patiño, a servant of God whose admirable virtues Potosí was enjoying at the time, and God came to her aid with a ray of his divine grace. And so great was Estefanía's sorrow that she began to weep streams of tears, with great sighs and sobs that seemed to tear out her soul, and when the sermon ended she threw herself at the priest's feet pleading for confession.

The priest exhorted her to penitence and absolved her, it being well known with what felicity women surrender themselves into the serpent's hands, due to flaws inherited from her who tempted Adam. Estefanía rose from the confessor's feet like another Magdalene and when she was on her way home—oh, happy sinner!— she earned the appearance of Most Holy Mary, who said to her:

"Daughter, thou art forgiven. I have pleaded for you to my Son, because in your childhood you prayed with my rosary."

(21)

1647: Santiago de Chile

Chilean Indians' Game Banned

The captain general, Don Martín de Mujica, proclaims the prohibition of the game of chueca, which the Araucanians play according to their tradition, hitting a ball with curved sticks on a
court surrounded by green boughs.

One hundred lashes for Indians who do not comply; and fines
for others, because the infamous chueca has spread widely among
the Creole soldiery.

The captain general's edict says that the ban is imposed *so
that sins so contrary to the honor of God Our Father may be
avoided* and because chasing the ball trains Indians for war: *The
game gives rise to disturbances and thus afterward the arrow flies
among them.* It is indecent, it says, that men and women foregather
for the chueca almost naked, *clad in nothing but feathers and skins
of animals on which they base their hopes of winning.* At the start
of the game they invoke the gods to favor their prowess and speed
their feet, and at the end, all in a big embrace, they drink oceans
of chicha.

(173)

1648: Olinda

Prime Cannon Fodder

He was a boy when they took him from his African village, shipped
him out from Luanda, and sold him in Recife. He was a man when
he fled from the canefields and took refuge in one of the black
bastions of Palmares.

As soon as the Dutch entered Brazil, the Portuguese promised
freedom to slaves who would fight the invaders. The runaways of
Palmares decided that the war was not theirs; it mattered little
whether those who held the lash in canefields and sugarmills were
Portuguese or Dutch. But he, Henrique Dias, went to volunteer.

Since then he commands a regiment of blacks who fight for the Portuguese Crown in northeastern Brazil. The Portuguese have ennobled him.

From Olinda, Captain Henrique Dias sends an intimidating letter to the Dutch army quartered in Recife. He says that his regiment, the Legion of the Henriques, consists of four nations: *Minas, Ardas, Angolans, and Creoles: These are so malevolent that they have and should have no fear; the Minas so wild that their reputation can subdue what they cannot reach with their arms; the Ardas so fiery that they want to cut everybody with a single blow; and the Angolans so tough that no work tires them. Consider, now, if men who have broken everything are not destined to break all Holland.*

(69 and 217)

1649: Ste. Marie des Hurons

The Language of Dreams

"Poor things," thinks Father Ragueneau, watching the Huron Indians surround with gifts and rituals a man who, last night, dreamed a mysterious dream. The community puts food in his mouth and dances for him; the young girls stroke him, rub him with ashes. Afterward, all seated in a circle, they set about interpreting the dream. They pursue the dream with flashed images or words and he keeps saying, "No, no" until someone says "river," and then among them all they succeed in capturing it: the river, a furious current, a woman alone in a canoe, she has lost the paddle, the river sweeps her away, the woman doesn't cry out, she smiles, looks happy. "Is it I?" asks one of the women. "Is it I?" asks another. The community invites the woman whose eyes penetrate the most obscure desires to interpret the symbols of the dream. While drinking herb tea, the clairvoyant invokes her guardian spirit and deciphers the message.

Like all the Iroquois peoples, the Hurons believe that dreams transfigure the most trivial things and convert them into symbols when touched by the fingers of desire. They believe that dreams are the language of unfulfilled desires and have a word, *ondinnonk*, for the secret desires of the soul that wakefulness does not recognize. Ondinnonks come forward in the journeys made by the soul while the body sleeps.

"Poor things," thinks Father Ragueneau.

For the Hurons, one who does not respect what dreams say commits a great crime. The dream gives orders. If the dreamer does not carry them out, the soul gets angry and makes the body sick or kills it. All the peoples of the Iroquois family know that sickness can come from war or accident, or from the witch who inserts bear teeth or bone splinters in the body, but also comes from the soul when it wants something that it is not given.

Father Ragueneau talks it over with other French Jesuits who preach in the area. He defends the Indians of Canada: *It's easy to call irreligion what is merely stupidity . . .*

Some priests see Satan's horns protruding from these superstitions and are scandalized because at the drop of a hat the Indians will dream against the Sixth Commandment and the next day plunge into therapeutic orgies. The Indians go about practically naked, looking at and touching each other in devilish liberty, and marry and unmarry whenever they want; and an order from a dream is all it takes to let loose the andacwandat fiesta, which is always the occasion for frenetic sinning. Father Ragueneau can't deny that the Devil can find fertile ground in this society without judges, or policemen, or jails, or property, where the women share command with the men and together they worship false gods, but he insists on the basic innocence of these primitive souls, still ignorant of God's law.

And when the other Jesuits tremble with panic because some Iroquois may dream one of these nights of killing a priest, Ragueneau recalls that that has already happened several times and that when it did, all that was necessary was to let the dreamer rip up a cassock while dancing his dream in an inoffensive pantomime.

"These are stupid customs," says Father Ragueneau, "but not criminal customs."

(153 and 222)

An Iroquois Story

It is snowing outside and in the center of the big house the old storyteller is talking, his face to the fire. Seated on animal skins, all listen as they sew clothing and repair weapons.

"The most splendid tree had grown in the sky," says the old man. "It had four big white roots, which extended in four directions. From this tree all things were born . . ."

The old man relates that one day wind completely uprooted the tree. Through the hole that opened in the sky fell the wife of the great chief, carrying a handful of seeds. A tortoise brought her soil on its shell so that she could plant the seeds, and thus sprouted the first plants that gave us food. Later that woman had a daughter, who grew and became the wife of the west wind. The east wind blew certain words in her ear . . .

The good storyteller tells his story and makes it happen. The west wind is now blowing on the big house; it comes down the chimney, and smoke veils all the faces.

Brother wolf, who taught the Iroquois to get together and listen, howls from the mountains. It is time to sleep.

One of these mornings, the old storyteller will not wake up. But someone of those who heard his stories will tell them to others. And later this someone will also die, and the stories will stay alive as long as there are big houses and people gathered around the fire.

(37)

Song About the Song of the Iroquois

When I sing
it can help her.
Yeah, it can, yeah!
It's so strong!

When I sing
it can raise her.
Yeah, it can, yeah!
It's so strong!

When I sing
her arms get straighter.
Yeah, it can, yeah!
It's so strong!

When I sing
her body gets straighter.
Yeah, it can, yeah!
It's so strong!

(197)

1650: *Mexico City*

The Conquerors and the Conquered

The family crest rears itself pompously in the ornamented iron over the gate, as if over an altar. The master of the house rolls up in a mahogany carriage, with his retinue of liveried attendants and horses. Within, someone stops playing the clavichord; rustlings of silks and tissues are heard, voices of marriageable daughters, steps on soft, yielding carpets. Then the tinkle of engraved silver spoons on porcelain.

This city of Mexico, city of palaces, is one of the largest in the world. Although it is very far from the sea, Spanish and Chinese ships bring their merchandise and silver shipments from the north end up here. The powerful Chamber of Commerce rivals that of Seville. From here merchandise flows to Peru, Manila, and the Far East.

The Indians, who built this city for the conquerors on the ruins of their Tenochtitlán, bring food in canoes. They may work here during the day, but at nightfall they are removed on pain of the lash to their slums outside the walls.

Some Indians wear stockings and shoes and speak Spanish in hope of being allowed to remain and thereby escape tribute and forced labor.

(148)

From the Náhuatl Song on the Transience of Life

We have but one turn at life.
In a day we go, in a night we descend
to the region of mystery.

We came here only to get to know each other.
We are here only in passing.
In peace and pleasure let us spend life.
Come and let's enjoy it!
Not those who live in anger:
broad is the earth.
How good to live forever,
never to have to die!

While we live, our spirit broken,
Here they harass us, here they spy on us.
But for all the misfortunes,
for all the wounds in the soul,
we must not live in vain!
How good to live forever,
never to have to die!

(77)

1654: Oaxaca

Medicine and Witchcraft

The Zapotec Indians, who before falling to earth were brightly colored songbirds, told a few secrets to Gonzalo de Balsalobre. After living among them for a time and after investigating the mysteries of religion and medicine, Don Gonzalo is writing in Oaxaca a detailed report that he will send to Mexico City. The report denounces the Indians to the Holy Inquisition and asks for punishment of the quackeries that monks and ordinary justice have been unable to suppress. A while back, Alarcón left the university to share for nine years the life of the Cohuixco Indian community. He got to know the sacred herbs that cure the sick; and later he denounced the Indians for devilish practices.

In the first period of the conquest, however, indigenous medicine aroused great curiosity in Europe, and marvels were attributed to America's plants. Fray Bernardino de Sahagún collected and published the wisdom of eight Aztec doctors, and King Philip II sent his personal physician, Francisco Hernández, to Mexico to make a thorough study of native medicine.

For the Indians, herbs speak, have sex, and cure. It is little plants, aided by the human word, that pull sickness from the body, reveal mysteries, straighten out destinies, and provoke love or forgetfulness. These voices of earth sound like voices of hell to seventeenth-century Spain, busy with inquisitions and exorcisms, which relies for cures on the magic of prayer, conjurations, and talismans even more than on syrups, purges, and bleedings.

(4)

1655: San Miguel de Nepantla

Juana at Four

Juana goes about constantly chatting with her soul, which is her internal companion as she walks on the bank of the stream. She feels all the happier because she has the hiccups, and Juana grows when she has the hiccups. She stops and looks at her shadow, which grows with her, and measures it with a branch after each little jump of her tummy. The volcanos also grew with the hiccups when they were alive, before their own fire burned them up. Two of the volcanos are still smoking, but they don't have the hiccups now. They don't grow anymore. Juana has the hiccups and grows. She gets bigger.

Crying, on the other hand, makes you smaller. For that reason old women and the mourners at funerals are the size of cockroaches. That isn't in her grandfather's books, which Juana reads, but she knows. These are things she knows from talking so much to her soul. Juana also talks to the clouds. To talk to the clouds you have to climb the hills or to the top branches of the trees.

"I am a cloud. We clouds have faces and hands. No feet."

(16 and 75)

1656: Santiago de la Vega

Gage

In a hammock stretched between two palms, the Anglican clergyman Thomas Gage dies in Jamaica.

Since the old days when he roamed the lands of America in a Catholic friar's cassock, preaching and spying and enjoying the chocolate and guava desserts, he dreamed of being the first English viceroy of Mexico. Back in London he switched sects and convinced Lord Cromwell that it was necessary and possible to fit out a good fleet to conquer the Spanish colonies.

Last year, Admiral William Penn's troops invaded the island of Jamaica. England seized from Spain the first bit of its American empire, and the inheritors of Columbus, marquises of Jamaica, lost the best of their revenues. Then the Reverend Thomas Gage delivered a patriotic Protestant sermon from the pulpit of the largest church in Santiago de la Vega, while the Spanish governor came in the arms of his slaves to surrender his sword.

(145)

1658: San Miguel de Nepantla

Juana at Seven

She sees her mother coming in the mirror and drops the sword, which falls with a bang like a gunshot, and Juana gives such a start that her whole face disappears beneath the broad-brimmed hat.

"I'm not playing," she says angrily as her mother laughs. She frees herself from the hat and shows her mustachios drawn with soot. Juana's feet move awkwardly in the enormous leather boots; she trips and falls and kicks in the air, humiliated, furious; her mother cannot stop laughing.

"I'm not playing," Juana protests, with tears in her eyes. "I'm a man! I'll go to the university, because I'm a man!"

The mother strokes her head. "My crazy daughter, my lovely Juana. I ought to whip you for these indecencies."

She sits beside her and says softly: "Better you were born stupid, my poor know-it-all daughter," and caresses her while Juana soaks her grandfather's huge cape with tears.

(16 and 75)

Juana Dreams

She wanders through the market of dreams. The market women have spread out dreams on big cloths on the ground.

Juana's grandfather arrives at the market, very sad because he has not dreamed for a long time. Juana takes him by the hand and helps him select dreams, dreams of marzipan or of cotton, wings to fly with in sleep, and they take off together so loaded down with dreams that no night will be long enough for them.

(16 and 75)

1663: Old Guatemala

Enter the Printing Press

Bishop Payo Enríquez de Ribera is one of the most fervent advocates of forced labor for Indians. Without the allotments of Indians, the bishop reasons, who will cultivate the fields? And if nobody cultivates the fields, who will cultivate souls?

When the bishop is preparing a document on the subject, he receives from Puebla the first printing press to reach Guatemala. The learned spiritual head of this diocese has had it brought with cases of type, typography and all, so that his theological treatise *Explicatio Apologetica* may be printed here.

The first book published in Guatemala is not written in Mayan or in Castilian but in Latin.

(135)

1663: The Banks of the Paraíba River

Freedom

The hounds' baying and the slave-hunters' trumpeting have long since faded away. The fugitive crosses a field of stubble, fierce stubble higher than himself, and runs toward the river.

He throws himself on the grass, face down, arms open, legs wide apart. He hears the accomplice voices of grasshoppers and cicadas and little frogs. "I am not a thing. My history is not the history of things." He kisses the earth, bites it. "I got my foot out of the trap. I'm not a thing." He presses his naked body to the dew-soaked ground and hears the sound of small plants coming through the earth, eager to be born. He is mad with hunger, and for the first time hunger gives him happiness. His body is covered with cuts, and he does not feel it. He turns toward the sky as if embracing it. The moon rises and strikes him, violent blows of light, lashes of light from the full moon and the juicy stars, and he gets up and looks for his direction.

Now for the jungle. Now for the great screen of greenness.

"You heading for Palmares, too?" the fugitive asks an ant crawling up his hand. "Guide me."

(43)

Song of Palmares

Rest, black man.
The white doesn't come here.
If he comes,
the devil will take him.
Rest, black man.
The white doesn't come here.
If he comes, he'll leave
with a taste of our cudgels.

(69)

1663: Serra da Barriga

Palmares

On some nights when there is lightning, the incandescent crest of this mountain range can be seen from the Alagoas coast. In its foothills the Portuguese have exterminated the Caeté Indians, whom the pope had excommunicated in perpetuity for eating the first Brazilian bishop; and this is where fugitive black slaves have found refuge, for the last many years, in the hidden villages of Palmares.

Each community is a fortress. Beyond the high wooden palisades and the pointed-stake traps lie vast planted fields. The farmers work with their weapons within reach; and at night, when they return to the citadel, they count bodies in case anyone is missing.

Here they have two harvests of corn a year, and also beans, manioc, sugar, potatoes, tobacco, vegetables, and fruits; and they raise pigs and chickens. The blacks of Palmares eat much more and better than the people of the coast, where all-devouring sugar-cane, produced for Europe, usurps all of everyone's time and space.

As in Angola, the palm is king in these black communities: with its fiber they weave clothing, baskets, and fans; the fronds serve as roof and bed; from the fruit, the flesh is eaten, wine is made, and oil for lighting is extracted; from the husk, cooking fat and smoking pipes are made. As in Angola, the chiefs perform the noble office of blacksmith, and the forge occupies the place of honor in the plaza where the people have their assemblies.

But Angola is multiple; still more Africa as a whole. The Palmarians come from a thousand regions and a thousand languages. Their only common tongue is the one heard from the mouths of the masters, accompanying lash-delivered orders on slave ships and in canefields. Sprinkled with African and Guaraní words, the Portuguese language is now a bond of communication for those it formerly humiliated.

Folga nêgo.
Branco não vem cá

Since the Dutch were expelled from Pernambuco, the Portuguese have launched more than twenty military expeditions against this land of the free. An informant writes from Brazil to Lisbon: *Our army, which could tame the pride of Holland, has produced no result against those barbarians on its many and frequent incursions into Palmares . . .*

The Dutch had no better luck. Its expeditions, too, were without glory. Both Dutch and Portuguese have burned down empty villages and gotten lost in the thickets, turning this way and that like madmen in the violent rains. Both have made war against a shadow, a shadow that bites and runs; and each time they have claimed victory. Neither has succeeded in crushing Palmares nor in stopping the flight of slaves who leave King Sugar and his court without labor, although the Dutch crucified rebellious blacks and the Portuguese flog and mutilate to instill fear and set an example.

One of the Portuguese expeditions against Palmares has just returned, empty-handed, to Recife. It was headed by a black captain, Gonçalo Rebelo, who had two hundred black soldiers under his command. They cut the throats of the few prisoners they could take.

(69)

1665: Madrid

Charles II

The new monarch rocks and weeps. They hold him up from behind with braces tied to armpits and waist. At four, he does not know how to talk or walk, and they have to tear him from the nipples of his fourteen wet nurses to sit him on the throne of Spain.

He weeps because the crown, slipping down over his eyes, hurts him, and because he wants to go back to play with the elves and drink the warm milk of the fairies.

The weakling survives by a miracle, or thanks to the fact that they never bathed him even when he was born, although his head and neck are covered with purulent scabs. (Nobody bathes at the court, ever since Domingo Centurión died of a cold nine years ago.)

"Arrorró," babbles the king and cradles his foot against his ear.

(201)

1666: New Amsterdam

New York

With a few shots from their guns the English bring down the flag that waves over the fortress and seize the island of Manhattan from the Dutch, who had bought it from the Delaware Indians for sixty florins.

Recalling the arrival of the Dutch over half a century ago, the Delawares say: *The great man wanted only a little, little land, on which to raise greens for his soup, just as much as a bullock's hide would cover. Here we first might have observed their deceitful spirit.*

New Amsterdam, the most important slave market in North America, now becomes New York; and Wall Street is named after the wall built to stop blacks from escaping.

(136)

1666: London

The White Servants

Three ships full of white servants slip down the Thames toward the sea. When they open their hatches in the remote island of Barbados, the living will go to the sugar, cotton, and tobacco plantations and the dead to the bottom of the bay.

Spirits they call the traffickers in white servants, very skilled in the magic of evaporating people: They send to the Antilles whores and vagabonds kidnapped in the poor quarters of London, young Catholics hunted down in Ireland and Scotland, and prisoners awaiting the gallows in the Brixton jail for having killed a rabbit on private property. Stored under lock and key in the holds of the ships, the drunks captured on the docks wake up; with them on the voyage to the Americas are some lads lured by sweets, and many adventurers deceived by the promise of easy fortunes. Over there on the plantations of Barbados or Jamaica or Virginia, the juice will be squeezed from them until they have paid their price and the price of the passage.

The white servants dream of becoming owners of land and blacks. When they recover their freedom, after years of hard penitence and unpaid toil, the first thing they do is buy a Negro to fan them in the siesta hour.

There are forty thousand African slaves in Barbados. Births are registered in the plantation account books. At birth, a little Negro is worth half a pound sterling.

(11 and 224)

1666: Tortuga Island

The Pirates' Devotions

Jean David Nau, known as El Olonés, has just sacked Remedios and Maracaibo. His cutlass has made mincemeat of many Spaniards. Due to the weight of the stolen wealth, his frigates return at half speed.

El Olonés lands. Between his boots, his one friend and confidant, companion of his adventures and misadventures, wags his tail and barks. Behind comes a pack of men newly released from the spider web of the rigging, hungry for taverns and women and solid ground underfoot.

On these sands hot enough to boil turtles' eggs, the pirates stand in silence through a long Mass. Patched-up bodies, jackets stiff with filth, greasy prophets' beards, faces like knives notched by the years: If anyone dares to cough or laugh during the Mass, they fell him with a shot and cross themselves. Each pirate is an arsenal. At his waist, four knives and a bayonet in alligator-hide sheaths, and two naked pistols, boarding sword knocking against the knee, musket slung across his chest.

After Mass, the booty is divided. First, the mutilated. Whoever has lost his right arm gets six hundred pesos or six slaves. The left arm is worth five hundred pesos or five slaves, which is also the price of either of the legs. Anyone who left an eye or a finger on the coasts of Cuba or Venezuela has the right to a hundred pesos or one slave.

They stretch out the day's work with long drafts of spiced rum and end it with the turtle barbecue grand finale. Beneath the sand and covered with embers, the chopped turtle meat has been slowly baked in its shell with egg yolks and spices—the supreme party dish of these islands. The pirates light their pipes reclining on the sand, and abandon themselves to smoke and nostalgia.

When night falls, they cover with pearls the body of a mulatto woman and whisper horror stories and marvels to her, tales of hangings and boardings and treasure, and swear into her ear that they won't be sailing again soon. They drink and love without removing their boots: boots that tomorrow will polish the stones of the port, seeking a ship for another raid.

(61 and 65)

1667: Mexico City

Juana at Sixteen

In ships, the bell marks off the quarter hours of the watches. In mines and canefields, it summons Indian serfs and black slaves to work. In churches, it marks the hours and announces Masses, deaths, and fiestas.

But in the tower over the palace of the viceroy of Mexico there is a silent bell. It is said that inquisitors took it from the bell tower of an old Spanish village, removed the clapper, and expatriated it to the Indies no one knows how many years back. Ever since the maestro Rodrigo constructed it in 1530, this bell had always been clean and obedient. They say it had three hundred tones, according to the bell ringer's whim, and the whole village was proud of it. Until one night its long and violent pealing made everybody jump out of bed. The bell was sounding the alarm, unleashed by fear or joy or who knows what, and for the first time no one understood it. A crowd gathered in the atrium as the bell pealed madly on, and the mayor and the priest went up to the tower and, frozen with fear, confirmed that no one was there. No human hand moved it. The authorities took the case to the Inquisition. The Holy Office tribunal declared the pealing of the bell to be totally null and void, and it was silenced forever and exiled to Mexico.

Juana Inés de Asbaje walks out of the palace of her protector, the viceroy Mancera, and crosses the great plaza followed by two Indians who carry her trunks. Reaching the corner, she stops and looks back at the tower, as if called by the voiceless bell. She knows its history. She knows that it was punished for singing all on its own.

Juana heads for the Santa Teresa la Antigua convent. She will no longer be a lady of the court. In the serene light of the cloister and the solitude of a cell she will seek what she cannot find outside. She would have liked to study the mysteries of the world at the university, but women are born condemned to the embroidery frame and the husband chosen for them. Juana Inés de Asbaje will become a barefoot Carmelite and will call herself Sor Juana Inés de la Cruz.

(58 and 213)

1668: Tortuga Island
The Dogs

No Indians remain in this islet north of Haiti. But the dogs brought by the Spaniards to hunt them down and punish them stay on. The mastiffs, which have multiplied and go about in packs devouring wild boars, dispute the dominion of this land with French corsairs. Night after night their howls are heard from the thickets. Within their ramparts, the pirates tremble in their sleep.

Tortuga Island belongs to the enterprise created by French minister Colbert to run the slave traffic and piracy. The enterprise has named Bertrand d'Ogeron as governor, a gentleman of shining prestige among buccaneers and freebooters.

From France the governor brings a cargo of poison. It will be used to kill a few horses whose bodies will be spread about the island, bellies full of venom. This way he expects to put an end to the threat of the wild dogs.

(65)

1669: Town of Gibraltar

All the Wealth in the World

Henry Morgan's men keep scratching along the shores of Lake Maracaibo, seeking the buried treasure that El Olonés could not take with him. For all the time and effort invested, El Olonés did not have days long enough nor ships' holds big enough to load it.

After the usual cannonade, the landing. The pirates jump from their skiffs and enter the smoking village with drawn swords.

No one there, nothing there.

In the middle of the plaza, a tattered lad receives them, laughing. The enormous hat that covers his eyes has a broken brim hanging down over his shoulder.

"Secret! Secret!" he cries. He moves his arms like a windmill, beating off imaginary flies, and never stops laughing.

When a sword point scratches his throat, he whispers: "Don't sleep with your feet bare, or the bats will eat them."

Thick with smoke and powder, the air boils. Morgan seethes with heat and impatience. They tie up the lad. "Where did they hide the jewels?" They beat him. "Where's the gold?" They open the first gashes in his cheeks and his chest.

"I am Sebastián Sánchez!" he yells. "I am the brother of the governor of Maracaibo! Very important person!"

They cut off half an ear.

They drag him along. The lad leads the pirates to a cave, through a wood, and reveals his treasure. Hidden beneath boughs are two clay plates, the rusted point of an anchor, an empty shell, some colored feathers and stones, a key, and three small coins.

"I am Sebastián Sánchez!" the owner of the treasure keeps repeating as they kill him.

(65 and 117)

1669: Maracaibo

The Broken Padlock

At dawn Morgan discovers that Spanish ships have appeared out of the night and closed the entrance to the lake. He decides to attack. Ahead of his fleet he sends a sloop at full sail headlong against the Spanish flagship. The sloop has the war flag flying in defiance and contains all of the pitch, tar, and sulphur that Morgan has found in Maracaibo, and cases of gunpowder stashed in every corner. Its crew are a few wooden dolls dressed in shirts and hats. The Spanish admiral, Don Alonso del Campo y Espinoza, is blown into the air without discovering that his guns have fired into a powder keg.

Behind it charges the pirate fleet. Morgan's frigates break the Spanish padlock with cannon fire and gain the open sea. They sail off stuffed with gold and jewels and slaves.

In the shadow of the sails struts Henry Morgan, clothed from head to foot in the booty from Maracaibo. He has a gold telescope and yellow boots of Córdoba leather; his jacket buttons are emeralds mounted by Amsterdam jewelers. The wind lifts the lacy foam of his white silk shirt and carries from afar the voice of the woman who awaits Morgan in Jamaica, the flaming mulatto who warned him on the docks, when he said good-bye: "If you die, I'll kill you."

(65 and 117)

1670: Lima

"Mourn for us,"

the Indians of the Potosí mines had said to him wordlessly. And last year Count Lemos, viceroy of Peru, wrote to the king in Spain: *There is no people in the world so exhausted. I unburden my conscience to inform Your Majesty with due clarity: It is not silver that is brought to Spain, but the blood and sweat of Indians.*

The viceroy has seen the mountain that eats men. From the villages Indians are brought in strung together with iron collars, and the more the mountain swallows, the more its hunger grows. The villages are being emptied of men.

After this report to the king, Count Lemos bans week-long work periods in the asphyxiating tunnels. Beatings of drums, proclamations in the streets: In the future, the viceroy orders, Indians will work from sunrise to sunset, because *they are not slaves to spend the night in the mines*.

No one pays any attention.

And now, in his austere palace in Lima, he receives a reply from the Council of the Indies in Madrid. The council declines to suppress forced labor in the silver and mercury mines.

(121)

1670: San Juan Atitlán
An Intruder on the Altar

In midmorning, Father Marcos Ruiz lets the donkey carry him to the village of San Juan Atitlán. Who knows whether the gentle music of water and bells borne on the breeze comes from village or from dream? The friar yawns and does not hurry the pace, that soporific swing.

Much twisting and turning are required to get to San Juan Atitlán, a village deep in the asperities of the countryside; and it is well known that the Indians grow their crops in the most obscure corners of the mountains to pay homage, in those hideaways, to their pagan gods.

The first houses, and Fray Marcos begins to wake up. The village is deserted; no one comes out to greet him. He blinks strenuously on arriving at the church, overflowing with people, and his heart gives a violent jump when he manages to shoulder his way in, and he rubs his eyes to see what is happening: In the church, flower-bedecked and perfumed as never before, the Indians are worshiping the village idiot. Seated on the altar, covered from head to foot with the sacred vestments, dribbling and squinting, the idiot is receiving offerings of incense and fruit and hot food amid a torrent of hardly recognizable orations and hymns. No one hears the indignant cries of Fray Marcos, who retreats on the run in search of soldiers.

The spectacle infuriates the pious clergyman, but his surprise does not last long. After all, what can one expect from these idolaters, who ask pardon of a tree when they go to cut it down and do not dig a well without first making excuses to the ground? Don't they confuse God with some stone or other, the sound of a running stream, or a drizzle of rain? Don't they call carnal sin play?

(71)

1670: Masaya

"The Idiot"

For a moment, the sun breaks through clouds, then hides again, ashamed or scared by the brilliance of people here below, for the land is lit up with joy: dialogue dance, dance theater, saucy musical skits: on the verge of intelligibility, "the Idiot" directs the fiesta. The characters, wearing masks, speak a language of their own, neither Náhuatl nor Spanish, a mestizo language that has grown up in Nicaragua. It has been fed by the thousand idioms that the people have developed for talking defiantly and inventing as they talk, fiery chili from the imaginations of a people making fun of its masters.

An ancient Indian, a coarse fast talker, occupies the center of the stage. It is "the Idiot," otherwise known as Macho Mouse, mocker of prohibitions, who never says what he says or listens to what he hears, and so manages to avoid being crushed by the powerful: When the rogue cannot win the game, he draws; when he can't achieve a draw, he confuses.

(9)

1670: Cuzco

Old Moley

The walls of the cathedral, obese with gold, overwhelm this dark Virgin with the black hair streaming from under her straw hat and a baby llama in her arms. Her simple image is surrounded by a foamy sea of filigreed gold. Cuzco's cathedral would like to vomit out of its opulent belly this Indian Virgin, Virgin of despair, as not long ago its doormen rejected an old barefooted woman who tried to enter.

"Leave her alone!" cried the priest from the pulpit. "Let this Indian woman come in, she is my mother!"

The priest is Juan de Espinosa Medrano, known to all as Old Moley because God has covered his face with moles. When Old Moley preaches, crowds flock to the cathedral. The Peruvian church has no better orator. Furthermore, he teaches theology in the San Antonio seminary and writes plays. *Love Your Own Death,* his comedy in the Spanish language, the language of his father, resembles the pulpit from which he pronounces his sermons: pompous verses twisted into a thousand arabesques, ostentatious and extravagant like the colonial churches. At the same time, he has written in Quechua, his mother's language, a sacramental mystery play of simple structure and stripped phraseology, on the theme of the prodigal son. In this, the Devil is a Peruvian landlord, the wine is chicha, and the biblical calf is a fat pig.

(18)

1671: Panama City

On Punctuality in Appointments

More than two years have passed since Henry Morgan reached Panama in a canoe and at the head of a fistful of men stormed the ramparts of Portobello with a knife between his teeth. With a very small force and no culverins or cannon, he seized this impregnable bastion; and for not burning it down, he collected a mountain of gold and silver in ransom. The governor of Panama, defeated and disillusioned by this unheard-of feat, sent to ask Morgan for a pistol of the type he had used in the assault.

"Let him keep it for a year," said the pirate. "I'll be back to get it."

Now he enters the city of Panama, advancing among the flames, with the English flag streaming from one hand and a cutlass grasped in the other. Two thousand men and several cannons follow him. The fire turns night into day, another summer overtopping the eternal summer of these coasts; it devours houses and convents, churches and hospitals, and licks the lips of the buccaneer who yells: *"I'm here for money, not for prayers!"*

After much burning and killing, he moves off followed by an endless caravan of mules loaded with gold, silver, and precious stones.

Morgan sends his apologies to the governor for the delay.

(61 and 65)

1672: London

The White Man's Burden

The duke of York, brother of the king of England, founded the Company of Royal Adventurers nine years ago. English planters in the Antilles bought their slaves from Dutch slavers; but the Crown could not permit the purchase of such valuable articles from foreigners. The new enterprise, set up for trade with Africa, had prestigious shareholders: King Charles II, three dukes, eight earls, seven lords, a countess, and twenty-seven knights. In homage to the duke of York, the captains burned the letters DY with hot irons onto the breasts of the three thousand slaves they carried yearly to Barbados and Jamaica.

Now the enterprise is to be called the Royal Africa Company. The English king, who holds most of the stock, encourages slave-buying in his colonies, where slaves cost six times as much as in Africa.

Behind the ships, sharks make the trip to the islands, awaiting the bodies that go overboard. Many die because there is not enough water and the strongest drink what little there is, or because of dysentery or smallpox, and many die from melancholy: they refuse to eat, and there is no way to open their jaws.

They lie in rows, crushed against each other, their noses touching the deck above. Their wrists are handcuffed, and fetters wear their ankles raw. When portholes have to be closed in rough seas or rain, the small amount of air rises to fever heat, but with portholes open the hold stinks of hatred, fermented hatred, fouler than the foulest stench of slaughterhouse, and the floor is always slippery with blood, vomit, and shit.

The sailors, who sleep on deck, listen at night to the endless moans from below and at dawn to the yells of those who dreamed they were in their country.

(127, 160, and 224)

Mandingo People's Song of the Bird of Love

But let me, oh, Dyamberé!
You who wear the belt with the long fringes,
let me sing to the birds,
the birds that listen to the departing princess
and receive her last confidences.
And you, maidens, sing, sing
softly
"la, la"—the beautiful bird.
And you, Master-of-the-terrible-gun,
let me look at the bird of love,
the bird that my friend and I love.
Let me, master-of-the-splendid-tunic,
lord of raiment more brilliant
than the light of day.
Let me love the bird of love!

(134)

1674: Port Royal

Morgan

He was almost a child when they sold him, in Bristol, to a dealer. The captain who took him to the Antilles exchanged him for a few coins in Barbados.

In these islands he learned to break with one ax blow any branch that hit his face; and that there is no fortune that does not have crime for father and infamy for mother. He spent years robbing galleons and making widows. Fingers wearing gold rings, he simply chopped off. He became chief of the pirates. Correction, buccaneers. *Admiral of buccaneers.* From his toadlike neck always hangs his buccaneer's license, which legalizes his function and keeps him from the gallows.

Three years ago, after the sack of Panama, they took him to London as a prisoner. The king removed his chains, dubbed him knight of the court, and named him lieutenant governor of Jamaica.

The philosopher John Locke has drawn up the instructions for good government of this island, which is the headquarters of English buccaneers. Morgan will see to it that neither Bibles nor dogs to hunt fugitive slaves will ever be lacking and will hang his brother pirates every time his king decides to be on good terms with Spain.

Newly landed at Port Royal, Henry Morgan takes off his plumed hat, downs a shot of rum, and by way of a toast empties the bowl over his many-rolled wig. The buccaneers shout and sing, waving swords.

The horse that takes Morgan to the government palace is shod with gold.

(11 and 169)

1674: Potosí

Claudia the Witch

With her hand she moved clouds and brought on or held off storms. In the twinkling of an eye she brought people back from far-off lands and also from death. She enabled a magistrate of the Porco mines to see his native Madrid in a mirror; and she served at the table of Don Pedro de Ayamonte, who came from Utrera, cakes freshly baked in an Utrera oven. She caused gardens to bloom in deserts and turned the savviest lovers into virgins. She saved hunted people who sought refuge in her house by changing them into dogs or cats. For bad times, a bright face, she'd say, and hunger she'd beat off with a guitar: She played her guitar and shook her tambourine to revive the sick and the dead. If you were mute she could make you speak, if you talked too much she could stop you. She made open-air love with an extremely black devil right out in the countryside. After midnight, she flew.

She had been born in Tucumán, and this morning she died in Potosí. On her deathbed, she called a Jesuit priest and told him to take from a drawer certain lumps of wax and remove the pins that were stuck in them, so that five priests whom she had made sick could get well.

The priest offered her confession and divine mercy, but she laughed and died laughing.

(21)

1674: Yorktown

The Olympian Steeds

James Bullocke, a tailor of Yorktown, has challenged Matthew Slader to a horse race. The county court fines him for his presumptuousness and warns him that it is *contrary to Law for a Labourer to make a race being a Sport for Gentlemen*. Bullocke must pay two hundred pounds of tobacco in casks.

People on foot, gentry on horseback: the halo of aristocracy is the dust cloud that hooves raise along the road. Horses' hooves make and unmake fortunes. For races on Saturday afternoons, or for horsey talk in the evenings, the knights of tobacco emerge from the solitude of the plantation in silken clothes and curly wigs, and over mugs of cider or brandy discuss and make bets while dice roll on the table. They bet money or tobacco or black slaves, or white servants of the kind that pay their fare from England with years of work; but only on big nights of glory or ruin do they bet horses. A good horse is the measure of the worth of its owner, a tobaccocrat of Virginia who lives and commands on horseback and on horseback will die, flying like the wind to the heavenly gates.

In Virginia there is no time for anything else. Three years ago Governor William Berkeley could proudly remark: *I thank God, there are no free schools nor printing, and I hope we shall not have either for a hundred years; for learning has brought disobedience and heresy, and sects into the world, and printing has divulged them.*

(35)

1676: Valley of Connecticut

The Ax of Battle

With the first snows, the Wampanoag Indians rise. They are tired of seeing the New England frontier run south and west on speedy feet, and by the end of winter they have ravaged the Valley of Connecticut and are fighting less than twenty miles from Boston.

The horse drags its rider along the ground, his foot caught in a stirrup. An arrow has killed him. The victims of the plunder, swift warriors, strike and disappear; and so push the invaders toward the coast where they landed years ago.

(153 and 204)

1676: Plymouth
Metacom

Half of the Indian population has died in the war. Twelve English towns lie in ashes.

At the end of summer, the English bring to Plymouth the head of Metacom, the Wampanoag chief: Metacom, that is, Satan, who tried to seize from the Puritan colonists the lands that God had granted them.

The High Court of Plymouth discusses: *What do we do with Metacom's son? Hang him or sell him as a slave?* Taking into account Deuteronomy 24:16, the first Book of Kings 11:17, II Chronicles 25:4, and Psalms 137 to 139, the judges decide to sell Metacom's son, aged nine, in the Antillean slave markets.

As further proof of generosity, the victors offer the Indians a small piece of what used to be theirs: In the future the Indian communities of the region, whether or not they fought with Metacom, will be enclosed in four reserves in Massachusetts Bay.

(153 and 204)

1677: Old Road Town
Death Here, Rebirth There

The body, which knows little, doesn't know it, nor does the soul that breathes; but the soul that dreams, which knows the most, does: The black man who kills himself in America revives in Africa. Many slaves of this island of St. Kitts let themselves die by refusing food or eating only earth, ashes, and lime; and others tie a rope around the neck. In the woods, among the lianas that drape from the great weeping trees hang slaves who by killing themselves not only kill their memories of pain but also set forth in white canoes on the long voyage back to their ancestral homes.

A certain Bouriau, owner of plantations, strolls through the foliage, machete in hand, decapitating the hanged:

"Hang yourselves if you like!" he advises the live ones. "Over there in your countries you won't have a head! You won't be able to see or hear or talk or eat!"

Another planter, Major Crips, the harshest castigator of men, enters the wood with a cartful of sugar pans and sugarmill pieces. He seeks and finds his escaped slaves, who have gathered together and are tying knots and choosing branches, and says to them:

"Keep it up, keep it up. I'll hang myself with you. I'll accompany you. I've bought a big sugarmill in Africa, and there you'll work for me."

Major Crips selects a big tree, a huge ceiba, ties the rope around his neck, and threads the slipknot. The blacks watch him in a daze, but his face is just a shadow beneath the straw hat, a shadow that says: "Let's go, everybody! Quick! I need hands in Guinea!"

(101)

1677: Pôrto Calvo

The Captain Promises Lands,
Slaves, and Honors

Early in the morning, the army moves off from Pôrto Calvo. The soldiers, volunteers, and draftees are marching against the free blacks of Palmares, who are going about the South of Pernambuco burning canefields.

Fernão Carrilho, senior captain of the Palmares war, addresses his troops after Mass: *"Great as is the host of our enemies, it is a host of slaves. Nature has created them more to obey than to resist. If we destroy them, we will have lands for our plantations, blacks for our service, and honor for our names. The blacks fight like fugitives. We will pursue them like lords!"*

(69)

1678: Recife

Ganga Zumba

Thanksgiving Mass in the mother church: the Governor of Pernambuco, Aires de Sousa de Castro, picks up the tails of his em-

broidered coat and kneels before the throne of the Most Holy.
Beside him, covered by an ample cape of red silk, kneels Ganga
Zumba, supreme chief of the Palmares federation.

Peal of bells, din of artillery and drums: The governor grants
to Ganga Zumba the title of sergeant at arms, and in proof of
friendship adopts two of his smallest children, who will take his
name. At the end of the peace talks held in Recife between del-
egates of the king of Portugal and representatives of Palmares, the
agreement is drawn up: The Palmares sanctuaries will be emptied.
All individuals born there are declared free, and those who have
the hot-iron brand will return to their owners.

"But I don't surrender," says Zumbí, Ganga Zumba's nephew.

Zumbí remains in Macacos, capital of Palmares, deaf to the
successive groups offering him pardon.

Of the thirty thousand Palmarinos, only five thousand accompany Ganga Zumba. For the others he is a traitor who deserves to
die and be forgotten.

"I don't believe in the word of my enemies," says Zumbí. "My
enemies don't believe it themselves."

(43 and 69)

Yoruba Spell Against the Enemy

When they try to catch a chameleon
under a mat,
the chameleon takes the color of the mat
and they can't tell which is which.
When they try to catch a crocodile
on the bottom of the river,
the crocodile takes the color of the water
and they can't distinguish him from the current.
When the Wizard tries to catch me
may I take on the agility of the wind
and escape with a puff!

(134)

1680: Santa Fe, New Mexico

Red Cross and White Cross

The knots in a rope of maguey announce the rebellion and indicate how many days to wait for it. The speediest messengers take it from village to village throughout New Mexico, until the Sunday of Wrath dawns.

The Indians of twenty-four communities rise. They are those that remain of the sixty-six that existed in these northern lands when the conquistadors arrived. The Spaniards succeed in suppressing the rebels in one or two villages.

"Surrender."

"I prefer death."

"You'll go to hell."

"I prefer hell."

But the avengers of pain advance destroying churches and forts, and after a few days are masters of the whole region. To wipe off the baptismal oils and get rid of the Christian names, the Indians plunge in the river and rub themselves with cleansing amole plants. Dressed up as monks, they drink to the recovery of their lands and their gods. They announce that they will never again work for others, that pumpkins will sprout all over the place, and that the world will be snowed under with cotton.

A noose is drawn around the city of Santa Fe, Spain's last redoubt in these remote regions. The chief of the Indians gallops up to the walls. He is armed with arquebus, dagger, and sword and wears a taffeta strip he found in a convent. He throws down at the foot of the wall two crosses, a white and a red one.

"The red cross is resistance. The white, surrender. Pick up whichever you choose!"

Then he turns his back on the besieged enemy and disappears in a puff of dust.

The Spaniards resist. But after a few days they raise the white cross. A while back they had come seeking the legendary golden cities of Cíbola. Now they begin the retreat southward.

(88)

1681: Mexico City

Juana at Thirty

After matins and lauds, she sets a top to spinning in the flour and studies the circles it draws. She investigates water and light, air and things. Why does an egg come together in boiling oil and separate in syrup? Forming triangles of pins, she seeks Solomon's ring. With one eye clamped to a telescope, she hunts stars.

They have threatened her with the Inquisition and forbidden her to open books, but Sor Juana Inés de la Cruz studies *the things that God created, which serve me as letters as this universal machine serves me as book.*

Between divine love and human love, between the fifteen mysteries of the rosary that hangs about her neck and the enigmas of the world, Sor Juana has set up a debate; and she passes many nights without sleep, praying, writing, when the endless war starts up again inside her between passion and reason. At the end of each battle, the first light of dawn enters her cell in the Jeronimite convent and helps Sor Juana remember what Lupercio Leonardo said, that one can both philosophize and cook supper. She creates poems on the table and puff pastry in the kitchen; letters and delicacies to give away, David's-harp music soothing to Saul as well as to David, joys of soul and mouth condemned by the advocates of pain.

"Only suffering will make you worthy of God," says the confessor, and orders her to burn what she writes, ignore what she knows, and not see what she looks at.

(49, 58, and 190)

1681: Mexico City

Sigüenza y Góngora

Since the end of last year, a comet has lit up the sky of Mexico. What evils does the angry prophet announce? What troubles will it bring? Will the sun like the great fist of God crash into the earth? Will the oceans dry up and no drop of water remain in the rivers?

"There is no reason why comets should be unlucky," says the wise man to the terrified people.

Carlos de Sigüenza y Góngora publishes his *Philosophical Manifesto Against the Stray Comets That the Empire Holds Over the Heads of the Timid*, a formidable indictment of superstition and fear. A polemic breaks out between astronomy and astrology, between human curiosity and divine revelation. The German Jesuit Eusebio Francisco Kino, who is visiting these regions, cites six biblical foundations for his affirmation that nearly all comets *are precursors of sinister, sad, and calamitous events*.

Kino disdainfully seeks to amend the theory of Sigüenza y Góngora, son of Copernicus, Galileo, and other heretics; and the learned Creole replies: "*Would you at least concede that there are also mathematicians outside of Germany, stuck though they may be among the reeds and bulrushes of a Mexican lake?*"

The Academy's leading cosmographer, Sigüenza y Góngora has intuited the law of gravity and believes that other stars must have, like the sun, planets flying around them. Calculating from eclipses and comets, he has fixed the dates of Mexico's indigenous history; and earth as well as sky being his business, he has also exactly fixed the longitude of this city (283° 23' west of Santa Cruz de Tenerife), drawn the first complete map of the region, and told it all in verse and prose works with the extravagant titles typical of his time.

(83)

1682: Accra

All Europe Is Selling Human Flesh

Not far from the English and Danish forts, a pistol shot away, rises the Prussian trading post. A new flag flies on these coasts, over the tree-trunk roofs of the slave depots and on the masts of ships that sail with full cargoes.

With their Africa Company the Germans have joined in the juiciest business of the period. The Portuguese hunt and sell blacks through their Company of Guinea. The Royal Africa Company operates for the English Crown. The French flag waves from ships of the Company of Senegal. Holland's Company of the West Indies is doing nicely. Denmark's enterprise specializing in the slave traffic is also called Company of the West Indies; and the Company of the South Sea lines the pockets of the Swedes.

Spain has no slave business. But a century ago, in Seville, the Chamber of Commerce sent the king a documented report explaining that slaves were the most lucrative of all merchandise going to America; and so they continue to be. For the right to sell slaves in the Spanish colonies, foreign concerns pay fortunes into the royal coffers. With these funds have been built, among other things, the Alcázars of Madrid and Toledo. The Negro Committee meets in the main hall of the Council of the Indies.

(127, 129, 160, and 224)

1682: Remedios

By Order of Satan

He trembles, twists, howls, dribbles. He makes the stones of the church vibrate. All around steams the red earth of Cuba.

"Satan, dog! Drunken dog! Talk or I'll piss on you!" threatens inquisitor José González de la Cruz, parish priest of Remedios, as he knocks down and kicks the black woman Leonarda before the main altar. Bartolomé del Castillo, notary public, waits without breathing. He clutches a thick bundle of papers in one hand, and with the other he waves a bird's quill in the air.

The Devil romps contentedly in the charming body of black Leonarda.

The inquisitor swings the slave around with a blow and she falls on her face, eats the dust, and bounces. She raises herself up, and turns, blazing and bleeding, handsome, on the checkerboard tiles.

"Satan! Lucifer! Nigger! Start talking, stinking shit!"

From Leonarda's mouth come flames and froth. Also noises that no one understands except Father José, who translates and dictates to the notary:

"She says she is Lucifer! She says there are eight hundred thousand devils in Remedios!"

More noises come from the black woman.

"What else? What else, dog?" demands the priest and lifts Leonarda by the hair.

"Talk, you shit!" He does not insult her mother because the Devil has none.

Before the slave faints, the priest shouts and the notary writes; "She says Remedios will collapse! She is confessing everything! I have him by the neck! She says the earth will swallow us up!"

And he howls: "A mouth of hell! She says Remedios is a mouth of hell!"

Everyone cries out. All the residents of Remedios jump about, screaming and shouting. More than one falls in a faint.

The priest, bathed in sweat, his skin transparent, and his lips trembling, loosens his grip on Leonarda's neck. The black woman collapses.

No one fans her.

(161)

1682: Remedios

But They Stay On

Eight hundred thousand devils. So there are more devils in the air of Remedios than mosquitos: 1,305 devils tormenting each inhabitant.

The devils are lame, ever since the Fall that all the world knows about. They have goats' beards and horns, bats' wings, rats' tails, and black skin. Circulating in Leonarda's body is more enjoyable to them because they are black.

Leonarda weeps and refuses to eat.

"If God wants to cleanse you," Father José tells her, "He will whiten your skin."

The plaintive song of cicadas and grasshoppers is that of souls in torment. Crabs are sinners condemned to walk crookedly. In the swamps and rivers live child-robbing goblins. When it rains, the scuffling of devils is heard from caves and crannies, furious because the flashes and sparks they have set off to burn down the skies are getting wet. And the harsh, nasal croak of frogs in the Boquerón fissure: is it foretelling rain, or is it cursing? Does the light that shines in the darkness come from the firefly? Those eyes, are they really the owl's? Against whom does the snake hiss?

The buzz of the blind nocturnal bat: if it brushes you with its wing, you will go straight to hell, which is down there beneath Remedios; there the flames burn but give no light, and eternal ice chatters the teeth of those who on earth sinned with randy heat.

"Stay back!"

At the smallest alarm, the priest makes one jump into the font of holy water.

"Satan, stay back!"

With holy water lettuces are washed. People yawn with their mouths shut.

"Jesus! Jesus!" the parishioners cross themselves.

There is no house unadorned by strings of garlic, no air that the smoke of sweet basil does not impregnate.

"They have feet but do not reach me, iron but do not wound me, nooses and do not bind me . . ."

But people stay on. No one leaves. No one abandons the town of Remedios.

(161)

1682: Remedios

By Order of God

The church bells, outlined against the sky, ring for service. All of Remedios turns out. The notary sits in his place to the right of the altar. The crowd presses in through the open doors.

There is a rumor that Father José is to hear testimony from God. It is hoped that Christ will unpin his right hand from the cross and swear to tell the truth, the whole truth, and nothing but the truth.

Father José advances to the main altar and opens the tabernacle. He raises the chalice and the host; and before the body and blood of the Lord, on his knees, formulates his request. The notary takes notes. God will show Remedios's inhabitants where they have to live.

If the Devil spoke through the mouth of Leonarda, Leonardo will be the vehicle for his invincible enemy.

With a bandage, the priest covers the eyes of Leonardo, a boy who does not reach to his waist, and Leonardo dips his hand in the silver pyx in which lie some bits of paper with names of places.

The boy picks one. The priest unfolds it and reads in a very loud voice: "Santa Maria de Guadalupe! Take note, notary!" And he adds triumphantly: "The Lord has had pity on us! He, in His infinite mercy, offers us protection! Up, people of Remedios! The time has come to go!"

And he goes.

He looks behind him. Few are following.

Father José takes everything along: chalice and host, lamp and silver candlesticks, images and wood carvings. But the barest handful of devout women and scared men accompany him to the promised land.

Slaves and horses drag their effects along. They take furniture and clothes, rice and beans, salt, oil, sugar, dried meat, tobacco, and also books from Paris, cottons from Rouen, and laces from Malines, all smuggled into Cuba.

The trek to Santa Maria de Guadalupe is long. Located there are the Hato del Cupey lands that belong to Father José. For years the priest has been seeking buyers for them.

(161)

1688: Havana

By Order of the King

All over Cuba it is the sole topic of conversation. Wherever people gather to gossip, bets are laid.

Will the people of Remedios obey?

Father José, abandoned by his faithful, remains alone and has to return to Remedios. But he continues his war, a stubborn holy war that has found echoes even in the royal palace. From Madrid, Charles II has ordered that the population of Remedios should move to the Hato del Cupey lands in Santa Maria de Guadalupe.

The government's captain general and the bishop of Havana announce that once and for all the king's will must be respected.

Patience is giving out.

The people of Remedios continue playing deaf.

(161)

1691: Remedios

Still They Don't Move

At dawn Captain Pérez de Morales arrives from Havana with forty well-armed men.

They stop at the church. One by one, the soldiers receive communion. Father José blesses their muskets and battle-axes.

They get the torches ready.

At noon, the town of Remedios is a big bonfire. From afar, on the road to his Hato del Cupey lands, Father José watches bluish smoke rise from the flaming rubble.

At nightfall, close to the ruins, the people emerge from hiding in the thickets.

Sitting in a circle, eyes fixed on the continuing clouds of smoke, they curse and remember. Many a time pirates have sacked this town. Some years back they carried off even the chalice of the Most Holy Sacrament, and a bishop was said to have died of disgust—a good thing, they said, that the scapulary hung on his breast at the time. But no pirate ever set fire to Remedios.

By the light of the moon, beneath a ceiba tree, the people hold a town council. They, who belong to this red-soiled clearing in the forest, resolve that Remedios shall be rebuilt.

The women clutch their young to their breasts and stare with the eyes of mother tigers ready to spring.

The air smells of burning but not of sulphur nor of Devil's dung.

The sounds rising among the trees are voices in discussion and a newly born babe wailing for some milk and a name.

(161)

1691: Mexico City
Juana at Forty

A stream of white light, limelight, sprays Sor Juana Inés de la Cruz, kneeling at center stage. Her back is turned, and she is looking upward. There bleeds an enormous Christ, arms open, on the lofty ramp lined with black velvet and bristling with crosses, swords, and flags. From the platform two prosecutors make their accusations.

Everything is black, and black the hoods that conceal the prosecutors' faces. However, one wears a nun's habit, and beneath the hood peep out the reddish rolls of a wig: it is the bishop of Puebla, Manuel Fernández de Santa Cruz, in the role of Sister Filotea. The other, Antonio Núñez de Miranda, Sister Juana's confessor, represents himself. His aquiline nose bulges from beneath the hood, moves as if it wanted to get free of its owner.

SISTER FILOTEA (*embroidering on a frame*): Mysterious is the Lord. Why, I ask myself, would He have put a man's head on the body of Sister Juana? So that she should concern herself with the wretched affairs of the earth? She does not deign to approach the Holy Scriptures.

THE CONFESSOR (*pointing at Sister Juana with a wooden cross*): Ingrate!

SISTER JUANA (*her eyes fixed on the Christ over the prosecutors' heads*): Indeed I repay badly the generosity of God. I only study to see whether studying will make me less ignorant, and I direct my footsteps toward the summits of Holy Theology; but I have studied many things and learned nothing, or almost nothing. The divine truths remain far from me, always far . . . I sometimes feel them to be so close yet know them to be so far away! Since I was a small child . . . at five or six I sought those keys in my grandfather's books, those keys . . . I read and read. They punished me and I read secretly, searching . . .

THE CONFESSOR (*to Sister Filotea*): She never accepted the will of God. Now she even writes like a man. I have seen the manuscripts of her poems!

SISTER JUANA: Searching . . . I knew quite early on that universities are not for women and that a woman who knows more than the Paternoster is deemed immodest. I had mute books for teachers and an inkpot for a schoolmate. When books were forbidden to me, as happened more than once in this convent, I studied the things of the world. Even cooking one can discover secrets of nature.

SISTER FILOTEA: The Royal and Pontifical University of the Pancake! The frying-pan campus!

SISTER JUANA: What can we women know except the philosophy of the kitchen? But if Aristotle had cooked, he would have written much more. That makes you laugh, does it? Well, laugh, if it pleases you. Men feel themselves to be very wise, just for being men. Christ, too, was crowned with thorns as King of Jests.

THE CONFESSOR (*erases his smile, hits the table with his fist*): Ever hear the like of that? The learned little nun! She can write little songs, so she compares herself with the Messiah!

SISTER JUANA: Christ also suffered from this unfairness. Is he one of *them*? So he must die! He is accused? So let him suffer!

THE CONFESSOR: There's humility for you!

SISTER FILOTEA: Really, my daughter, you scandalize God with your vociferous pride . . .

SISTER JUANA: My pride? (*Smiles sadly*) I used that up long ago.

THE CONFESSOR: The common people applaud her verses, so she thinks herself one of the elect. Verses that shame this house of God, exaltation of the flesh . . . (*coughs*) Evil arts of the male animal . . .

SISTER JUANA: My poor verses! Dust, shadow, nothing. Vain glory, all the applause . . . Did I ask for it? What divine revelation forbids women to write? By grace or curse, it was Heaven that made me a poet.

THE CONFESSOR (*looks at the ceiling and raises his hands in supplication*): She dirties the purity of the faith, and Heaven is to blame for it.

SISTER FILOTEA (*puts embroidery frame aside and clasps hands over stomach*): Sister Juana has much to sing to the human spirit, little to the divine.

SISTER JUANA: Don't the Gospels teach us that the celestial expresses itself in the terrestrial? A powerful force pushes my hand . . .

THE CONFESSOR (*waving the wooden cross, as if to strike Juana from afar*): Force of God, or force of the king of the proud?

SISTER JUANA: . . . and I'll continue writing, I'm afraid, as long as my body makes a shadow. I fled from myself when I took the habit, but I brought myself along, wretch that I am.

SISTER FILOTEA: She bathes in the nude. There are proofs.

SISTER JUANA: Oh, Lord, put out the light of my understanding! Leave only what suffices to keep Thy Law! Isn't the rest superfluous for a woman?

THE CONFESSOR (*screaming harshly like a crow*): Shame on you! Mortify your heart, ingrate!

SISTER JUANA: Put me out. Put me out, my God!

(*The play continues, with similar dialog, until 1693*).

(58 and 75)

1691: *Placentia*

Adario, Chief of the Huron Indians, Speaks to Baron de Lahontan, French Colonizer of Newfoundland

Nay, you are miserable enough already, and indeed I can't see how you can be more such. What sort of men must Europeans be? What species of creatures do they retain to? The Europeans, who must be forc'd to do good, and have no other prompter for the avoiding of Evil than the fear of punishment . . .

Who gave you all the countries that you now inhabit? By what right do you possess them? They always belonged to the Algonquins before. In earnest, my dear brother, I'm sorry for thee from the bottom of my soul. Take my advice, and turn Huron; for I see plainly a vast difference between thy condition and mine. I am master of myself and my condition. I am master of my own body, I have the absolute disposal of myself, I do what I please, I am the first and the last of my nation, I fear no man, and I depend only upon the Great Spirit. Whereas, thy body, as well as thy soul, are doomed to a dependence upon thy great Captain, thy Vice-Roy disposes of thee, thou hast not the liberty of doing what thou hast a mind to; thou art afraid of robbers, false witnesses, assassins, etc., and thou dependest upon an infinity of persons whose places have raised them above thee. Is it true or not?

(136)

1692: *Salem Village*

The Witches of Salem

"Christ knows how many devils there are here!" roars the Reverend Samuel Parris, pastor of the town of Salem, and speaks of Judas, the devil seated at the Lord's table, who sold himself for thirty coins, £3/15/0 in English pounds, the derisory price of a female slave.

In the war of the lambs against the dragons, cries the pastor, no neutrality is possible nor any sure refuge. The devils have planted themselves in his own house: a daughter and a niece of the Reverend Parris have been the first ones tormented by the army of devils that has taken this Puritan town by storm. The little girls fondled a crystal ball, wanting to know their fate, and saw death. Since that happened, many young girls of Salem feel hell in their bodies, the malignant fever burns them inside and they twist and turn, roll on the ground frothing at the mouth and screaming blasphemies and obscenities that the Devil puts on their lips.

The doctor, William Griggs, diagnoses evil spells. A dog is given a cake of rye flour mixed with the urine of the possessed girls, but the dog gobbles it up, wags his tail, and goes off to sleep in peace. The Devil prefers human habitations.

Between one convulsion and the next, the victims accuse.

Women, and poor ones, are the first sentenced to hang. Two whites, one black: Sarah Osborne, a bent old woman who years ago cried out to her Irish servant, who slept in the stable, and made her a place in her bed; Sarah Good, a disorderly beggar who smokes a pipe and grumbles when given alms; and Tituba, a black West Indian slave, mistress of a hairy devil with a long nose. The daughter of Sarah Good, a young witch aged four, is in Boston prison with fetters on her feet.

But the agonized screams of Salem's young girls do not cease, and charges and condemnations multiply. The witch-hunt spreads from suburban Salem Village to the center of Salem Town, from the town to the port, from the accursed to the powerful. Not even the governor's wife escapes the accusing finger. From the gallows hang prosperous farmers and businessmen, shipowners trading with London, privileged members of the Church who enjoy the right to Communion.

A sulphurous rain is reported over Salem Town, Massachusetts' second port, where the Devil, working harder than ever, goes about promising the Puritans cities of gold and French footwear.

(34)

1692: Guápulo

Nationalization of Colonial Art

In the sanctuary of Guápulo, a village overlooking Quito, Miguel de Santiago begins to show his canvases.

In homage to the local Virgin, who is a great miracle worker, Miguel de Santiago offers these mountains and plains, this cordillera and this sky, landscapes that would have little life if the people who move in them did not light them up: local people moving through local settings in procession or alone. The artist no longer copies works from Madrid or Rome about the life of St. Augustine. Now he paints the luminous city of Quito surrounded by volcanos, the towers of these churches, the Indians of Pujilí and Machángara Canyon, Bellavista Hill and the Valley of Guápulo; and the suns behind the mountains, the rising bonfire-smoke clouds, and the misty rivers that never stop singing all belong here.

Nor is it only Miguel de Santiago. The anonymous hands of indigenous or mestizo artisans sneak contraband llamas into their Christmas paintings instead of camels, and pineapples and palms and corncobs and avocados into church-façade greenery carvings; and even head-banded suns up close to the altars. On all sides there are pregnant Virgins, and Christs that grieve like men, like men of these parts, for the sadness of this world.

(215)

1693: Mexico City

Juana at Forty-Two

Lifelong tears, springing from time and pain, soak her face. She sees the world as profoundly and sadly clouded. Defeated, she bids it farewell.

For days she has been confessing the sins of her whole existence to the implacable Father Antonio Núñez de Miranda, and the rest is all penitence. With her own blood as ink she writes a letter to the Divine Tribunal, asking forgiveness.

Her *light sails and heavy keels* will no longer sail the seas of poetry. Sister Juana Inés de la Cruz abandons her human studies and renounces literature. She asks God for the gift of forgetfulness and chooses silence, or accepts it, and so America loses its best poet.

Her body will not survive long this suicide of the soul. *Let life be ashamed of lasting so long for me . . .*

(16, 49, and 58)

1693: Santa Fe, New Mexico

Thirteen Years of Independence

Thirteen years have passed since the bells of Santa Fe went mad celebrating the death of the God of the Christians and of Mary, his mother.

Thirteen years the Spaniards have taken to reconquer these wild lands of the North. While that truce of independence lasted, the Indians recovered their liberty and their names, their religion and their customs, but they also introduced into their communities the plow and the wheel and other instruments that the Spaniards brought.

For the colonial troops, the reconquest has not been easy. Each pueblo of New Mexico is a huge, tightly shut fortress, with board walls of stone and adobe several stories high. In the Rio Grande Valley live men not accustomed to obedience or servile labor.

(88)

Song of the New Mexican Indians to the Portrait That Escapes from the Sand

So I might cure myself,
the wizard painted,
in the desert, your portrait:
your eyes are of golden sand,
of red sand now your mouth,

of blue sand your hair
and my tears are of white sand.
All day he painted.
You grew like a goddess   .
on the immensity of the yellow canvas.
The wind of the night will scatter your shadow
and the colors of your shadow.
By ancient law nothing will remain for me.
Nothing, except the rest of my tears,
the silver sands.

(63)

1694: Macacos

The Last Expedition
Against Palmares

The great Indian-hunter, killer of Indians over many leagues, was born of an Indian mother. He speaks Guaraní, very little Portuguese. Domingos Jorge Velho is captain of the *mamelukes* of São Paulo, mestizos who have sown terror over half of Brazil in the name of their colonial lords and in ferocious exorcism of one half of their blood.

In the past six years, Captain Domingos has hired out his services to the Portuguese Crown against the Janduim Indians, rebelling in the hinterlands of Pernambuco and in Rio Grande do Norte. After a long campaign of carnage he arrives victorious at Recife, and there is contracted to demolish Palmares. They offer him fat booty in lands and blacks to sell in Rio de Janeiro and Buenos Aires and also promise him infinite amnesties, four religious orders' habits, and thirty military grades to distribute among his men.

With telescope slung over his naked chest, his greasy jacket open, Captain Domingos parades on horseback through the streets of Recife at the head of his mestizo officers and his rank-and-file Indian cutters of Indian throats. They ride amid clouds of dust and whiffs of gunpowder and rum, to applause and the fluttering of white handkerchiefs: this Messiah will save us from the rebellious blacks, the people believe or hope, convinced that the runaways are to blame for the lack of hands in the sugarmills as well as for the diseases and droughts that are devastating the Northeast, since God will not send health or rain while the Palmares scandal endures.

And the great crusade is organized. From all directions come volunteers, impelled by hunger, seeking sure rations. The prisons empty out, as even the jailbirds join the biggest army yet mobilized in Brazil.

The Indian scouts march ahead and the black porters bring up the rear. Nine thousand men cross the jungle, reach the mountains, and climb toward the summit, where the Macacos fortifications stand. This time they bring cannons.

The siege lasts several days. The cannons wreck the triple bulwark of wood and stone. They fight man to man on the edge of the abyss. There are so many dead that there is no place left to fall down, and the slaughter continues in the scrub. Many blacks try to flee, and slip down the precipice into the void; many choose the precipice and throw themselves off it.

Flames devour the capital of Palmares. From the distant city of Pôrto Calvo, the huge bonfire can be seen burning throughout the night. *Burn even the memory of it.* Hunting horns unceasingly proclaim the victory.

Chief Zumbí, wounded, has managed to escape. From the lofty peaks he reaches the jungle. He wanders through green tunnels, seeking his people in the thickets.

(38, 43, and 69)

Lament of the Azande People

The child is dead;
let us cover our faces
with white earth.
Four sons I have borne
in the hut of my husband.
Only the fourth lives.

I want to weep,
but in this village
sadness is forbidden.

(134)

1695: Serra Dois Irmãos

Zumbí

Jungle landscape, jungle of the soul. Zumbí smokes his pipe, his eyes locked on the high red rocks and caves open like wounds, and does not see that day is breaking with an enemy light, nor that the birds are flocking off in terrified flight.

He does not see the traitor approaching. He sees his comrade Antonio Soares and rises to embrace him. Antonio Soares buries a dagger several times in his back.

The soldiers fix the head on a lance point and take it to Recife, to putrefy in the plaza and teach the slaves that Zumbí was not immortal.

Palmares no longer breathes. This broad space of liberty opened up in colonial America has lasted for a century and resisted more than forty invasions. The wind has blown away the ashes of the black bastions of Macacos and Subupira, Dambrabanga and Obenga, Tabocas and Arotirene. For the conquerors, the Palmares century whittles down to the instant when the dagger polished off Zumbí. Night will fall and nothing will remain beneath the cold stars. Yet what does the wakeful know compared with what the dreamer knows?

The vanquished dream about Zumbí; and the dream knows that while one man remains owner of another man in these lands, his ghost will walk. He will walk with a limp, because Zumbí had been lamed by a bullet; he will walk up and down time and, limping, will fight in these jungles of palms and in all the lands of Brazil. The chiefs of all the unceasing black rebellions will be called Zumbí.

(69)

1695: São Salvador de Bahia

The Capital of Brazil

In this radiant city, there is a church for every day of the year, and every day a saint's day. A glow of towers and bells and tall palms, of bodies and of air sticky with *dendê* oil: today a saint is celebrated, tomorrow a lover, in the Bahia of All Saints and of the not-so-saintly. São Salvador de Bahia, seat of the viceroy and the archbishop, is the most populated of all Portuguese cities after Lisbon, and it envies Lisbon its monumental monasteries and golden churches, its incendiary women and its fiestas and masquerades and processions. Here strut mulatto prostitutes decked out like queens, and slaves parade their masters on litters down leafy avenues amid palaces of delirious grandeur. Gregorio de Matos, born in Bahia, thus portrays the noble gentry of the sugar plantations:

In Brazil the gentlefolk
are not all that gentle;
their good manners, not all that good:
So where do they belong?
In a pile of money.

Black slaves are the brick and mortar of these castles. From the cathedral pulpit Father Antonio Vieira insists on gratitude toward Angola, because without Angola there would be no Brazil, and without Brazil there would be no Portugal, *so that it could be very justly said that Brazil has its body in America and its soul in Africa*: Angola, which sells Bantu slaves and elephants tusks; Angola, as the father's sermon proclaims, *with whose unhappy blood and black but happy souls Brazil is nourished, animated, sustained, served, and preserved.*

At almost ninety this Jesuit priest remains the worst enemy of the Inquisition, advocate of enslaved Indians and Jews, and most persistent accuser of the colonial lords, who believe that work is for animals and spit on the hand that feeds them.

(33 and 226)

1696: Regla

Black Virgin, Black Goddess

To the docks of Regla, poor relation of Havana, comes the Virgin, and she comes to stay. The cedar carving has come from Madrid, wrapped in a sack, in the arms of her devotee Pedro Aranda. Today, September 8, is fiesta day in this little town of artisans and sailors, always redolent of shellfish and tar; the people eat meat and corn and beans and manioc, Cuban dishes, and African dishes, ecó, olelé, ecrú, quimbombó, fufú, while rivers of rum and earthquakes of drums welcome the black Virgin, *the little black one*, patron protector of Havana Bay.

The sea is littered with coconut husks and boughs of sweet basil, and a breeze of voices sings as night falls:

Opa ule, opa ule,
opa é, opa é,
opa opa, Yemayá.

The black Virgin of Regla is also the African Yemayá, silvered goddess of the seas, mother of the fish and mother and lover of Shangó, the womanizing and quarrel-picking warrior god.

(68 and 82)

1697: Cap Français

Ducasse

Gold escudos in hard cash, doubloons, double doubloons, big-shot gold and little-shot gold, gold jewelry and dishes, gold from chalices and crowns of virgins and saints: Filled with gold are the arriving galleons of Jean-Baptiste Ducasse, governor of Haiti and chief of the French freebooters in the Antilles. Ducasse has humbled Cartagena with his gun salvos; he has reduced to dust the cliff ramparts of the fortress, colossal lions of rock that rear up from the sea, and has left the church without a bell and the governor without rings.

To France goes the gold of the sacked Spanish colony. From

Versailles, Ducasse receives the title of admiral and a bushy wig of snow-white rolls worthy of the king.

Before becoming governor of Haiti and admiral of the royal fleet, Ducasse operated on his own, stealing blacks from Dutch slave ships and treasure from galleons of the Spanish fleet. Since 1691, he has been working for Louis XIV.

(11 and 61)

1699: Madrid

Bewitched

Although the herald has not blown his trumpet to announce it, the news flies through the streets of Madrid. The inquisitors have discovered who bewitched King Charles. The witch Isabel will be burned at the stake in the main plaza.

All Spain has been praying for Charles II. On waking, the monarch has been taking his posset of powdered snake, infallible for giving strength, but in vain: The penis has continued in a state of stupefaction, unable to make children, and from the royal mouth froth and foul breath have continued to emerge, and not one word worth hearing.

The curse did not come from a certain cup of chocolate with gallows bird's testicles, as some witches of Cangas had claimed; nor from the talisman that the king wore round his neck, as the exorcist Fray Mauro believed. Someone suggested that the king had been bewitched by his mother with tobacco from America or benzoin pills; and it was even rumored that the palace *maître d'hôtel*, the duke of Castellflorit, had served the royal table a ham larded with the fingernails of a Moorish or Jewish woman burned by the Inquisition.

The inquisitors have at last found the mess of pins, hairpins, cherrystones, and His Majesty's blond hairs that the witch Isabel had hidden near the royal bedroom.

The nose hangs down, the lip hangs down, the chin hangs down; but now that the king has been debewitched, his eyes seem to have lit up somewhat. A dwarf raises the candle to look at the portrait Carreño did of him years ago.

Meanwhile, outside the palace there is no bread or meat, fish or wine, as if Madrid were a besieged city.

(64 and 201)

1699: Macouba

A Practical Demonstration

To put some gusto into his slaves' work in this land of sluggishness and drowsiness, Father Jean-Baptiste Labat tells them he was black before coming to Martinique and that God whitened him as a reward for the fervor and submission with which he served his masters in France.

The black carpenter of the church is trying to make a difficult dovetailing of a beam and cannot get the angle right. Father Labat draws some lines with a ruler and compass, and he orders: "Cut it here."

The angle is right.

"Now I believe you," says the slave, looking him in the eyes. "No white man could do that."

(101)

1700: Ouro Prêto

All Brazil to the South

In the old days, the map showed Bahia close to the newly discovered mines of Potosí, and the governor general reported to Lisbon that *this land of Brazil and Peru are all one*. To turn the Paranapiacaba Mountains into the Andes cordillera, the Portuguese brought two hundred llamas to São Paulo and sat down to wait for the silver and gold to appear.

A century and a half later, the gold has turned up. The riverbeds and streams on the slopes of the Espinhaço Mountains are full of shiny stones. The São Paulo *mamelukes* found the gold when they were out hunting Cataguaz Indians.

The wind spread the news all through Brazil, and a multitude responded. To get gold in the Minas Gerais region, all you had to do was gather a handful of sand or pull up a tuft of grass and shake it.

With gold has come hunger. The price of a cat or a dog in the camps is 115 grams of gold, which is what a slave gets for two days' work.

(33 and 38)

1700: St. Thomas Island

The Man Who Makes Things Talk

Lugubrious bells and melancholy drums are sounding in this Danish island of the Antilles, a center for contraband and piracy. A slave walks up to the execution stake. Vanbel, the big boss, has condemned him because this black fellow turns on rain when he feels like it, kneeling before three oranges, and because he has a clay idol that answers all his questions and clears him of all doubts.

Smiling from ear to ear and with his eyes fixed on the stake surrounded by firewood, the condemned man approaches.

Vanbel intercepts him: "So you won't be chatting with your doll anymore, you black sorcerer!"

Without looking at him, the slave answers softly: "I can make that cane of yours talk."

"Stop!" Vanbel cries to the guards. "Unbind him!"

And before the waiting crowd he throws him his cane.

"Do it," he says.

The slave kneels. With his hands, he fans the cane stuck in the ground, makes a few turns around it, kneels again, and strokes it.

"I want to know," says the master, "whether the galleon that's due here has sailed yet. When it will arrive, who is aboard, what has happened . . ."

The slave takes a few steps backward.

"Come closer, sir," he suggests. "It will tell you."

His ear close to the cane, Vanbel hears that the ship sailed some time ago from Helsingør, in Denmark, but that on reaching the tropics a storm broke its small topsail and carried off the mizzensail. Vanbel's neck quivers like a frog's belly. The onlookers see him turn white.

"I don't hear anything," says Vanbel as the cane proceeds to tell him the names of the captain and the sailors.

"Nothing!" he screams.

The cane whispers to him: *The ship will arrive in three days.*

Its cargo will make you happy, and Vanbel explodes, tears off his wig, shouts: "Burn that Negro!"

He roars: "Burn him!"

He howls: "Burn that sorcerer!"

(101)

Bantu People's Song of the Fire

Fire that men watch in the night,
in the deep night.
Fire that blazest without burning, that shinest
without blazing.
Fire that fliest without a body.
Fire without heart, that knowest not
home nor hast a hut.
Transparent fire of palm leaves:
a man invokes thee without fear.
Fire of the sorcerers, thy father, where is he?
Thy mother, where is she?
Who has fed thee?
Thou art thy father, thou art thy mother,
Thou passest and leavest no trace.
Dry wood does not engender thee,
thou hast not cinders for daughters.
Thou diest and diest not.
The errant soul turns into thee, and no one
knows it.
Fire of the sorcerers, Spirit
of the waters below and the air above.
Fire that shinest, glowworm that lightest up
the swamp.
Bird without wings, thing without body, Spirit
of the Force of Fire.
Hear my voice:
a man invokes thee
without fear.

(134)

1700: Madrid

Penumbra of Autumn

He could never dress himself alone, or read fluently, or stand up by himself. At forty, a little old man without descendants, he lies dying surrounded by confessors, exorcists, courtiers, and ambassadors who dispute the throne.

The doctors, defeated, have removed the newly dead doves and the sheep's entrails from on top of him. Leeches no longer cover his body. They are not giving him rum to drink or the water of life brought from Malaga, because nothing is left but to wait for the convulsion that will tear him from the world. By the light of torches a bleeding Christ at the head of the bed presides over the final ceremony. The cardinal sprinkles holy water from the hyssop. The bedchamber smells of wax, of incense, of filth. The wind beats at the shutters of the palace, badly fastened with cord.

They will take him to the Escorial morgue, where the marble coffin with his name on it has awaited him for years. That was his favorite journey, but it is some time since he visited his own tomb or even stuck his nose outside. Madrid is full of potholes and garbage and armed vagabonds; and the soldiers, who keep alive on the thin soup of the monasteries, do not put themselves out to defend the king. The last times that he dared to go out, the Manzanares washerwomen and the street urchins ran after the carriage and hurled insults and stones at it.

Charles II, his bulging eyes red, trembles and raves. He is a small piece of yellow flesh that runs out beneath the sheets as the century also runs out, and so ends the dynasty that conquered America.

(201 and 211)

(End of the first volume of
Memory of Fire)

The Sources

1. Abbad y Lasierra, Augustín Iñigo. *Historia geográfica civil y natural de la isla de San Juan Bautista de Puerto Rico*. Río Piedras: Universidad, 1979.
2. Acosta Saignes, Miguel. *Vida de los esclavos negros en Venezuela*. Havana: Casa de las Américas, 1978.
3. Acuña, René, *Introducción al estudio del Rabinal Achí*. Mexico City: UNAM, 1975.
4. Aguirre Beltrán, Gonzalo. *Medicina y magia: El proceso de aculturación en la estructura colonial*. Mexico City: Instituto Nacional Indigenista, 1980.
5. Alegría, Fernando. *Lautaro, joven libertador de Arauco*. Santiago de Chile: Zig-Zag, 1978.
6. Alemán, Mateo. *Guzmán de Alfarache* (Benito Brancaforte, ed.). Madrid: Cátedra, 1979.
7. Alonso, Dámaso. *Cancionero y romancero español*. Estella: Salvat, 1970.
8. Alvarado, Pedro de. *Cartas de relación*, BAE, Vol. XXII. Madrid: M. Rivadeneyra, 1863.
9. Álvarez Lejarza, Emilio. *El Güegüence*, Managua, Distribuidora Cultural, 1977.
10. Amaral, Álvaro do. *O Padre José de Anchieta e a fundação de São Paulo*. São Paulo: Secretaría de Cultura, 1971.
11. Arciniegas, Germán. *Biografía del Caribe*. Buenos Aires: Sudamericana, 1951.
12. ———. *Amerigo y el Nuevo Mundo*. Mexico: Hermes, 1955.
13. ———. *El Caballero de El Dorado*. Madrid: Revista de Occidente, 1969.
14. Arguedas, José María. *Dioses y hombres de Huarochirí* (includes text by Pierre Duviols). Mexico: Siglo XXI, 1975.
15. ——— (with F. Izquierdo). *Mitos, leyendas y cuentos peruanos*. Lima: Casa de la Cultura, 1970.
16. Arias de la Canal, Fredo. *Intento de psicoanálisis de Juana Inés*. Mexico City: Frente de Afirmación Hispanista, 1972.
17. Armellada, Cesáreo de, and Carmela Bentivenga de Napolitano. *Literaturas indígenas venezolanas*. Caracas: Monte Ávila, 1975.
18. Arrom, José Juan. *El teatro hispanoamericano en la época colonial*. Havana: Anuario Bibliográfico Cubano, 1956.
19. ———. *Certidumbre de América*. Havana: Anuario Bibliográfico Cubano, 1959.
20. Arteche, José de. *Elcano*. Madrid: Espasa-Calpe, 1972.
21. Arzáns de Orsúa y Vela, Bartolomé. *Historia de la Villa Imperial*

de Potosí (Lewis Hanke and Gunnar Mendoza, eds.). Providence: Brown University Press, 1965.

22. Asturias, Miguel Ángel. *Leyendas de Guatemala*. Madrid: Salvat, 1970.

23. Balboa, Silvestre de. *Espejo de paciencia* (prologue by Cintio Vitier). Havana: Arte y Literatura, 1975.

24. Ballesteros Gaibrois, Manuel. *Vida y obra de fray Bernadino de Sahagún*. León: Inst. Sahagún, 1973.

25. Barrera Vázquez, Alfredo, and Silvia Rendón. *El Libro de los Libros de Chilam Balam*. Mexico: Fondo de Cultura Económica, 1978.

26. Bascuñán, Francisco Núñez de Pineda y. *Cautiverio feliz*. Santiago de Chile: Editorial Universitaria, 1973.

27. Bataillon, Marcel, and André Saint-Lu. *El Padre Las Casas y la defensa de los indios*. Barcelona: Ariel, 1976.

28. Benítez, Fernando. *Los primeros mexicanos: La vida criolla en el siglo XVI*. Mexico: Era, 1962.

29. ———. *La ruta de Hernán Cortés*. Mexico City: FCE, 1974.

30. ———. *Los indios de México*, Vol. V. Mexico City: Era, 1980.

31. Bowser, Frederick P. *El esclavo africano en el Perú colonial (1524–1650)*. Mexico City: Siglo XXI, 1977.

32. Boxer, C. R. *Race Relations in the Portuguese Colonial Empire (1415–1825)*. Oxford: Clarendon, 1963.

33. ———. *The Golden Age of Brazil (1695–1750)*. Berkeley: University of California, 1969.

34. Boyer, Paul, and Stephen Nissenbaum. *Salem Possessed: The Social Origins of Witchcraft*. Cambridge, Mass.: Harvard University, 1978.

35. Breen, T. H. *Puritans and Adventurers: Change and Persistence in Early America*. New York and Oxford: Oxford University, 1980.

36. Bridenbaugh, Carl. *Jamestown 1544–1699*. New York and Oxford: Oxford University, 1980.

37. Bruchac, Joseph. *Stone Giants and Flying Heads*. Trumansburg, N.Y.: Crossing, 1979.

38. Buarque de Holanda, Sergio. "A época colonial" in *História Geral da Civilização Brasileira (I)*. Rio de Janeiro and São Paulo: Difel, 1977.

39. Cabeza de Vaca, Álvar Núñez. *Naufragios y comentarios*. Madrid: Espasa-Calpe, 1971.

40. Cadogan, Leon. *La literatura de los guaraníes*. Mexico City: Joaquín Mortiz, 1965.

41. Carande, Ramón. *Carlos V y sus banqueros*. Barcelona: Crítica, 1977.

42. Cardenal, Ernesto. *Antología de poesía primitiva*. Madrid: Alianza, 1979.

43. Carneiro, Edison. *O quilombo dos Palmares*. Rio de Janeiro: Civ-ilização Brasileira, 1966.
44. Carpentier, Alejo. *El arpa y la sombra*. Madrid: Siglo XXI, 1979.
45. Carvajal, Gaspar de. *Relación del nuevo descubrimiento del famoso río Grande de las Amazonas*. Mexico City: FCE, 1955.
46. Cervantes Saavedra, Miguel de. *El ingenioso hidalgo don Quijote de la Mancha*. Barcelona: Sopena, 1978.
47. Chacón Torres, Mario. *Arte virreinal en Potosí*. Seville: Escuela de Estudios Hispanoamericanos, 1973.
48. Chang-Rodríguez, Raquel. *Prosa hispanoamericana virreinal* (includes text by Mogrovejo de la Cerda). Barcelona: Hispam, 1978.
49. Chávez, Ezequiel A. *Ensayo de psicología de Sor Juana Inés de la Cruz*. Barcelona: Araluce, 1931.
50. Cieza de León, Pedro de. *La crónica del Perú*, BAE, Vol. XXVI. Madrid: M. Rivadeneyra, 1879.
51. Civrieux, Marc de. *Watunna: Mitología makiritare*. Caracas: Monte Ávila, 1970.
52. Colón, Cristóbal. *Diario del descubrimiento* (with notes by Manuel Alvar). Las Palmas: Cabildo de Gran Canaria, 1976.
53. ———. *Los cuatro viajes del Almirante y su testamento*. Madrid: Espasa-Calpe, 1977.
54. Cora, María Manuela de. *Kuai-Mare: Mitos aborígenes de Venezuela*. Caracas: Monte Ávila, 1972.
55. Corona Núñez, José. *Mitología tarasca*. Mexico: FCE, 1957.
56. Cortés, Hernán. *Cartas de relación*, BAE, Vol. XXII. Madrid: M. Rivadeneyra, 1863.
57. Cossío del Pomar, Felipe. *El mundo de los incas*. Mexico: FCE, 1975.
58. Cruz, Juana Inés de la. *Páginas escogidas* (Fina García Murruz, ed.). Havana: Casa de las Américas, 1978.
59. D'Ans, André Marcel. *La verdadera Biblia de los cashinahua*. Lima: Mosca Azul, 1975.
60. Davies, Nigel. *Los aztecas*. Barcelona: Destino, 1977.
61. Deschamps, Hubert. *Piratas y filibusteros*. Barcelona: Salvat, 1956.
62. Díaz del Castillo, Bernal. *Verdadera historia de los sucesos de la conquista de la Nueva España*, BAE, Vol. XXVI. Madrid: M. Rivadeneyra, 1879.
63. Di Nola, Alfonso M. *Canti erotici dei primitivi*. Rome: Lato Side, 1980.
64. Elliott, J. H. *La España imperial*. Barcelona: V. Vices, 1978.
65. Exquemelin, Alexandre O. *Piratas de América*. Barcelona: Barral, n.d.
66. Eyzaguirre, Jaime. *Historia de Chile*. Santiago: Zig-Zag, 1977.

67. ———. *Ventura de Pedro de Valdivia.* Madrid: Espasa-Calpe, 1967.
68. Franco, José Luciano. *La diáspora africana en el Nuevo Mundo.* Havana: Ciencias Sociales, 1975.
69. Freitas, Decio. *Palmares, la guerrilla negra.* Montevideo: Nuestra América, 1971.
70. Friede, Juan. *Bartolomé de las Casas: precursor del anticolonialismo.* Mexico: Siglo XXI, 1976.
71. Fuentes y Guzmán, Francisco Antonio de. *Obras históricas.* Madrid: BAE, 1969 and 1972.
72. Gage, Thomas. *Viajes en la Nueva España,* Havana: Casa de las Américas, 1980.
73. Gandía, Enrique de. *Indios y conquistadores en el Paraguay.* Buenos Aires: García Santos, 1932.
74. ———. *Historia de la conquista del río de la Plata y del Paraguay (1535–1556).* Buenos Aires: García Santos, 1932.
75. Garcés, Jesús Juan. *Vida y poesía de Sor Juana Inés de la Cruz.* Madrid: Cultura Hispánica, 1953.
76. Garcilaso de la Vega, Inca. *Comentarios reales de los incas.* Madrid: BAE, 1960.
77. Garibay K., Ángel María (ed.). *Poesía indígena de la altiplanicie.* Mexico: UNAM, 1972.
78. Gerbi, Antonello. *La naturaleza de las Indias Nuevas.* Mexico City: FCE, 1978.
79. Gibson, Charles. *Los aztecas bajo el dominio español (1519–1810).* Mexico City: Siglo XXI, 1977.
80. Godoy, Diego. *Relación a Hernán Cortés,* BAE, Vol. XXII. Madrid: M. Rivadeneyra, 1863.
81. Gómara, Francisco López de. *Primera y segunda parte de la Historia General de las Indias,* BAE, Vol. XXII. Madrid: M. Rivadeneyra, 1863.
82. Gómez Luaces, Eduardo. *Historia de Nuestra Señora de Regla* (booklet). Havana: Valcayo, 1945.
83. Gortari, Eli de. *La ciencia en la historia de México.* Mexico City: FCE, 1963.
84. Gow, Rosalind, and Bernabé Condori. *Kay Pacha.* Cuzco: Centro de Estudios Rurales Andinos, 1976.
85. Graham, R. B. Cunningham. *Pedro de Valdivia.* Buenos Aires: Inter-Americana, 1943.
86. Granada, Daniel. *Supersticiones del río de la Plata.* Buenos Aires: Guillermo Kraft, 1947.
87. Gridley, Marion E. *The Story of the Haida.* New York: Putnam's, 1972.
88. Hackett, Charles Wilson. "The Revolt of the Pueblo Indians of New

Mexico in 1680," *Quarterly of the Texas State Historical Association*, Vol. XV, No. 2, October 1911.

89. Hammond, George P., and Agapito Rey. *The Rediscovery of New Mexico (1580–1594)*. Albuquerque: University of New Mexico, 1966.

90. Hanke, Lewis. *Bartolomé de las Casas*. Buenos Aires: EUDEBA, 1968.

91. Harris, Olivia, and Kate Young (eds.). *Antropología y feminismo*. Barcelona: Anagrama, 1979.

92. Henestrosa, Andrés. *Los hombres que dispersó la danza*. Havana: Casa de las Américas, 1980.

93. Hernández Sánchez-Barba, M. *Historia de América*. Madrid: Alhambra, 1981.

94. Jara, Álvaro. *Guerra y sociedad en Chile*. Santiago de Chile: Editorial Universitaria, 1961.

95. ———. "Estructuras coloniales y subdesarrollo en Hispanoamérica," *Journal de la Société des Américanistes*, Vol. LXV. Paris, 1978.

96. Jerez, Francisco de. *Verdadera relación de la conquista del Perú y provincia del Cuzco*, BAE, Vol. XXVI. Madrid: M. Rivadeneyra, 1879.

97. Kirkpatrick, F. A. *Los conquistadores españoles*. Madrid: Espasa-Calpe, 1970.

98. Konetzke, Richard. *América Latina (II): La época colonial*. Madrid: Siglo XXI, 1978.

99. ———. *Descubridores y conquistadores de América*. Madrid: Gredos, 1968.

100. Krickeberg, Walter. *Mitos y leyendas de los aztecas, incas, mayas y muiscas*. Mexico City: FCE, 1971.

101. Labat, Jean-Baptiste. *Viajes a las islas de la América* (Francisco de Oraá, ed.). Havana: Casa de las Américas, 1979.

102. Las Casas, Bartolomé de. *Brevísima relación de la destrucción de las Indias*. Barcelona: Fontamara, 1979.

103. ———. *Historia de las Indias*. Mexico City: FCE, 1951.

104. ———. *Apologética historia de las Indias*. Mexico City: UNAM, 1967.

105. Lafone Quevedo, Samuel A. "El culto de Tonapa" in Valera Santillán and Santacruz Pachacuti, *Tres relaciones de antigüedades peruanas*. Asunción: Guarania, 1950.

106. Leal, Rine. *La selva oscura*. Havana: Arte y Literatura, 1975.

107. León-Portilla, Miguel. *El reverso de la Conquista. Relaciones aztecas, mayas e incas*. Mexico City: Joaquín Mortiz, 1964.

108. ———. *Los antiguos mexicanos*. Mexico City: FCE, 1977.

109. ———. *Culturas en peligro*. Mexico City: Alianza Editorial Mexicana, 1976.

110. ———. *La filosofía náhuatl*. Mexico City: UNAM, 1958.
111. Lévi-Strauss, Claude. *Lo crudo y lo cocido (Mitológicas, I)*. Mexico City: FCE, 1978.
112. ———. *De la miel a las cenizas (Mitológicas, II)*. Mexico City: FCE, 1978.
113. ———. *El origen de las maneras de mesa (Mitológicas, III)*. Mexico City: Siglo XXI, 1976.
114. ———. *El hombre desnudo (Mitológicas, IV)*. Mexico City: Siglo XXI, 1976.
115. Lewin, Boleslao. *La Inquisición en Hispanoamérica*. Buenos Aires: Proyección, 1962.
116. Lewis, D. B. Wyndham. *Carlos de Europa, emperador de Occidente*. Madrid: Espasa-Calpe, 1962.
117. Leydi, Roberto, Arrigo Polillo, and Tommaso Giglio. *Piratas, corsarios y filibusteros*. Barcelona: Maucci, 1961.
118. Lipschutz, Alejandro. *El problema racial en la conquista de América*. Mexico City: Siglo XXI, 1975.
119. ———. *Perfil de Indoamérica de nuestro tiempo*. Santiago de Chile: Andrés Bello, 1968.
120. Lockhart, James, and Enrique Orte. *Letters and People of the Spanish Indies: The Sixteenth Century*. Cambridge: Cambridge University Press, 1976.
121. Lohmann Villena, Guillermo. *El conde de Lemos, virrey del Perú*. Madrid: Escuela de Estudios Hispanoamericanos, 1946.
122. ———. *El arte dramático en Lima durante el Virreinato*. Madrid: Escuela de Estudios Hispanoamericanos, 1945.
123. López, Casto Fulgencio. *Lope de Aguirre, el Peregrino*. Barcelona: Plon, 1977.
124. López-Baralt, Mercedes. "Guamán Poma de Ayala y el arte de la memoria en una crónica ilustrada del siglo XVII," *Cuadernos Americanos*. Mexico City: May–June 1979.
125. ———. "La crónica de Indias como texto cultural: policulturalidad y articulación de códigos semióticos multiples en el arte de reinar de Guamán Poma de Ayala" (unpublished manuscript).
126. ———. *El mito taíno: Raíz y proyecciones en la Amazonia continental*. Río Piedras: Huracán, 1976.
127. Mannix, Daniel P., and M. Cowley. *Historia de la trata de negros*. Madrid: Alianza, 1970.
128. Marañón, Gregorio. *El conde-duque de Olivares (La pasión de mandar)*. Madrid: Espasa-Calpe, 1936.
129. Marchant, Alexander. *From Barter to Slavery*. Baltimore: Johns Hopkins, 1942.
130. Mariño de Lobera, Pedro. *Crónica del Reino de Chile*. Santiago de Chile: Editorial Universitaria, 1979.

131. Marmolejo, Lucio. *Efemérides guanajuatenses,* Vol. I. Guanajuato: Universidad, 1967.

132. Marriott, Alice, and Carol K. Rachlin. *American Indian Mythology.* New York: Apollo, 1968.

133. Martínez, José Luis. *El mundo antiguo, VI: América antigua.* Mexico City: Secretaría de Educación, 1976.

134. Martínez Fivee, Rogelio (ed.). *Poesía anónima africana.* Madrid: Miguel Castellote, n.d.

135. Martínez Peláez, Severo. *La patria del criollo.* San José, Costa Rica: EDUCA, 1973.

136. McLuhan, T. C. (ed.). *Touch the Earth (A Self-portrait of Indian Existence).* New York: Simon and Schuster, 1971.

137. Medina, José Toribio. *Historia del Tribunal de la Inquisición de Lima (1569–1820).* Santiago de Chile: Fondo Histórico y Bibliográfico J.T. Medina, 1956.

138. ———. *Historia del Tribunal del Santo Oficio de la Inquisición en Chile.* Santiago: Fondo J.T. Medina, 1952.

139. ———. *Historia del Tribunal del Santo Oficio de la Inquisición en México.* Santiago: Elzeviriana, 1905.

140. ———. *El Tribunal del Santo Oficio de la Inquisición en las provincias del Plata.* Santiago: Elzeviriana, 1900.

141. Méndez Pereira, Octavio. *Núñez de Balboa.* Madrid: Espasa-Calpe, 1975.

142. Mendoza, Diego de. *Chronica de la Provincia de S. Antonio de los Charcas.* . . . Madrid: n.p., 1664.

143. Montoya, Antonio Ruiz de. *Conquista espiritual hecha por los religiosos de la Compañía de Jesús en las provincias del Paraguay, Paraná, Uruguay y Tape,* Bilbao: El Mensajero, 1892.

144. Morales, Ernesto. *Leyendas guaraníes.* Buenos Aires: El Ateneo, 1929.

145. Morales Padrón, Francisco. *Jamaica española.* Seville: Escuela de Estudios Hispanoamericanos, 1952.

146. More, Thomas. *Utopía* (bilingual edition with introduction by Joaquim Mallafré Gabaldá). Barcelona: Bosch, 1977.

147. Mörner, Magnus. *Historia social latinoamericana (Nuevos enfoques).* Caracas: Universidad Católica Andrés Bello, 1979.

148. ———. *La Corona española y los foráneos en los pueblos de indios de América.* Stockholm. Instituto de Estudios Ibero-Americanos, 1970.

149. Mousnier, Roland. *Historia general de las civilizaciones.* Los siglos XVI y XVII. Barcelona: Destino, 1974.

150. Murra, John V. *La organización económica del Estado inca.* Mexico City: Siglo XXI, 1978.

151. ———. *Formaciones económicas y políticas del mundo andino.* Lima: Instituto de Estudios Peruanos, 1975.

152. Nabokov, Peter (ed.). *Native American Testimony*. New York: Harper and Row, 1978.
153. Nash, Gary B. *Red, White, and Black: The Peoples of Early America*. Englewood Cliffs, N.J.: Prentice-Hall, 1974.
154. Nebrija, Elio Antonio de. *Vocabulario español-latino* (facsimile ed.). Madrid: Real Academia Española, 1951.
155. Oberem, Udo. "Notas y documentos sobre miembros de la familia del Inca Atahualpa en el siglo XVI," *Estudios etno-históricos del Ecuador*, Casa de la Cultura Ecuatoriana, Núcleo del Guayas, 1976.
156. ———. *Los quijos*. Otavalo: Instituto Otavaleño de Antropología, 1980.
157. Ocaña, Diego de. *Un viaje fascinante por la América hispana del siglo XVI* (annotated by Fray Arturo Alvarez). Madrid: Studium, 1969.
158. Oliva de Coll, Josefina. *La resistencia indígena ante la conquista*. Mexico City: Siglo XXI, 1974.
159. Ortiz, Fernando. *Contrapunteo cubano del tabaco y el azúcar*. Havana: Consejo Nacional de Cultura, 1963.
160. ———. *Los negros esclavos*. Havana: Ciencias Sociales, 1975.
161. ———. *Historia de una pelea cubana contra los demonios*. Havana: Ciencias Sociales, 1975.
162. Ortiz Rescaniere, Alejandro. *De Adaneva a Inkarrí*. Lima: Retablo de Papel, 1973.
163. Otero, Gustavo Adolfo. *La vida social del coloniaje*. La Paz: La Paz, 1942.
164. Otero Silva, Miguel. *Lope de Aguirre, príncipe de la libertad*. Barcelona: Seix Barral, 1979.
165. Oviedo y Baños, José de. *Los Bélzares: El tirano Aguirre. Diego de Losada*. Caracas: Monte Avila, 1972.
166. Oviedo y Valdés, Gonzalo Fernández de. *Historia general y natural de las Indias*. Madrid: Real Academia de la Historia, 1851.
167. Palma, Ricardo. *Tradiciones peruanas* (1st and 2nd ed.). Buenos Aires: Espasa-Calpe, 1938 and 1940.
168. Pané, Ramón. *Relación acerca de las antigüedades de los indios* (José Juan Arrom, ed.). Mexico City: Siglo XXI, 1974.
169. Parry, J.H., and Philip Sherlock. *Historia de las Antillas*. Buenos Aires: Kapelusz, 1976.
170. Paz, Ramón. *Mitos, leyendas y cuentos guajiros*. Caracas: Instituto Agrario Nacional, 1972.
171. Peixoto, Afranio. *Breviario da Bahía*. Rio de Janeiro: Agir, 1945.
172. Pereira Salas, Eugenio. *Apuntes para la historia de la cocina chilena*. Santiago de Chile: Editorial Universitaria, 1977.
173. ———. *Juegos y alegrías coloniales en Chile*. Santiago: Zig-Zag, 1947.

174. Péret, Benjamin. *Anthologie des mythes, légendes et contes populaires d'Amérique.* Paris: Albin Michel, 1960.
175. Pérez Embid, Florentino. *Diego de Ordás, compañero de Cortés y explorador del Orinoco.* Seville: Escuela de Estudios Hispanoamericanos, 1950.
176. Phelan, John Leddy. *The Kingdom of Quito in the Seventeenth Century.* Madison: University of Wisconsin, 1967.
177. ———. *The Millennial Kingdom of the Franciscans in the New World.* Berkeley: University of California, 1970.
178. Plath, Oreste. *Geografía del mito y la leyenda chilenos.* Santiago de Chile: Nascimento, 1973.
179. Poma de Ayala, Felipe Guamán. *Nueva corónica y buen gobierno* (facsimile ed.). Paris: Institut d'Ethnologie, 1936.
180. Portigliotti, Giuseppe. *Los Borgia.* Madrid: J. Gil, 1936.
181. Portuondo, Fernando. *El segundo viaje del descubrimiento* (letters of Michele de Cúneo and Alvarez Chanca). Havana: Ciencias Sociales, 1977.
182. Prado, Juan José. *Leyendas y tradiciones guanajuatenses.* Guanajuato: Prado Hnos., 1953.
183. Quevedo, Francisco de. *Obras completas.* Madrid: Aguilar, 1974.
184. Quintana, Manuel J. *Los conquistadores.* Buenos Aires: Suma, 1945.
185. ———. *Vida de Francisco Pizarro.* Madrid: Espasa-Calpe, 1959.
186. Ramos Smith, Maya. *La danza en México durante la época colonial.* Havana: Casa de las Américas, 1979.
187. Real, Cristóbal. *El corsario Drake y el imperio español.* Madrid: Editora Nacional, n.d.
188. Recinos, Adrián (ed.). *Popol Vuh. Las antiguas historias del Quiché.* Mexico City: FCE, 1976.
189. Reichel-Dolmatoff, Gerardo and Alicia. *Estudios antropológicos.* Bogotá: Inst. Colombiano de Cultura, 1977.
190. Reyes, Alfonso. *Medallones.* Buenos Aires: Espasa-Calpe, 1952.
191. Rivet, Paul. *Etnographie ancienne de l'Équateur.* Paris: Gauthier-Villars, 1912.
192. Roa Bastos, Augusto (ed.). *Las culturas condenadas.* Mexico City: Siglo XXI, 1978.
193. Rodrigues, Nina. *Os africanos no Brasil.* São Paulo: Cía. Editora Nacional, 1977.
194. Rodríguez Fresle, Juan. *El carnero de Bogotá,* Bogotá: Ed. Colombia, 1926.
195. Rodríguez Marín, Francisco. *El Quijote: Don Quijote en América.* Madrid: Hernando, 1911.
196. ———. *Cantos populares españoles.* Seville: Alvarez, 1882–83.
197. Rothenberg, Jerome. *Shaking the Pumpkin: Traditional Poetry of the Indians of North America.* Garden City, N.Y.: Doubleday, 1972.

198. Rowse, A.L. *The England of Elizabeth*. London: Cardinal, 1973.
199. Rubio Mañé, J. Ignacio. *Introducción al estudio de los virreyes de Nueva España (1535–1746)*. Mexico City: UNAM, 1959.
200. Sahagún, Bernardino de. *Historia general de las cosas de la Nueva España* (annotated by Ángel Ma. Garibay K.). Mexico City: Porrúa, 1969.
201. Salas, Horacio. *La España barroca*, Madrid: Altalena, 1978.
202. Salazar Bondy, Sebastián (ed.). *Poesía quechua*. Montevideo; Arca, 1978.
203. Sapper, Karl. "El infierno de Masaya" in *Nicaragua en los cronistas de Indias* (anthology). Managua: Banco de América, 1975.
204. Segal, Charles M., and David C. Stineback. *Puritans, Indians and Manifest Destiny*. New York: Putnam's, 1977.
205. Sejourné, Laurette. *América Latina, I: Antiguas culturas precolombinas*. Madrid: Siglo XXI, 1978.
206. ———. *Pensamiento y religión en el México antiguo*. Mexico City: FCE, 1957.
207. Sheehan, Bernard. *Savagism and Civility*. Cambridge: Cambridge University, 1980.
208. Sodi, Demetrio. *La literatura de los mayas*. Mexico City: Mortiz, 1964.
209. Teitelboim, Volodia. *El amanecer del capitalismo y la conquista de América*. Havana: Casa de las Américas, 1979.
210. Tibón, Gutierre. *Historia del nombre y de la fundación de México*. Mexico City: FCE, 1975.
211. Tizón, Héctor. *La España borbónica*. Madrid: Altalena, 1978.
212. Toscano, Salvador. *Cuauhtémoc*. Mexico City: FCE, 1975.
213. Valle-Arizpe, Artemio de. *Historia de la ciudad de México según los relatos de sus cronistas*. Mexico City: Jus, 1977.
214. Vargas, José María. *Historia del Ecuador: Siglo XVI*. Quito: Universidad Católica, 1977.
215. ——— (ed.). *Arte colonial de Ecuador*. Quito: Salvat Ecuatoriana, 1977.
216. Velasco, Salvador. *San Martín de Porres*. Villava: Ope, 1962.
217. Vianna, Helio. *História do Brasil*. São Paulo: Melhoramentos, 1980.
218. Vicens Vives, J. (ed.). *Historia de España y América*. Barcelona: Vicens Vives, 1977.
219. Von Hagen, Víctor W. *El mundo de los mayas*. Mexico City: Diana, 1968.
220. ———. *Culturas preincaicas*. Madrid: Guadarrama, 1976.
221. Wachtel, Nathan. *Los vencidos: Los indios del Perú frente a la conquista española (1530–1570)*. Madrid: Alianza, 1976.
222. Wallace, Anthony F.C. "Dreams and the Wishes of the Soul: A Type

of Psychoanalytic Theory Among the Seventeenth-Century Iroquois," *The American Anthropologist*, Vol. 60, No. 2, 1958.

223. Watt, Montgomery. *Historia de la España islámica*. Madrid: Alianza, 1970.

224. Williams, Eric. *Capitalismo y esclavitud*. Buenos Aires: Siglo XX, 1973.

225. Wolf, Eric. *Pueblos y culturas de Mesoamérica*. Mexico City: Era, 1975.

226. Zavala, Silvio. *El mundo americano en la época colonial*. Mexico City: Porrúa, 1967.

227. ————. *Ideario de Vasco de Quiroga*. Mexico City: El Colegio de México, 1941.

Index

Accra, 261
Achocalla, 205
Acla, 62–63
Ácoma, 156
Ácoma Indians, 157
Adamarca River, 89
Adario, Chief, 269
Agüeynaba, Chief, 55–56
Aguirre, Francisco de, 102
Aguirre, Lope de, 133, 134–37
Alagoas, 175, 241
Albuquerque, Rodrigo de, 164, 165
Alemán, Mateo, 179
Alexander VI, Pope, 47–48
Alfinger, Ambrosio, 81
Alfonso the Wise, 181
Algiers, 93, 163
Algonquin Indians, 269
the Alhambra, 53
Almagro, Diego de, 91, 107, 114
Altamirano, Bishop, 178–79
Alvarado, Miguel de, 131
Alvarado, Pedro de, 77, 78, 91–92, 102–3, 150, 215
Álvarez, Alonso, 146
Álvar the Miracle Worker: see Cabeza de Vaca, Álvar Núñez
Amazon jungle, 14, 75, 171
Amazon River, 105, 133, 134
the Amazons, 105
Amonio, 200–201
Amsterdam, 207
Anchieta, José de, 161–62
Andalusia, 48, 58
Andrés, Father, 59
Angola, 242, 276
Angolan people, 233
Angulo, Isabel de, 161
Anne, St., 193
Anthony, St., 194

the Antilles, 50, 138, 244, 252, 253, 277
Antwerp, 61
Aranda, Pedro, 277
Araucanian Indians, 101, 119, 120, 126, 127, 128, 138, 169, 176, 181, 208–12, 232
Arauco Fortress, 138
Archidona, 151
Arda people, 233
Arequipa, 177, 205
Arias de Avila, Pedro, 62–63
Arica, 172, 177
Arobe, Francisco de, 168
Arotirene, 275
Arzáns de Orsúa y Vela, Bartolomé, 164, 230
Asmodeo, 199–201
Asunción, 124, 125, 152
Atahualpa, Alonso, 159
Atahualpa, Francisco, 152, 158–59
Atahualpa, Inca, 87–88, 89–90, 92
Augustine, St., 59, 271
Avila, Alonso de, 96, 143
Avila, Francisco de, 181, 226
Avila Mountains, 144
Ayamonte, Pedro de, 254
Aylmer, John, 220
Aymaco, 56
Azande Indians, 274
Aztec Indians, 5, 19, 40–41, 48, 54–55, 63, 67, 68, 69, 70, 79, 130, 237

Babalú, 194
Bacon, Francis, 153
Bad Luck Island, 82, 97
Balboa, Silvestre de, 178–79
Balboa, Vasco: see Núñez de Balboa, Vasco

Balsalobre, Gonzalo de, 237
Bantu people, 276, 281
Barbados, 244, 252, 253
Barbara, St., 193, 194
Barcelona, 46, 92
Barquisimeto, 118, 136
Beatriz (Alvarado's wife), 103–4
Becerrillo (dog), 56, 58
Bellavista Hill, 271
Benalcázar, Sebastián de, 92, 99–100
Berkeley, William, 255
Bernal, Lorenzo, 138
Beto (Indian priest), 151, 152
Bezerra, Bartolomeu, 175
Bío-Bío River, 169, 176, 209
Board of Theologians, 227–28
Bogotá, 139
Bogotá, Valley of, 99
Boleyn, Anne, 153
Bonda, 170
Bopé-joku, 32
Borgia, Rodrigo, 47–48
Bororo Indians, 32
Bosch, Hieronymus, 62
Botoque, 21–22
Bouriau (plantation owner), 256–57
Bravo, Francisco, 212–13
Brazil, 161–62, 175, 194, 225, 227, 232, 273–74, 275, 276, 279
Brussels, 70
Buenos Aires, 124, 152, 273
Bullocke, James, 255
Buría mines, 118
Buritaca, 170

Cabeza de Vaca, Álvar Núñez, 82, 97, 104, 106
Cabot, Sebastian, 152
Cabrera, Alonso, 152
Cabrera, Nuño de, 125
Cacaria, 189
Cachapoal River, 101
Cádiz, 104, 228

Caeté Indians, 241
Cáicihu, Chief, 41
Cajamarca, 87, 88, 89
Cakchiquele Indians, 12, 78
Calderón, Francisca de, 179
Campeche, 107
Campo y Espinoza, Alonso de, 248
Cañaribamba, 159
Cañete, 127
Cañete, Marquis of, 136
Cangas, 278
Caonabó, 50–51
Cápac Huanca Pariacaca, 181
Cap Français, 277
Caracas, 144
Carducci (engineer), 227
Carib Indians, 38
Caricari, Lake, 205
Carirí Indians, 29
Carrilho, Fernão, 257
Cartagena, 139, 277
Carvajal, Francisco, 108–9, 113–14, 115
Cashinahua Indians, 7, 8–9
Castellflorit, duke of, 278
Castillo, Alonso del, 97
Castillo, Bartolomé del, 262
Castillo, Blas de, 101
Castillo, María del, 213–14
Castro del Río, 163
Cataguaz Indians, 279
Catherine, St., 223
Cauillaca, 21
Caupolicán, Chief, 119, 127, 128
Cauri, 158
Cempoala, 64
Centeno, Diego, 113
Centurión, Domingo, 243
Cervantes, Miguel de, 163, 185
Chaco, 75
Chagres River, 168
Chapman, George, 182
Chapultepec, 66, 67, 77
Charlemagne, 62

Charles II, king of England, 252
Charles II, king of Spain, 243, 265, 278, 282
Charles V, Holy Roman Emperor, 62, 70, 81, 88, 92–94, 123, 129, 130
Chaves, Diego de, 131
Chengue, 170
Chiapas, 108, 110, 206
Chibcha Indians, 99, 100
Chilam Balam, 42
Chile, 75, 101, 111, 113, 116, 119, 126, 169, 178, 208, 211
Chilipirco mountain, 127
Chillán, 208
Chiloé Island, 31
Chinchón, Count, 213, 214
Choco Indians, 14
Chonea, 170
Chontal Indians, 19
Choquenca, 170
Cibao, 50
Cíbola, 103, 156, 259
Ciénaga, 170
Cinto, 170
Cisneros, Archbishop, 52, 53
Cisneros, Bernardo, 189
Claudia the Witch, 254
Cloud, 5
Cohuixco Indians, 237
Colbert, Jean-Baptiste, 247
Colhuacan, 132
Columbus, Bartholomew, 51
Columbus, Christopher, 45–47, 48, 49, 50, 51–52, 53, 54, 63, 72, 106
Columbus, Diego, 72
Comanche Indians, 23
Cominca, 170
Company of Guinea, 261
Company of Royal Adventurers, 252
Company of Senegal, 261
Company of the West Indies (Holland), 261
Company of the West Indies

(Denmark), 261–62
Concepción, 138
Concepción convent, 214
Coniraya, 21
Conlapayara, 105
Connecticut, 221, 255
Constantinople, 93
Copacabana, 154
Copernicus, Nicolaus, 261
Córdoba, 180, 224
Coro, 99
Corona, Mateo de la, 131
Coronado, Francisco: see Vázquez de Coronado, Francisco
Cortés, Hernán, 64–65, 67–69, 70, 76, 79, 97, 130, 131, 145, 150
Cortés, Martín, 145
Cortés, Martín, marquis of the Valley of Oaxaca, 142–43, 145
Cotton, John, 221
Council of the Indies, 84, 143, 156, 218, 249, 262
Creole people, 204, 233
Criolla, Fabiana, 192–93
Crips, Major, 257
Cromwell, Oliver, 239
Cruz, Juana Inés de la, 238, 239–40, 245–46, 260, 266–68, 271–72
Cuareca, 58
Cuauhcapolca, 75
Cuauhtémoc, Emperor, 67, 71, 72, 79–80
Cuba, 57, 82, 178, 194, 207, 262, 265
Cubagua, 106
Cubilete mountain, 115
Cuchacique, Chief, 169, 170
Culiacán, 97
Cuneo, Miquele de, 49–50
Cuyes, 159
Cuzapa Valley, 140
Cuzco, 39, 49, 74, 88, 90, 91, 94, 96, 102, 110, 120, 122, 160, 173, 180, 182, 250

Dale, Thomas, 191
Dambrabanga, 275
Daodama, 170
Daona, 170
Dávila, Benito, 101
Delaware Indians, 243
Denmark, 261–62, 280
Desana Indians, 171
Dias, Henrique, 232–33
Díaz, Alonso, 136
Díaz del Castillo, Bernal, 65
Dibocaca, 170
Dieguillo (pirate), 219–20
D'Ogeron, Bertrand, 247
Domingo, 149
Donne, John, 182
Dorantes, Andrés, 97
Drake, Francis, 153
Ducasse, Jean-Baptiste, 277
Durama, 170
Dürer, Albrecht, 70
Dursino, 170
the Dutch, 207, 219–20, 225–26,
    232–33, 242, 243, 261

Elcano, Juan Sebastián de, 73
El Dorado, 99, 100, 104, 133, 162
Elegguá, 194
Elizabeth I, queen of England,
    138–39, 153
the English, 138–39, 261; see also
    London; specific colonies
Enríquez, Juan, 114
Enríquez, Pedro Luis, 161
Enríquez de Ribera, Payo, 240
Erasmus of Rotterdam, 181
Escobedo, Rodrigo de, 46
Esmeraldas River, 168
Españarrí, 148
Espejo, Antonio de, 156, 157
Espinhaço Mountains, 279
Espinosa Medrano, Juan de (Old
    Moley), 251
Esquivel, Diego de, 120, 121–23

Estebanico (black Arab), 97
Estefanía, 230–32
Estremadura, 58, 67
Explicatio Apologetica
    (Enríquez de Ribera), 240
Exú, 194

Federmann, Nicolás de, 99, 100
Ferdinand II of Aragon, 46, 47,
    51, 59
Fernández de Enciso, Martín,
    59–60
Fernández de Oviedo, Gonzalo, 57,
    60–61, 80, 98
Fernández de Santa Cruz, Manuel,
    266–68
First Father, 11, 12–13, 18
Florence, 53
Florida, 72, 82
Francisca (Alvarado's wife), 103
Franco, Miguel, 149
Frankfurt, 61
the French, 174, 227, 247, 261,
    277–78, 279
Frió, Cabo, 104
Függer (German banker), 62

Gabriel, archangel, 178
Gabriellino, 47
Gage, Thomas, 203, 204, 206,
    216–17, 219–20, 238–39
Gairaca, 170
Galileo, 261
Ganga Zumba, 258
Garay, Juan de, 152
García, Bartolomé, 124
García, Juana, 139–40
García Óñez de Loyola, Martín, 169
Garcilaso de la Vega, Inca, 180
Gasca, Pedro de, 112–13
General History of New Spain
    (Sahagún), 156
George, St., 194
the Germans, 62, 274, 261

Gibraltar, 247
Giron, Gilbert, 178, 179
Gluskabe, 5–6
González de Avila, Gil, 75
González de Cellorigo, Martín, 174
González de la Cruz, José,
    262–63, 264–66
González de Nájera, Alonso, 178
Good, Sarah, 270
Granada, 52
Griggs, William, 270
Guachaca, 170
Guahaba, 57
Guaicaipuro, 144
Guami (Indian priest), 151, 152
Guanahaní, 45
Guanajuato, 115, 149
Guápulo, 271
Guaraní Indians, 11, 18, 227
Guarao Indians, 52
Guarapari, 161
Guarinea, 170
Guatemala, 77, 91, 102, 103, 132,
    204, 212, 214, 216, 240
Guatemala City, 103
Guauravo River, 55
Guayrá, 227
Guerrero, Gonzalo, 96–97
Guevara, Isabel de, 124
Guillo, Diego, 219–20
Guinea, 138, 168
Guiomar, Queen, 118
Guyana, 162–63
Guzmán, Fernando de, 133, 134
Guzmán, Juan de, 217

Haida Indians, 8
Haiti, 26, 50, 51, 57, 246, 277–78
Hato del Cupey, 265
Hatuey, Chief, 57
Havana, 145, 159, 265
Hawkins, John, 138–39, 149
Helsingør, 280
Henry VIII, king of England, 153

Hernández, Alonso, 94
Hernández, Francisco, 237
Heyn, Piet, 207
History of the Indies (Las Casas),
    147
Hithloday, Rafael, 61
Holland: see the Dutch
Hopi Indians, 157
Huaina Cápac, 74–75
Huancavélica, 173
Huánuco, 185
Huaquechula, 69
Huarochirí, 34
Huáscar, 89
Huelén, 101
Huémac, 66, 67
Huexotzingo, 48, 70, 131–32, 156
Huexotzingo Indians, 70
Huitzilopochtli, 41, 71
Huron Indians, 233–34, 269

Iconology (Ripa), 176
Iglulik Indians, 16
Ignatius, St., 161, 169
Iguazú Mountains, 19
Iguazú River, 106
Imperial River, 210
Inca Indians, 39, 48, 54, 75, 87–90,
    93, 94, 96, 107, 141, 147, 180, 184
Inkarrí, 148
Innocent IV, Pope, 146
the Inquisition, 53, 137, 146–47,
    148–49, 155, 160–61, 179, 207,
    213, 217, 224, 237, 276, 278
Inuit Indians, 38
Irala, Governor, 124
Iroquois Indians, 233–36
Isabel (witch), 278
Isabella I of Castile, 46, 47, 51
Isidore, St., 59
Isidro, St., 195
Islam: see Muslims
Itapicurú River, 175
Izmachí forest, 40

Jalisco, 132
Jamaica, 81, 238, 239, 244, 248, 252, 253–54
James I, king of England, 190
Jamestown, 228
Janduim Indians, 273
Jerez de la Frontera, 220
Jeriboca, 170
Jerónimo, St., 193
Jesús, Mariana de, 229
Jews, 53, 217
Jiménez de Quesada, Gonzalo, 99, 100
Jirijara Indians, 118
John the Baptist, St., 194
Juana: see Cruz, Juana Inés de la
Juana I la Loca, 59
Juan Diego, 84
Juruá River, 36
Jurupari, 9

Kadiueu Indians, 13
Kalina Indians, 9
Kanaima, 38–39
Kayapó Indians, 21–22, 35
Kekchi Indians, 19
Kino, Eusebio Francisco, 261
Kumokums, 33

Labat, Jean-Baptiste, 279
La Concepción, 51
Lagares, Bartolomé de, 161
Lahontan, Baron de, 269
La Imperial, 126, 169
La Isabela, 50
Landa, Diego de, 137
La Paz, 154
Las Cangrejeras, 208
Las Casas, Bartolomé de, 58, 84–85, 107–8, 110, 123, 124, 143–44, 147
La Serena, 116
Lautaro, 119, 127
Lázaro, 213

Lazarus, St., 194
Legion of the Henriques, 233
Lemos, Count, 248–49
Leonarda, 262–63
Leonardo, 264
Leonardo, Lupercio, 260
Leonardo da Vinci, 53
Leoncico (dog), 58–59
León Mullohuamani, Cristóbal de, 182
Lima, 105, 108–9, 116, 122, 123, 126, 140, 155, 160, 177, 183, 184, 192, 194, 198, 199, 213, 222, 224, 226, 248
Lisbon, 276
Locke, John, 253
London, 153, 162, 182, 190, 244, 252, 253, 270
Lord of Shells, 4–5
Losada, Diego de, 118
Los Teques, 144
Louis XIV, king of France, 278
Love Your Own Death (Espinosa Medrano), 251
Loyola, Ignacio de: see Ignatius, St.
Luanda, 193, 232
Lurín, 28
Lurín River, 140
Luther, Martin, 62, 93, 136

Mabodamaca, Chief, 56
Macacos, 258, 273–74, 275
Macchiavelli, Niccolò, 62
Machángara Canyon, 271
Machu Picchu, 96, 107
Macouba, 279
Macusi Indians, 23
Madrid, 81, 143, 147, 159, 185, 195, 207, 217, 227, 243, 277, 278, 279, 282
Magdalena River, 99
Magellan, Ferdinand, 74
Makiritare Indians, 3
Malaga, 282

Maldonado, Juan, 204, 213, 214
Maldonado, Juana, 214–16
Maldonado de Saavedra, Melchor,
  224
Mal Hado Island, 82, 97
Malinche (Cortés's Indian woman),
  65, 68, 69, 76–77, 145
Mamatoco, 170
Mamazaca, 170
Manco Cápac: see Manco Inca
Manco Inca, 90, 94, 96
Mandingo people, 253
Manhattan, 243
Mani, 30–31
Maní, 137
Manoc Inca, 107
Manzanares River, 227
Manzanillo, 178
Maracaibo, 244, 248
Maracaibo, Lake, 247
Maravilla, Hernando, 155
Margarita Island, 134
Mariana, Father, 196
Mariño de Lobera, Pedro, 126
Maroma, 170
Martelli (engineer), 227
Martial, St., 159
Martínez, Domingo, 125
Martinique, 279
Masaca, 170
Masanga, 170
Masaya, 250
Masaya volcano, 100–101
Masinga, 170
Masinguilla, 170
Massachusetts, 220–21, 256, 269
Matanzas, 207
Matos, Gregorio de, 276
Maulicán, 209, 210–11
Mauracataca, 170
Mauro, Fray, 278
Maya Indians, 3, 12, 28, 40,
  76, 137
Mayna Indians, 18

Mbororé, 226
Mby'a-guaraní Indians, 12
Méndez, Diego, 107
Mendieta, Jerónimo de, 150, 151
Mendiguaca, 170
Mendoza, Felipe de, 124, 131
Mendoza, Pedro de, 152
Menéndez de Avilés, Pedro, 228
Meneses, Hernando de, 131
Menomenee Indians, 6
Metacom, 256
Mexico, 41, 63, 65, 103, 156, 203,
  204, 228
Mexico City, 84, 95, 115, 123, 130,
  142, 145, 146, 148, 154, 174, 202,
  203, 236, 245, 260, 266, 271;
  see also Tenochtitlán
Mezquital, 189
Michael, St., 194
Michaelangelo, 62
Michmaloyan, 128
Michoacán, 132
Miguel, King, 117–18
Mina people, 233
Minas Gerais, 279
Mixco, 217
Moctezuma, Emperor, 54, 64, 65,
  66–67, 68, 70, 142
Modoc Indians, 33
Mogrovejo de la Cerda, Juan de,
  199–201
Molina, Alonso de, 81–82
Molucca Indians, 73–74
Montesinos, Antonio de, 57–58
More, Thomas, 61, 132
Morga, Antonio de, 218–19
Morgan, Henry, 247, 248, 251–52,
  253–54
Moseten Indians, 10
Motocintle, 212
Motolinía, Toribio de, 95–96
Mujica, Martín de, 232
Muslims, 52–53, 62, 92–93, 217
Mystic Fort, 221

Nabía, Antonia, 155
Nahuanje, 170
Narváez, Pánfilo de, 82
Nasuk, 13
Nau, Jean David (El Olonés),
    244–45, 247
Navajo Indians, 157
Navidad fort, 50
Ñeambiú, 19
Nebrija, Elio Antonio de, 50
Negro Committee, 262
Negro River, 9
New Amsterdam, 243
New Cádiz, 106
Newfoundland, 269
New Mexico, 259, 272
New York, 243
Nicaragua, 206, 250
Nicaragua, Chief, 75–76
Nivakle Indians, 13, 35–36
Nochistlán, Rock of, 102
Nooktas Indians, 27
Nueva Valencia del Rey, 134, 136
Núñez de Balboa, Vasco, 58, 59,
    62–63
Núñez de Miranda, Antonio,
    266–68, 271
Núñez de Pineda y Bascuñán,
    Francisco, 208–9, 210–12
Núñez Vela, Blasco, 115
The Nun Lieutenant
    (Pérez de Montalbán), 214

Oaxaca, 17, 132, 237
Obatalá, 193
Obenga, 275
Ocaña, Diego de, 168–69
Océlotl, Martín, 128
Ochoa, Juan, 194–95
Ogum, 194
Ojeda, Alonso de, 50–51
Old Meanie, 36–37
Old Road Town, 256
Olinda, 232

Olonés, El, 244–45, 247
Omapacha, 182
Ona Indians, 36
Opechancanough, Chief, 191–92,
    228
Ordaz, Diego de, 83
Orellana, Francisco de, 105
Origua, 170
Orinoco River, 38, 52, 83
Osborne, Sarah, 270
Oshún, 193
Our Lady of Guanajuato, 149–50
Ouro Prêto, 279
Oviedo: see Fernández de Oviedo,
    Gonzalo
Oxalá, 193
Oxley, Henry, 160
Ozama River, 51

Pachacamac, 28
Pacific Ocean, 59
Painala, 76
Palawiyang Indians, 37
Palmares, 175, 232, 241–42, 257,
    258, 273–74, 275
Palos, 96
Panama, 58, 94, 111, 134, 168,
    200, 253
Panama City, 167, 251
Pané, Ramón, 51
Pánuco, 132
Paraguay, 124, 125, 227
Paraguay River, 20
Paraíba River, 240
Paraná, 29
Paranapiacaba Mountains, 279
Paraná River, 124
Paria, Gulf of, 28, 52
Parris, Samuel, 269–70
Pasto, 48
Patiño, Francisco, 231
Paul III, Pope, 98, 146
Paullo (Inca leader), 96
Pedrarias the Buried: See Arias de
    Avila, Pedro

Pedro, Maese, 115
Peña, Lorenzo de la, 161
Penn, William, 239
Pequot Indians, 221–22
Pérez de Montalbán, Juan, 214
Pérez de Morales, Captain, 265
Pernambuco, 242, 257, 273
Peru, 21, 34, 115, 116, 133, 134, 135, 158, 172, 181, 205, 206, 226
Peter, St., 59
Philip II, king of Spain, 110, 129, 131, 136, 137, 147, 156, 163, 174, 184, 228, 237
Philip III, king of Spain, 184, 185, 195–96
Philosophical Manifesto Against the Stray Comets (Sigüenza y Góngora), 261
Piaroa Indians, 83
Pichincha volcano, 229
Pinel, Juan, 111, 112
Pinola, 216
Pius V, Pope, 143
Pizarro, Francisco, 63, 81, 87–89, 90, 94, 96, 105, 107, 114
Pizarro, Gonzalo, 104–5, 108–9, 112, 115
Placentia, 269
Plate River, 104
Plymouth, England, 138
Plymouth, Massachusetts, 221, 256
Pocahontas, 191
Poma de Ayala, Guamán, 184–85
Ponce de León, Juan, 55, 56, 72
Popocatépetl volcano, 69, 83
Porres, Martín de, 222–23
Portilla, Juan de la, 161
Portobello, 168, 199, 251
Pôrto Calvo, 257, 274
Port Royal, 253
the Portuguese, 174, 232–33, 241, 242, 257–58, 261, 273, 276

Potosí, 110, 117, 120, 121, 153, 154, 164, 168, 172, 173, 186–89, 205, 224, 230, 248, 254
Powhatan, 191
Prieto, Juan, 117
Puebla, 240
Puerto Príncipe, 178
Puerto Rico, 55, 56
Puerto Viejo, 91
Pujilí, 271
Puná, 160
the Puritans, 220–21, 256, 270
Putapichun, Chief, 209–10

Quetzalcóatl, 65, 66, 67
Quetzaltenango, 77
Quevedo y Villegas, Francisco de, 175, 201–2
Quiché Indians, 12, 28, 40, 78
Quijo Indians, 151–52
Quillacinga Indians, 48–49
Quintero, 116
Quiroga, Vasco de, 132
Quito, 75, 89, 91, 92, 94, 100, 104, 151, 158, 167, 218, 229, 271

Ragueneau, Father, 233–34
Raleigh, Walter, 162–63
Rebelo, Gonçalo, 242
Recife, 175, 232, 242, 257, 273, 275
Redbeard (pirate), 93
Regla, 277
Remedios, 244, 262–66
Repocura, 210, 211
Reyes, Gaspar de los, 149
Ribera, Alonso de, 176–77
Rímac River, 199
Riobamba, 91, 94
Rio de Janeiro, 273
Rio Grande do Norte, 273
Rio Grande Valley, 272
Ripa, Cesare, 176
Robles, Martín de, 136
Rodrigo, Martín, 115

Rojas, Alonso de, 229
Rolfe, John, 190–91
Rome, 47, 98, 176
Rosales, Floriana, 164–66
Royal Africa Company, 252, 261
Ruiz, Marcos, 249–50
Ruiz, Pedro, 101
Rumiñahui, General, 92

Sacasa, 170
Sahagún, Bernardino de, 155–56, 237
Ste. Marie des Hurons, 233
St. Kitts, 256
St. Thomas Island, 280
Salamanca, 50
Salazar, Bernardo de, 206
Salazar, Diego de, 56
Salcedo (soldier), 55–56
Salem Village, 269
Salvador (heroic slave), 179
Samayac, 204
Sánchez, Juan, 101
Sánchez, Sebastián, 247–48
Sánchez Farfán, Julio, 164, 165–66
Sánchez Gallque, Andrés, 168
San Francisco monastery, 203, 205
San Juan Atitlán, 249
San Lorenzo, 166
Sanlúcar de Barrameda, 82, 197
San Marcos de Arica, 205
San Miguel, Gulf of, 59
San Miguel de Nepantla, 238, 239
San Miguel de Tucumán, 224
San Pablo, 226
San Pedro de Omapacha, 182
San Pedro River, 117
Santa Catarina, 189
Santa Cruz Island, 49
Santa Fe, 259, 272
Santa Lucía, 101
Santa María de Guadalupe, 264, 265
Santa María del Darién, 60
Santa Marta, 81, 99, 169, 170

Santiago, apostle, 150–51, 185
Santiago, Miguel de, 271
Santiago de Chile, 101, 127, 155, 176, 180, 232
Santiago de la Vega, 238
Santiago Papasquiaro, 189
Santo Domingo, 51, 57, 72, 81, 84, 94, 98, 138, 140
São Paulo, 273, 279
São Salvador de Bahia, 225, 276
Sarmiento, Juan, 149
Scorpion Islands, 78
Sebastian, St., 151
Segura de la Frontera, 69
Sepúlveda, Juan Ginés de, 123–24
Serra da Barriga, 241
Serra de Leguízamo, Mancio, 160
Serra Dois Irmãos, 275
Serrana Island, 85
Serrano, Pedro, 85–87, 93
Seville, 45, 73, 93, 163, 172, 178, 179, 197, 199, 201, 262
Shakespeare, William, 153, 182–83
Shangó, 194, 277
Shipaiás Indians, 25
Sigüenza y Góngora, Carlos de, 261
Silva, José Asunción, 192
Simon, St., 146, 159
Sinaloa, 97
Sinú River, 59
Sioux Indians, 41–42
Slader, Matthew, 255
Small Syphilitic God, 4–5
Soares, Antonio, 275
Solar, Antonio, 140
Soto, Hernando de, 88
Sousa de Castro, Aires de, 257–58
Spain, 52–53
Suárez, Inés, 101, 102, 116
Sublimis Deus (papal bull), 98
Subupira, 275
Sucre River, 219
Suliman, Sultan, 93
the Swedes, 262

Tabocas, 275
Tagus River, 227
Taíno Indians, 26, 41
Tairama, 170
Taironaca, 170
Tairona Indians, 170–71
Takelma Indians, 20
Tambisa, 151
Tapajós River, 105
Tarascan Indians, 10
Tecayehuatzin, 48
Tecum Umán, Captain, 77
Tehuantepec, 132
The Tempest (Shakespeare),
   182–83
Tenochtitlán, 41, 54, 63, 65,
   67, 70, 71, 76, 80, 83, 95;
   see also Mexico City
Teocalhueyacan, 68
Teotihuacán, 4
Tepeaca, 69
Tepehuanes Indians, 189–90
Tepeyac, 84
Tereupillán, 211–12
Tetón, Juan, 128
Teuctepec, 54
Texcoco, 70, 128, 156
Tierra del Fuego, 36
Tillamook Indians, 31
Titicaca, Lake, 23, 39, 154
Tituba (slave), 270
Tlatelolco, 64, 71, 155, 156
Tlaxcala, 48, 70, 129
Tlazoltéotl, 66
Tocuyo, 118
Toledo, 80
Toltec Indians, 5, 19
Tonantzin, 84
Torama, 170
Torres, Alonso de, 112
Torres, Luis de, 46
Torres, Simón de, 167
Tortuga Island, 244, 246–47
Tovar, Hernando del, 189

Treatise on Necessary Policy
   (González de Cellorigo), 174
Trinidad, 190, 193
Trujillo, 197
Tucapel, 119
Tucumán, 254
Tukano Indians, 9
Tukuna Indians, 34–35
Tula, 19, 156
Tulán, 40
Tumbes, 81, 94
Tunis, 93
Túpac Amaru, 147, 169
Tuxkahá, 79

Ubinas volcano, 205–6
Uceda, duke of, 195–96
Uitoto Indians, 12
Ulúa, Valley of, 96
Underhill, John, 221–22
Urquía, 144
Urubamba River, 96
Utatlán, 78
Utopia, 61
Utopia (More), 132

Vaca de Castro, Cristóbal, 115
Valderrábano (scribe), 59
Valdivia, Pedro de, 101, 102, 111–12,
   113, 116, 118, 119–20, 177
Valladolid, 54, 110, 117, 174
Valle, Jual del, 189
Valparaíso, 111, 116
Valverde, Vincente de, 87–88
Vanbel, 280–81
Vancouver Island, 15
Vázquez, Antonio, 226
Vázquez, Juan Bautista, 159
Vázquez, Tomás, 136
Vázquez de Coronado,
   Francisco, 157
Vázquez de Espinosa, Antonio,
   197–98
Vega, Lope de, 195

Velasco, Luis de, 228
Velázquez, Diego, 65
Velho, Jorge, 273
Venezuela, 81, 118, 134
Veracruz, 64, 95, 213
Verapaz, 204
Vespucci, Amerigo, 54, 61
Vieira, Antonio, 225–26, 276
Vilcabamba, 107
Villa de los Bergantines, 133
Virginia, 182, 190, 191, 221, 228,
    244, 255
Virginia Company, 182, 190
Virgin of Copacabana, 154
Virgin of Guadelupe,
    84, 187–88
Virgin of Regla, 277
Virgins of Candelaria, 193

Waiwai Indians, 9
Wall Street, 243
Wampanoag Indians, 255–56
Wanakauri, Mount, 39
Waterdrinker, 41–42
Wawenock Indians, 5
Welser (German banker), 62, 81,
    100
Wilcabamba Mountains, 147
Winthrop, John, 220–21
Wiracocha, 39

Xaquixaguana, 90, 112, 113, 114
Xochimilco, 150, 151

Yagan Indians, 36
Yanaoca, 205
Yarovilcas Indians, 184
Yarutini, 181
Yauyoa, 141
Yobuënahuaboshka, 7
York, duke of, 252
Yorktown, 255
Yoruba Indians, 258
Yucatán, 4, 42, 65, 76, 96

Yupanqui, Francisco Tito, 154
Yuste, 129

Zaca, 170
Zacatecas, 115, 189, 190
Zamora, 204
Zape, 189
Zapotec Indians, 24, 26, 237
Zárate (lawyer), 109
Zuazo, Alonso, 78, 79
Zumárraga, Bishop, 84
Zumbí, Chief, 258, 274, 275

About the Author

Eduardo Galeano is one of the world's most distinguished writers. He is the author of *Mirrors: Stories of Almost Everyone; Voices of Time; Upside Down; Soccer in Sun and Shadow; The Book of Embraces; We Say No; Days and Nights of Love and War; Walking Words; Open Veins of Latin America;* and the three volumes of this trilogy: *Genesis, Faces and Masks,* and *Century of the Wind.* His work has served as inspiration around the world to cultural historians, political organizers, composers, and artists alike; it has been translated into twenty-eight languages.

Born in Montevideo in 1940, Galeano lived for years in Argentina and Spain, in exile from the Uruguayan military dictatorship, before returning to Montevideo, where he lives today. He is the recipient of many international prizes, including the inaugural Lannan Prize for Cultural Freedom, the American Book Award, the Casa de las Américas Prize, and the First Distinguished Citizen of the region by the countries of Mercosur.

About the Translator

Born in London in 1904, Cedric Belfrage came to the U.S. in 1925 and began writing about movies in Hollywood. He was a cofounder of the *National Guardian* in 1948 and its editor until 1955, when a brush with McCarthy led to his deportation. He wrote ten books and novels published in this country, including *Away from It All; Abide with Me; My Master Columbus;* and *The American Inquisition, 1945-1960.* He lived with his wife, Mary, in Cuernavaca, Mexico, until his death in 1990.